G000162265

BURGUNDY

Anthony Turner and Christopher Brown

BURGUNDY

B. T. Batsford Ltd *London*

First published 1977
© Anthony Turner and Christopher Brown 1977
ISBN 0 7134 0889 8
Phototypeset by Trident Graphics Ltd, Reigate, Surrey
Printed by Thomson Litho Ltd, East Kilbride, Scotland
for the publishers
B. T. Batsford Ltd, 4 Fitzhardinge Street, London W1H 0AH

Contents

List of Illustrations

(between pages 96 and 97)

List of Maps

Foreword

This foreword would not be complete without my grateful thanks to the following people who, in many different ways, contributed towards the creation of this book: Bernard Dussaucy, Michel Tanazacq, Annie and Paul Lance, Martine Bailly, Nicole and Robert Thion, and the Lassallian Brothers of L'Ecole Saint-Joseph, Dijon, for their companionship and hospitality during my four years in Burgundy; René Paris, for the use of his ideal cellar and for limitless supplies of *gnôle*; Jean Lafarges, Guy Cheeseman and M. René Chasles for their invaluable help with the photographs; Dr John Martin Robinson for his expertise on French classical art; Michael Sissons, for getting the book off the ground, Michael Stephenson for bringing it to completion; Sally Brown and Lawrence Reynolds for their comments and suggestions on the text; and finally my parents, for their encouragement and unfailing patience.

I would like to thank Jean Lafarges for photographs 1-4, 6-10, 12, 14-16, 19, 20, 23; Guy Cheeseman for 5 and the Seine et Loine Tourisme for 11, 13, 17, 18, 21, 22.

A.B.T.

This book, which is intended to help the visitor to Burgundy get the most from him holiday, was itself the result of a holiday. In the autumn of 1972, I went to visit an old friend, Anthony Turner, who was teaching English at the Ecole St Joseph in Dijon. Such was my enjoyment of that holiday that I visited him on a number of other occasions. From his enthusiasm for the knowledge of Burgundy, and my wish to know more about the art and architecture of the region, this book was born. I had already studied 15th century Burgundian art at Oxford, and the writing of this book entailed the immensely pleasurable task of extending my knowledge into earlier and later periods. This book, however, is largely the work of Anthony Turner, who lived in Dijon for four years, from 1971 until 1975. The sections on history and topography are almost entirely by him, and while I enjoyed many of the meals he mentions and drank a good number of the wines, the descriptions of Burgundian food and wine are also his. My contribution has been limited to the discussion of the art and architecture of Burgundy, and even here, many of his suggestions and ideas have been incorporated into the text, which was subsequently revised by him.

C.P.H.B.

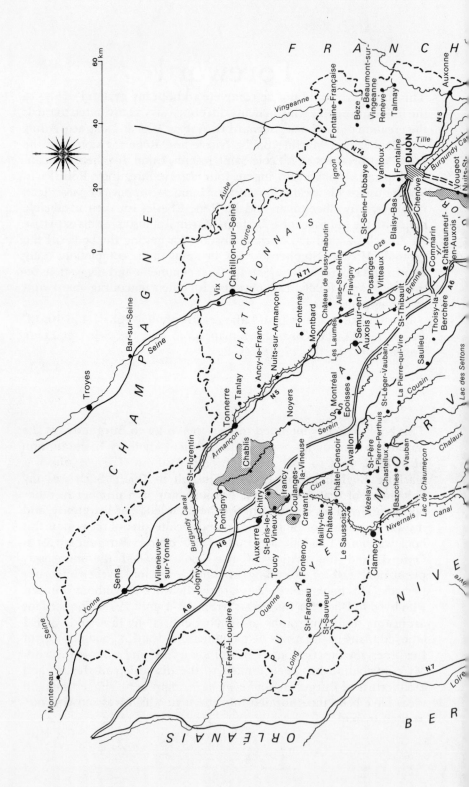

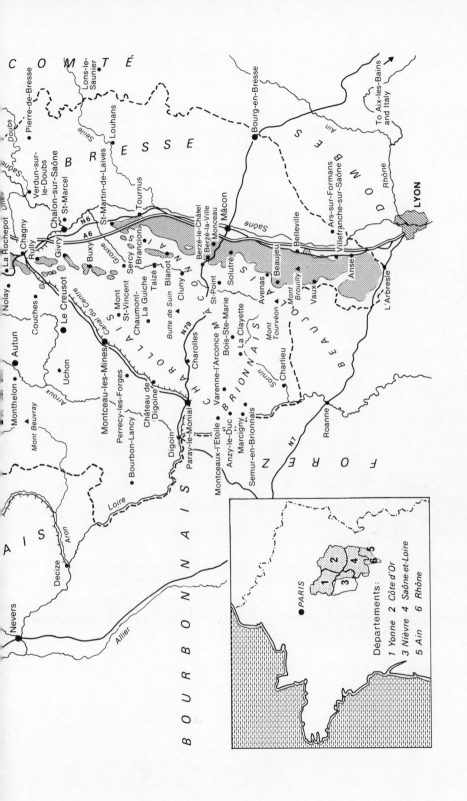

Introduction

'Burgundy has a centre but no frontiers.' This is the classic description of one of the most captivating but elusive areas of provincial France. Unlike Normandy, Brittany, Alsace, Auvergne or Provence, Burgundy does not admit of an easy geographical definition. No mountains fence it round, no great river serves as its axis. The waters do not pass through it so much as flow out from it in all directions. The heart of Burgundy is a divide, from one side of which the rivers drain into the Atlantic, and from the other into the Mediterranean. But far from separating north and south, this 'barrier' brings them closer together. It is a limestone bridge between the granite massifs of the Vosges to the north-east and the Morvan to the south-west, and as such has provided a convenient link between northern France and the Rhône valley from the earliest times.

In the heat of summer, the cicadas sing as far north as Nuits-Saint-Georges; at Tournus, the steep slate roofs of the north give place to the curved red tiles of Provence; and in the same district, the *langue d'oïl* once gave place to the *langue d'oc*. Michelet saw Burgundy as the binding element of France, harmonising the Germanic and Mediterranean cultures; and yet Burgundy itself seems to lack a unifying theme. Wine is an obvious suggestion—the very name of Burgundy conjures up a jovial, bibulous image, and the 'provincial anthem', *La Bourguignonne,* is a drinking song popular all over France. But wine is only one voice of the fugue. This book trespasses into the Beaujolais, but in Burgundy proper the vine occupies only 1.5% of the land, and contributes less than 10% of total agricultural production.

The province does not form a physical region, but is a cluster of individual *pays* or districts, each with its own character: the northern plateaux and river-valleys (Puisaye, Auxerrois, Tonnerrois and Châtillonnais), which rightfully belong to the Paris Basin; the highlands of the Morvan; the Auxois, a depression flanking the Morvan on the east; the Côte d'Or, a scarp rising abruptly from a subsided river-plain and backed by a range of hills; the Mâconnais, a sort of southward continuation of the Côte, but without the latter's clear-cut outlines; the Charollais and Brionnais, soft, undulating countryside sloping towards the Loire; and Bresse, which occupies most of the broad plain of the River Saône on the east.

Without physical unity and without community of economic interest, it is hardly surprising that Burgundy does not have a common popular culture like Brittany or Languedoc. The chorus of *La Bourguignonne* runs, '*Je suis fier d'être Bourguignon*', but regional pride is somewhat less aggressive than that of the average Yorkshireman; the Burgundians are Frenchmen first and Burgundians second. There is no convenient stereotype, though physically the people are more Nordic than Mediterranean, and in temperament stolid rather than excitable. An Englishman would feel more at home with them than with the abrasive Provençaux.

The regional accent survives at its best among the *vignerons* of the Côte. 'R's' are trilled, though this is a feature of many French provincial dialects (the Englishman's bugbear, the guttural 'r', originated in the Paris area). Far more distinctive is the lengthening of 'a's' and 'o's' as if each one carried a circumflex accent, so that to her doting Burgundian parents, Marie-Claude becomes '*Maarrie-Clôôde*'. Where place-names are concerned, 'x', as in Auxerre, Auxonne and Aloxe-Corton, is pronounced '*ss*'. But these peculiarities are far from universal among Burgundians, and 'standard' French is gaining ground all the time as a result of education, broadcasting and increased mobility.

Burgundy is a creation of history, expanding and contracting with the political fortunes of kings, dukes and bishops. As the opening quotation suggests, despite the fluctuating frontiers, the nucleus has never been in doubt. The centre referred to by Maurice Chaume is the capital, Dijon, but we can enlarge it to include all the *pays* bordering on the great watershed, corresponding to the whole of the present-day departments of Côte d'Or and Saône-et-Loire. The unity of Burgundy is historic, but its sense of identity does not spring from a culture evolved in isolation; it springs rather from a common experience of a multitude of outside influences. Burgundy is a crossroads—not a destination, but a staging-post on the way to everywhere else.

1   History

The earliest known human remains date back to the Upper Palaeolithic (Aurignacian period, before 15,000 B.C.), but the population of hunters and gatherers would have been too sparse and too nomadic to allow talk of 'politics'. It was the penetration of the western Mediterranean by the Greeks and the rise of the Etruscan civilisation that really put our area on the map. Demand for the tin used in bronze-working opened an overland trade-route from Cornwall, passing up the Seine valley, crossing the limestone 'bridge', and descending the Saône and Rhône valleys to the sea. The Greeks were established at Massilia (Marseille) around 600 B.C., and the Etruscans may have been using a variant of the route (through Switzerland and over the Brenner) even earlier than that.

500 B.C. is the first date for which we have firm archaeological evidence. Around that year, a Celtic princess died and was buried with a rich display of grave-goods—many of them Greek—at Vix, near Châtillon-sur-Seine. This was the most spectacular of many finds that give ample proof of the wealth and power of the Hallstatt occupants of Latisco, the stronghold commanding the Seine-Saône corridor. The absence of written records has obscured the events of the following 400 years, although the Aedui and Senones, who dominated the region in Caesar's time, were among the Gauls who invaded Italy and sacked Rome in 390 B.C. It may have been this adventure which led to the first introduction of vine-plants, as opposed simply to the finished product.

In the end, it was the tribal politics of the area that drew the Romans out of their *Provincia* into 'Long-haired' Gaul. The Sequani, rivals of the Aedui to the east, had called in the German chieftain Ariovistus to help them. Worse still, the Helvetii of Switzerland were evacuating their territory, and Ariovistus planned to seize it and install his Suebi permanently on the left bank of the Rhine. The Aedui appealed to the Romans, their 'brothers' and long-standing allies. The crisis was ruthlessly exploited by Julius Caesar, who assumed the proconsulship of Gaul in 58 B.C. He blocked the migration of the Helvetii, drove Ariovistus back over the Rhine, and finished by extending Roman domination to the whole of central and northern Gaul. Despite the near-success of the revolt of Vercingetorix, Gallic independence came to an end at Alesia (Alise-Sainte-Reine) in 52 B.C.

It is not till the last days of the western Roman Empire that the name 'Burgundy' appears; it derives from a group of invaders, whom the Romans called Burgundiones. The first known home of this Germanic tribe was on the shores of the Baltic, where the island of Bornholm (Burgundarholm) preserves their memory. By the fifth century they had crossed into Roman territory in the wake of the Vandals and others, and were settled on the middle Rhine. In 436 they were crushingly defeated by Attila's Huns, and their king, Gunther, perished in the rout. So resounding was the disaster that it passed into legend, becoming one of the themes of the *Nibelungenlied*. The remnants of the tribe were settled in the area around Geneva and became Roman allies. By 470 they had recovered sufficiently to take Lyon, and thereafter they expanded irresistibly. By the end of the century, they had extended their control over large areas of eastern France and most of Switzerland, and had advanced down the Rhône to Arles and Avignon. This, then, was the first Burgundy—an area much too big for our purposes, since modern Burgundy is only a fragment of this original kingdom.

The Burgundiones formed a close-knit military caste settled in small enclaves and mixing little with the Gallo-Roman inhabitants. Even when they adopted Christianity, they isolated themselves from their Catholic subjects by choosing the Arian version. They made a poor social impression at first, with their long hair bleached with lime and perfumed with rancid butter, but were Romanized more quickly than the other barbarian invaders. Gundebald, who ruled the Burgundian kingdom at its apogee around the year 500, produced an adaptation of the Roman penal code for the benefit of his German subjects.

The moment of glory was short. Already under pressure from the Franks during Gundebald's lifetime, the Burgundian kingdom collapsed after his death. In the following centuries, the 'Merovingian nightmare' descended upon Burgundy as upon the rest of Gaul until the establishment of Charlemagne's empire. But it was only when Charlemagne's grandsons divided the inheritance in 843 that Burgundy began to assume its present contours. Everything south of Lyon and east of the Saône went to Lothair; the rest, the north-west corner of the old Burgundian kingdom, went to Charles the Bald. This 'lower Burgundy' evolved into a French duchy, while the rest, after a period of anarchic independence, fell into the orbit of the Holy Roman Empire in 1032; the Imperial county of Burgundy, facing the French duchy across the Saône, was the future province of Franche-Comté.

One effect of the Viking and corsair raids of the 9th century was to turn Burgundy into a major religious centre. Embattled Christendom saw the inaccessible French province as a safe refuge from the fury of the Norsemen. Retreating from the areas most exposed to seaborne attack, the monks brought with them the relics whose protection had become one of their most important raisons d'être. The significance of a handful of dry bones is lost on us, but we forget that the notion of a physical resurrection was taken very seriously then. To be enrolled among the saints was, by definition, to be assured of Paradise; so that on the Last Day, all relics would be claimed by the saints and become an integral part of the kingdom of Heaven. Man was alone, and defenceless without supernatural aid; relics were a tangible link with the eternal world, and both liturgy and government drew their strength from them.

In addition to the relics of numerous local martyrs, Burgundy acquired those of St Vorles, St Vivant, St Philibert and even (for a time) St Martin in the course of the 9th century. Mâcon Cathedral had owned the remains of St Vincent of Saragossa since the 7th century, and St Germanus, the most popular French confessor saint after St Martin, had lived and was buried at Auxerre. With one notable exception (the winter of 886-7, when Bèze, Flavigny, Vézelay and Auxerre were sacked), Burgundy was spared the horrors of the Norse invasion. As they withdrew to this oasis of security, the monks created a unique concentration of intellectual activity and religious tradition. It was in this fertile Burgundian soil that the great reform movement led by the abbey of Cluny (founded in 910) took root and flourished; and when the barbarian tide subsided, this revitalising force was released over all Christendom.

The Hungarian onslaught of 937, which devastated Tournus, was only a temporary setback. In the fervid, sometimes hysterical atmosphere of the years leading up to the millennium, Cluny and the other Burgundian abbeys played a major part in the rebirth of Europe. They stand out as symbols of the return of spring after the long winter of the Dark Ages and the great invasions. The visible expression of the new spirit was in building. 'Shortly after the year 1000, it happened that the churches were rebuilt throughout almost the entire world, principally in Italy and Gaul; and although most of them were quite adequate and lacked nothing, great emulation seized each Christian people to surpass the others in magnificence. It was as if the world, shaking off its old age, were everywhere donning a white mantle of churches.' Those are the words of Ralph

Glaber, himself a monk of Saint-Bénigne at Dijon and one of the most engaging personalities of the age. By his own admission he was a difficult character who had been thrown out of several monasteries. Abbot William of Volpiano took him in at Saint-Bénigne and absorbed this excess energy by setting him to write the chronicles of his time. Apart from his famous reference to the 'white mantle of churches', Glaber has left us a lurid account of the famine of 1030-3 in southern Burgundy. The relish with which he describes the outbreak of cannibalism shows a true journalist's instinct.

Meanwhile, other monks worked steadily to clear the land, organise agriculture, improve communications and encourage trade. They saw their real work as the ceaseless spiritual battle against the unseen enemy, but their economic and cultural rôle was crucial well into the twelfth century. New relics, notably those of Lazarus and Mary Magdalene, enhanced the already considerable cult in Burgundy.

Even as Cluniac fervour declined, the Cistercian reform ensured that Burgundian monasteries retained the leadership of Christendom. Just as four of the first six abbots of Cluny had been canonised, so were the first three abbots of Cîteaux—a fair measure of their order's prestige. But their memory was eclipsed by an even more dynamic figure and a Burgundian by birth, St Bernard. As abbot of Clairvaux, it was he who transformed a purely local protest against the worldliness of Cluny into an international movement. His austerity, arrogance and aggressiveness have been stressed at the expense of the new strain of tenderness that he helped to introduce by his writings. The lyrical mysticism that earned St Bernard the title of *doctor mellifluus* belied his muscular exterior. His love of music, and the veiled eroticism of his devotion to the Virgin, brought him closer to the frank sensuality of his contemporary Suger of Saint-Denis than he would have cared to admit. The twelfth century's rediscovery of the feminine virtues coincided with the full flowering of Romanesque. It is no accident that Lord Clark, in his personal view of civilisation, should have picked Cluny, Vézelay and Autun for particular mention; all in Burgundy, within a few miles of each other, they are the style's greatest monuments. Artistic links paralleled political ones: Vézelay was one of the principal starting-points for the Santiago pilgrimage zealously promoted by Cluny.

The prosperity which the monasteries had helped to create ultimately deprived them of their central position in the medieval world. The monastic ideal of a static society serving God carried less and less weight in the growing towns. The centre of gravity moved northwards out of Burgundy, and the initiative passed to the new civic authorities and the bishops, while the abbeys slid into a backwater. This shift in power and resources brought with it a new style, Gothic; the thirteenth and fourteenth centuries were the age of splendid city churches like Notre-Dame de Dijon and great cathedrals like Sens and Auxerre.

All this time, Burgundy was taking shape as a political entity. The duchy emerges from the shadows in 1016, when a 14-year feudal war ended with the bishop of Langres surrendering Dijon to King Robert the Pious of France. Duke Robert I succeeded his brother Henry in 1031, when the latter came to the French throne. Robert chose Dijon as his capital, and was the true founder of the new line—a bewildering collection of Hugues and Eudes, with two Roberts and a Philip thrown in for good measure—which was to rule Burgundy for 330 years. They are known as the Capetian dukes by reason of their descent from Hugh Capet, who supplanted the last Carolingian king and was the father of Robert the Pious.

History has largely forgotten the Capetians. Their painstaking creation of a secular power has been eclipsed by the great age of the Church, and whenever 'the dukes of Burgundy' are mentioned, one invariably thinks of their Valois successors. And yet they were far from colourless; Robert I, as fierce as his contemporary William the Conqueror, set the tone by divorcing his wife in scandalous circumstances, killing his father-in-law in the heat of an argument, and then going to Rome on foot to receive absolution. One duke renounced the world and became a monk at Cluny, while another earned the name of 'Peacemaker'; but in general their piety, though sincere, was intermittent. 'The clergy are puffed up with pride,' grumbled Hugues IV, but nonetheless followed St Louis on his ill-fated crusade to Egypt. All the early dukes distinguished themselves against the infidel, whether the Moslems of Spain and Palestine, or the Albigensian heretics of southern France. Closer to home, however, they quarrelled just as enthusiastically with the Church and were periodically excommunicate.

When the western counter-attack petered out in the thirteenth century, militant Christianity gave place to courtly love and a nostalgia for chivalry. In these less uncouth times, the dukes became more devious in their attempts to expand. Hugues IV, for example, appears as purchaser in over 600 conveyances. By the turn of the fourteenth century, the dukes of Burgundy were playing to a wider audience. Two of them married into the French royal family, and all cut grand figures as courtiers, more at home in their Parisian mansions than in their gloomy provincial castles. Suddenly, this orderly progress was turned to confusion.

In 1361, the young duke Philip of Rouvres died of the plague and the Capetian line became extinct. After the short and hapless reigns of Philip the Fair's three sons, the Capetian royal house had also died out and in 1328 Philip of Valois had become king. The feudal dispute with the duke of Aquitaine (alias Edward III of England) had been complicated by the latter's rival claim to the French throne, and had flared up into the Hundred Years' War in 1337. France's performance had been disappointing: there had been two major military defeats, Crécy and Poitiers; at the second of these, in 1356, King John of France and a large portion of the French nobility had been taken prisoner by the Black Prince; in 1358 there had been a peasants' revolt and open revolution in Paris; and most of Edward's territorial claims had had to be met by the treaty of Brétigny in 1360. The duchy of Burgundy reverted to the crown against a background of terror and disruption spread by the Black Death and by the *Grandes Compagnies* of disbanded mercenaries turned freelance. All this, however, was just a discordant prelude to Burgundy's second golden age.

In 1364 the duchy was given in apanage to Philip, fourth son of King John the Good. For over a century, he and his three successors ruled with a splendour that outshone the French court, and indeed all others. Through their domination of the Low Countries, they became the richest princes in Europe and almost succeeded in restoring Burgundy to the status of a kingdom. To their very real power they harnessed a genius for self-publicity; they styled themselves 'the great dukes of the West', and encouraged the use of ringing surnames—'the Bold', 'the Fearless', 'the Good', 'the Rash' (the last sounding better in French, 'le Téméraire')—which have invested them ever since with an aura of romance. 'The whole history of the house of Burgundy,' wrote Huizinga, meaning the four Valois dukes, 'is like an epic of overweening and heroic pride,' and it captured the imagination of fifteenth-century Europe.

At the outset, no-one could have guessed that Burgundy was to develop into a threat to the very existence of the kingdom of France. The Capetian dukes had extended their domain and brought their unruly vassals to order, but the duchy as constituted in 1364 could never have given its masters the virtual independence that the Valois dukes were to enjoy. The system of giving slices of royal territory to the king's younger sons was partly to blame, since these apanages, although theoretically not hereditary, tended to become so. But it was an unforeseeable sequence of events that turned Burgundy into a more than ordinary menace to national security.

While scarcely more than a boy, Philip had distinguished himself at the battle of Poitiers. After the French defeat, he struck an English nobleman who had spoken disrespectfully to King John. Father and son were shipped off to England to await ransom in comfortable captivity. At a banquet attended by both monarchs, Philip slapped the face of a butler who had dared to offer a dish to the king of England before the king of France (the former being the latter's vassal in respect of Aquitaine, according to the French). This startling gesture drew from Edward III the remark, 'Truly, cousin, you are indeed Philip the Bold!' The revival of the dukedom of Burgundy was intended as a signal act of generosity to reward Philip for his spirit.

The last Captian, Philip of Rouvres, had been briefly married to Margaret of Flanders, the most desirable heiress in Europe. On her father's death, her husband stood to inherit not only the rich and densely populated province of Flanders, but also Artois, Nevers, Rethel and Franche-Comté. To prevent such a prize from falling into the hands of an English prince, Philip's elder brother, now king as Charles V, reluctantly permitted the young duke to press his suit. The count of Flanders made it a condition of his consent that his future son-in-law's apanage should be made hereditary. Undeterred by Margaret's ugliness, Philip married her at Ghent in 1369. He still had fifteen years to wait for the coveted counties.

Meanwhile, circumstances had given Philip an even greater rôle to play. Charles V had died in 1380, and the duke of Burgundy became the leading figure of the council of regency that governed France during the minority of Charles VI. The regency had only been suspended for a few months when it was unexpectedly prolonged by the onset of the king's paranoid delusions (of which the belief that he was made of glass is the most famous). Philip the Bold remained the effective ruler of France until his death in 1404.

Like all great noblemen of the Middle Ages, Philip saw it as his first duty to the world to spend, and his greatest glory to be able to spend lavishly. Very little property was liquid, and power, not yet being associated with money in people's minds, depended largely on the awe one could inspire by magnificent display. In these circumstances, the true aristocrat could not afford to worry about *whose* money he was spending. To get married, Philip borrowed 40,000 *livres* and still had to pawn his jewels in order to throw a farewell banquet for the corporation of Ghent. Later, he founded a chivalrous order, but had to return his own insignia to the goldsmith because he could not pay for them. As regent, not content with his personal resources, he pocketed nearly half the royal revenue to help him maintain his state. And yet when he died, his heirs had to pawn his gold and silver plate to pay for the funeral.

His successor was John the Fearless, who had won his sobriquet in the muddle-headed Balkan crusade against the Turks in 1396. Whereas most of his companions were massacred at Nicopolis, he was fortunate enough to be captured and ransomed. As duke, his reputation for slyness surpassed even that of his father, doubtless owing to his pinched, weasel-like features and shifty eyes. In an age when most men wore their hearts on their sleeves, he was a master of dissimulation. The mainspring of his policy was the desire to regain the position held by his father on the council of regency, which had now passed under the control of the king's brother Louis of Orléans. The hatred and rivalry of the royal cousins reached its climax in 1407, when John had Louis ambushed in a dark alley and bludgeoned to death.

France was plunged into a ferocious conflict between the 'Burgundians' and the partisans of the count of Armagnac, who now headed the Orléanist faction. The chief beneficiaries were the English. At first they played off one side against the other, but the accession of Henry V in 1413 brought a full-scale renewal of the Hundred Years' War. The crushing victory of Agincourt in 1415 was followed by a systematic conquest of Normandy while France was still hopelessly divided. In 1418, John the Fearless won control of Paris in a coup which involved the wholesale slaughter of Armagnacs in the capital. On 10 September 1419 a meeting was held on the bridge of Montereau at which John hoped to force the Dauphin Charles to join his parents in Paris and accept Burgundian 'protection'. Instead, the duke's skull was cleft with a hatchet by one of the Dauphin's knights. The Armagnacs claimed that John had laid violent hands on the prince, but the assassination was in fact premeditated with Charles's connivance.

The new duke, Philip the Good, was determined to exact exemplary vengeance for his father's murder. He formed an alliance with Henry V—a thing John the Fearless had never done—which was to be the foundation of English power in France. The treaty of Troyes (1420), to which Henry, Philip and Queen Isabella of France were signatories, declared the Dauphin to be the illegitimate product of the queen's adultery and recognised Henry as the true heir to the throne; in addition, Henry was to marry Charles VI's daughter and act as regent until his father-in-law's death. The Dauphin (who became Charles VII in 1422) withdrew to the safety of Bourges, and while the Burgundian alliance held firm, the English ruled the whole of northern France. It was Philip the Good who turned Joan of Arc over to the English after her capture at Compiègne. Only the death of his brother-in-law the duke of Bedford (regent in France during the minority of Henry VI) and Charles VII's concession of virtual independence at the treaty of Arras (1435) brought Philip back into the Valois camp.

Unlike his predecessors, Philip did not seek domination in France. The treaty of Arras confirmed him in possession of the counties of Auxerre and Mâcon in Burgundy proper, but his grasping policy was directed more towards enlarging his domains in the Low Countries. Secure in the knowledge that whoever ruled in Paris needed his support (at least until the Wars of the Roses removed the English threat), he sought a political capital outside France. In official documents he continued to refer to Dijon as his capital, but half his territories were in the Holy Roman Empire, and after the treaty of Arras he styled himself 'duke by the grace of God' (and not of the king of France). The centre of gravity moved north to the Netherlands, the true source of Philip's wealth and power.

There, in his palaces of Lille, Ghent, Brussels, Bruges and Hesdin, the duke of Burgundy rose to new heights of ostentation. In terms of costume, banquets and entertainments, his was the most brilliant court in Europe. On 14 January 1429, in honour of his wedding to Isabella of Portugal, Philip instituted the Order of the Golden Fleece. Created in honour of God, the Virgin Mary and St Andrew (patron saint of the Valois dukes), it rapidly became the most prestigious of all orders of chivalry and remained so until the present century. After the abdication of Philip's great-great-grandson, the Emperor Charles V, the Golden Fleece was divided into two branches, Austrian and Spanish. The present Grand Masters are the Archduke Otto von Habsburg and Don Juan respectively. The greatest artists of the day worked for Philip the Good and his entourage: the musicians Binchois and Dufay, the writers Chastellain and La Marche, the painters Rogier van der Weyden and Jan van Eyck (who was an honoured courtier, entrusted with several important diplomatic missions).

But the modern notion of art for its own sake had not yet arrived. The painters and sculptors were still only decorators, the musicians still only makers of background music and embellishers of church liturgy, the writers principally employed to glorify the deeds of the duke and the pomp of his court. Philip the Good may have had a serious interest in art, but in his collections, objects of genuine value and beauty were mixed up with tasteless knick-knacks. He also had a surprising passion for fairground novelties: distorting mirrors, bridges that collapsed when they were stepped on, and buried conduits 'for wetting the ladies from underneath'.

Court fêtes created a world of make-believe in reaction to the profound pessimism of the fifteenth century. The banquet of the Vow of the Pheasant, held at Lille in 1454, has become legendary. Constantinople had fallen to the Turks in the previous year, and Philip the Good used the banquet to publicise his intention of leading a crusade for its recapture. The knights present all took fanciful oaths connected with the project, the duke himself swearing to challenge the Grand Turk to single combat. The *tableaux vivants,* which were a feature of such pageants, here included Olivier de la Marche as Holy Church, making his appearance in a tower on the back of an elephant, led by a huge Turk. The tables were loaded with extraordinary decorations: a fully-rigged carrack, a meadow surrounded by trees with a fountain, rocks and a statute of St Andrew, the castle of Lusignan with the fairy Mélusine, a bird-shooting scene near a windmill, a wood in which wild beasts prowled, and a church with an organ and singers, whose songs alternated with the music of a 28-piece orchestra concealed in a pie. The climax of the feast came when Golden Fleece King-at-Arms brought in a live pheasant decked in a golden necklace garnished with pearls and other precious stones; it was on this bird that the knights took their oaths.

Philip was affable (though occasionally hot-tempered), pleasure-loving and, where women were concerned, *'durement lubrique'*. He had 30 known mistresses and 17 acknowledged bastards, two of whom succeeded each other as bishops of Utrecht, while others were knights of the Golden Fleece. And yet, in common with most men of his time, Philip oscillated violently between self-indulgence and severe piety. At times he would eat and drink nothing but bread and water for days on end, and he always spent hours at his prayers.

Despite the move to Flanders and Brabant, Burgundians were still highly influential at court. Notable among them were the Thoisy family, the Lord Steward Philippe Pot, and above all Nicholas Rolin of Autun, Chancellor for forty years until his death in 1462. The duchy itself, however, enjoyed only the reflected splendour of the ducal court while suffering the very real hardship of the duke's wars. Charles VII and his advisers were no more interested in a lasting settlement at Arras than they had been at Montereau. The discharge of royal mercenaries in 1435 meant a revival of the *Grandes Compagnies* of the previous century, and the duchy of Burgundy fell prey to the *Ecorcheurs*—so called because where others merely fleeced, they flayed alive. With the king's tacit approval, the bandits raped, looted and burnt for nine years. The damage was made good, but the duchy's vulnerability had been demonstrated alarmingly.

The last act of the melodrama was played out between the sons of Charles VII and Philip the Good. Louis XI mounted the French throne in 1461, and Charles the Rash became duke in 1467; both had quarrelled with their fathers, both had had periods of exile before their accessions, but there the resemblance ends. Charles was a conscientious ruler who undid his own best work by his impulsiveness, a dreamer who allowed fantasy to blind him to practical realities. His court surpassed even Philip the Good's in magnificence. The ceremony which attended the duke's meals and every other aspect of his daily life verged on the megalomanic; the complex protocol excited such admiration that Olivier de la Marche was requested to write a treatise to serve as a model for the court of the duke's brother-in-law, Edward IV of England. Like his father, Charles was a generous patron of the arts. He would not retire at night without listening to chivalrous romances or the exploits of classical heroes for at least two hours. He was not only an accomplished player on several instruments, but had been taught composition by Dufay. He had a remarkable capacity for work and was austere in his personal life. He was the only one of the Valois dukes to water his wine, and was strongly criticised by his courtiers for failing to take a mistress.

Louis XI, on the other hand, although superstitious to the point of eccentricity, was modern enough to realise that money, and not knightly prowess, was the measure of power. With his immense reserves of patience and cunning, he was more than a match for his erratic opponent. As his father had been a Philip in name, Charles the Rash was determined to be an Alexander in deed. His aims were to solve the problem of his divided dominions and to re-establish the Burgundian kingdom. The second objective was very nearly realised in 1473, when Charles forced the Emperor Frederick III to promise him the title of king as part of a bargain involving the marriage of the duke's daughter to Frederick's son Maximilian. Frederick had second thoughts and escaped by night before the agreement could be ratified.

Charles's first objective seemed to have been attained by the annexation of Lorraine in 1475, but the success was short-lived Ultimately, the independence won by the treaty of Arras was only secure while France remained weak and disunited; by pulling away the main prop of the English occupation, the treaty had given Burgundy the shadow of power and deprived it of the substance. A belated realisation of this fact led to a renewal of the English connexion in 1468, with the marriage of Charles to Margaret of

York. But by 1475, Louis' astute deplomacy was beginning to pay off. Charles's aggressive policies had made him many enemies, whom Louis was only too pleased to subsidise. Edward IV was bribed to abandon his plans for invading France, and Swiss mercenaries in French pay soundly defeated the Burgundians at Grandson and Morat in 1476. The duke's 'rash fierce blaze of riot' was at an end. Even Lorraine slipped out of his grasp. In a desperate attempt to retrieve the situation, Charles laid siege to Nancy, the capital of the disputed province. On 5 January 1477, encouraged by the arrival of a Swiss relief force the defenders made a sortie in which the Burgundians were routed and the duke killed.

The corpse of Charles the Rash was found later in a frozen pond, stripped of its armour and half-eaten by wolves. The remains were unrecognisable except for the long fingernails known to have been affected by the duke. The new Burgundian 'kingdom' vanished even more quickly and completely than its predecessor 900 years earlier. Charles's sole heir was his 19-year-old daughter Mary. The 'universal spider', Louis XI, could not believe his good fortune; invoking the Salic Law (by which women could not inherit), he seized as much of the Burgundian possessions as his armies could occupy. The duchy, Franche-Comté, Artois and Picardy all fell into his web. Mary hastily revived the plan for her marriage to Maximilian of Habsburg, who helped her retain Flanders and most of her non-French domains. He even recovered Artois and Franche-Comté from Louis' successor, Charles VIII. The duchy of Burgundy, however, reverted permanently to the French crown, and its history thereafter is that of France.

After some initial hestitation, and despite an outbreak in 1630 when the cry of *'Vive l'Empereur!'* was heard in Dijon, the province was content with the privileges granted it by Louis XI in return for its submission. Apart from the usual grumbles about taxation, the Burgundians were satisfied with their lot under the French crown, and there was no genuine separatist sentiment. During the dreadful winter of 1709, when the mob at Dijon cried, 'Let us do to our king what the English did to theirs!', they were only voicing the whole nation's feelings. Today, particularism is limited to a faint nostalgia for Burgundy's last days as the centre of the European stage. The unfading popularity of the Valois dukes is a striking tribute to their success in creating their own legend. Every year, on the Sunday nearest St Andrew's Day (30 November), a special mass is celebrated in Dijon Cathedral; and the four dukes even feature incongruously in Dijon's Christmas illuminations.

By comparison with the age of the Valois dukes, the five centuries that have elapsed since the death of Charles the Rash seem uneventful. They are dominated not by the feudal nobility, but by the middle class of merchants and lawyers who built the many fine town houses in Dijon. In particular, the officers of the Parlement or High Court of Dijon came to form a new aristocracy which not only patronised the arts and sciences, but even produced its own saint— St Jeanne de Chantal, foundress of the Order of the Visitation. Burgundy's religious vocation was also maintained by St Marguerite-Marie Alacoque, who initiated the cult of the Sacred Heart (St Madeleine-Sophie Barat, foundress of the Sacred Heart convent schools, was also born in Burgundy, at Joigny).

Before the Revolution of 1789, the only national convulsion to shake the province was the Wars of Religion. From the massacre of Vassy in 1562 till the Edict of Nantes in 1598, the conflict between Catholic and Huguenot was exploited by nobles who resented the growth of royal power. Burgundy was never a particular stronghold of the Reformed faith, but many of its churches were devastated by Calvinist iconoclasts. The leadership of the *Fronde*, a rebellion against the government of Cardinal Mazarin, was assumed in 1650 by the Prince of Condé, governor of Burgundy. However, the *Fronde* developed into an aristocratic movement which quickly exhausted the enthusiasm of the common people, and there was hardly any fighting in the province.

During the revolutionary years 1789-93, Burgundy was spared the worst excesses of terror and counter-terror, but suffered no less than the rest of France from other futile gestures. A childish obsession with 'the symbols of tyranny' led to deliberate campaigns of public vandalism. Religious communities were suppressed, and monastery buildings were sold off to speculators who generally demolished them for the value of the stone. Cluny was the most notable and heart-breaking casualty.

A more constructive act of the Revolution was to reform the administration by dividing France into 90 *départements* named after rivers or other purely geographical features. Anxious to eliminate every last trace of the Ancien Régime, the government thus abolished even the names of the old provinces. As well as its States and Parlement, Burgundy lost its identity. However, a more extreme proposal, that the new departments should be created by laying a grid over a map of France, was not adopted. In many cases, the outer boundaries of groups of departments corresponded with the *ci-devant* provincial frontiers, though this was only partially true of Burgundy. In 1960 General de Gaulle grouped the departments into regions for the purposes of more efficient economic planning.

One of these groups consisted of the departments of Côte d'Or, Saône-et-Loire, Yonne and Nièvre, and in 1964 the name of 'Burgundy' was revived for it. The Prefect of Côte d'Or, residing at Dijon, has overall responsibility for the whole region.

This book's Burgundy does not coincide exactly with any of the historical Burgundies—neither that of the Burgundiones, nor of the Capetian dukes, nor of the Valois, nor of the Ancien Régime, nor of modern French planners. Instead, we have adopted the policy of the courts that formulated the *appellation contrôlée* wine laws in the 1930s: to have regard to 'honest and established local usage'. The application of this principle deprives us of most of Nièvre, which is officially included in modern Burgundy. Only the Morvan, in the east of the department, satisfies our requirements. The rest belongs really to the Loire country, as does its one notable wine, Pouilly-Fumé. The department of Yonne is a ragbag thrown together in 1790 from snippets of Burgundy and several other Ancien Régime provinces. It had been incorporated entirely in the kingdom of the Burgundiones, though until 1964 only the sentiment of the people and 'honest and established local usage' kept it in Burgundy. A fifteenth-century edict refers to all wine produced above Sens bridge as burgundy, while more recently Colette, who was born in Puisaye in west Yonne, was proud to describe herself as *Basse-Bourguignonne*. Côte d'Or and Saône-et-Loire are not in question, as they have been the nucleus of every Burgundy since the 5th century.

We have only deviated from our rule twice. In the case of Bresse, we have included the southern part because the northern part is in Burgundy and the boundary is artificial. In any case, Bourg-en-Bresse was irresistible. The reasons for our inclusion of the Beaujolais are vinous, and are explained in the appropriate chapter.

2 Wine

*O Burgundy, happy for your name
alone, and surely worthy as well,
as one who may claim to be called
Mother of Mankind because she has
such milk in her breasts!*

Desiderius Erasmus

However one argues for Burgundy as an historical entity, for most foreigners and even many Frenchmen its name means wine. A few remarks about the vine, its history and its cultivation in Burgundy might not be out of place here, since wherever the traveller begins his tour of the province, he will need to know some basic facts about its wine.

Nobody knows when the first vine was planted in Burgundy. All we can be sure of is that burgundy has a far longer continuous history than its great rival bordeaux. One long-established theory is that Greek traders from Massilia (Marseille), who for many years imported the finished product from the Aegean in amphorae, were eventually persuaded to bring plant cuttings. Another suggestion is that the vine arrived with the Roman conquest, some time after 52 B.C. Reliable texts are infuriatingly scarce. The monk Gregory of Tours, writing in the 6th century, tells us that the people of Beaune made a wine which they preferred to the finest vintages of Ascalon in Palestine (the Château Lafite-Rothschild of its time). Long before, the rhetorician Eumenes of Augustodunum (Autun), in a panegyric addressed to Constantine in 312, had spoken of vinestocks 'whose age we do not know'. Columella, writing in the middle of the 1st century, mentions that in Gaul the vine was grown in nearly all regions, and that every district possessed varieties peculiar to it. If Columella is not exaggerating, it is difficult to see how the Gauls could have developed a range of different varieties in only 100 years, the life-span of two vine plants.

M. Pierre Forgeot sets aside both these hypotheses and argues that the Gauls themselves, who invented the wooden barrel to replace the fragile amphora, were perfectly capable of introducing the vine to

The *Pays* of Burgundy

their own land. Round about 400 B.C. the Gauls were crossing the Alps in force, among them the Aedui, within whose territory lay the Côte de Beaune. They sacked Rome, destroyed the Etruscan empire, and settled in the Po valley, known to the Romans thereafter as Cisalpine Gaul. Large vineyards already existed there, and the Gauls must have learnt all the techniques of viticulture—propagation, pruning and grafting—that had been known to the Mediterranean world for centuries. There is evidence of a reflux movement of Gauls as the Romans expanded northwards in the 3rd century B.C. M. Forgeot's tentative conclusion, drawn from circumstantial rather than documentary evidence, is that the returning Aedui had established the vine in the neighbourhood of Beaune by 150 B.C. Why does Caesar not mention the fact? Probably because vines were not grown on a commercial scale, but were reserved for the private requirements of Gallic notables. Eumenes' remarks prove, however, that commercial production was well established by the middle of the 3rd century.

With the end of the Dark Ages and the beginning of that of the great monasteries, we leave the realm of conjecture behind. The story has already been told of how the monks took the lead in repairing the ravages of the invasions, of how they cleared the land and put agriculture on an organised basis. The vine has always been one of the most profitable cash crops, and was bound to find favour with shrewd estate managers. It was also, in its own right, one of the most acceptable of all gifts to princes and church dignitaries. The Cluniacs extended the vineyards of the Mâconnais during the 10th and eleventh centuries, while the Cistercians of Pontigny did the same for Chablis in the twelfth. Both congregations had considerable holdings along the Côte d'Or, along with the abbeys of Bèze, Tart, Saulieu and Saint-Vivant, and the cathedral chapters of Langres and Autun.

By the end of the reign of Philip Augustus (1223), the vineyards of Beaune were reputed to produce the finest red wine in France. The transfer of the Papal court to Avignon in 1309 gave another boost to the sales and prestige of burgundy, since the rivers Saône and Rhône gave easy access to this vital international centre. Later on, Petrarch was to accuse the wines of Burgundy of causing the cardinals to prolong the 'Babylonian Captivity' when a return to Rome had become feasible.

It was the wine not only of popes but of kings. On several occasions it graced the coronation feasts at Rheims. The Valois dukes, with their unerring flair for publicity, played the advantage for all it was worth and styled themselves 'lords of the finest wines in

Christendom', and took practical steps to ensure that the product lived up to the claims made for it. Their control of the Low Countries created a rich and densely populated captive market for the wines of the duchy, and established a tradition that survives today. The Belgians are ahead of everyone except the Swiss and the French themselves in their per capita consumption of burgundy.

The growth of the wine trade was checked by the return of the Papacy to Rome and the dismemberment of the Burgundian state after the death of Charles the Rash. Business boomed again under Louis XIV, traditionally as a result of the operation for fistula which the king underwent in 1680. The royal physician Fagon prescribed the wines of Nuits and Vosne to restore his patient's strength, and so brought burgundy back into vogue at court. No doubt weightier factors came into play, such as the expulsion of the Huguenots in 1685; the refugees created foreign demand in the countries where they settled. The first firms of merchants established themselves at Beaune and Nuits at the beginning of the eighteenth century, and looked immediately to the Netherlands and northern France for new markets.

The Revolution ended the domination of the nobility and the religious orders over the vineyard. Their lands were confiscated and auctioned off. The properties generally fell into the hands of operators who broke them up into small lots for resale. At the same time the law of primogeniture was rescinded, with the result that the eldest son had to share his father's estate with his younger brothers. These factors produced the fragmentation which is such a feature of the Burgundy vineyard today. In any one field of vines, the individual proprietor usually owns no more than a few rows. For example, the 150-odd acres of the Clos de Vougeot are divided between no fewer than 65 separate proprietors; the 67 acres of the Chambertin between 25 owners, and the 15.5 acres of the Montrachet between 12. The average size of property for the Côte d'Or, which grows the best wines, works out at 1.5 acres per proprietor.

This situation is completely different from that in Bordeaux, where all the most famous vineyards remain grouped round the château where their wines are made and bottled, the whole estate being in the hands of a single proprietor. The predominantly *parlementaire* landlords of Bordeaux largely escaped expropriation during the Revolution, and in any case their creation of vast centralised vineyard properties was peculiar to the Bordelais. The Burgundian system has the disadvantage that no single person is responsible for maintaining the reputation of a great name like Chambertin or Musigny. But for anyone fortunate enough to live in the area, there is the pleasure of hunting for bargains and comparing the almost infinite variety of wines available; every grower produces a wine slightly different from his neighbours', even from the same plot of land. This pursuit is the excuse for the ritual *descente de cave,* which any *vigneron* who bottles his own wine (as most now do, at least a part of it) is only too pleased to arrange for the prospective buyer. In the cool depths of the cellar, in an atmosphere heavy with the smell of fermenting wine, the *vigneron* knocks the bung from the top of a cask and reaches inside with his *pipette* or *chanfleure,* a large glass tube which uses the vacuum principle (operated by closing or opening the upper end of the tube with the thumb) to draw, retain or release liquid. A generous sample is emptied from the pipette into the visitor's glass or *tastevin.* The latter, the traditional instrument for this activity, is a small, shallow, silver or silver-plated cup used originally by medieval merchants for tasting wine as they toured the Côte. Its shape and robustness made it easily portable, while the bosses and ridges on the inner surface captured and reflected the maximum amount of light in candle-lit cellars.

There will almost certainly by several different wines to sample, as the fragmentation of the vineyard means that a *vigneron*'s property is scattered over a wide area, quite often outside his home village. The talk is of the differing characteristics of each wine, the merits of past vintages (the classic 1947, produced with difficulty in an unseasonably hot autumn, or the disastrous 1968, which oxydised even as they ran it out of the vats), and the prospects for the next. Last of all come the wines already in bottle, and perhaps, for a very honoured guest, something from the *vigneron's* own private reserve.

Wine-growing in Burgundy is still very much a family affair, and business is done almost entirely by personal contact. It is as well to know someone, or at least to know someone who knows someone, to gain the entrée. Otherwise, the tourist's best policy is to spend a little time in one of the villages, have a good meal, strike up a conversation with the *patron* of the restaurant, and introduce the subject of wine. The hard sell has scarcely touched this corner of the world—the *dégustation* is the *vigneron's* courtesy.

The vine is vulnerable to many pests and diseases, condemning the *vigneron* to constant watchfulness; but special mention should be made of the phylloxera, because of the shattering and lasting effect it has had on viticulture. The sap-sucking aphid known as *phylloxera vastatrix* (the devastator) is a visitor from America, probably imported in a consignment of fruit landed at Marseille. Its feeding causes nodules to form on the roots of young vines, which then die.

It made its first appearance in the department of Gard in 1863, and reached the Beaujolais in 1874. By 1878 it was at Meursault, and within a few years the entire Burgundy vineyard was in danger of being wiped out. American vines, however, are resistant to the insect's bites, and this fact suggested the possibility of grafting French vines on to American roots. This was the solution adopted generally when the prejudices of purists had been overcome, though some of the more exalted *crus* maintained costly chemical treatments well into this century. Today, all French vines are grafted.

Three major factors contribute towards the individuality of a natural wine: climate, soil and *cépage* or variety of grape. There are only four principal *cépages* grown in Burgundy, two each for red and white, two 'noble' and two 'semi-fine'.

The *pinot noir* produces all the fine red wines of the Côte d'Or, and is the rock on which Burgundy's reputation is founded. Its history goes back at least to the Roman era. In a letter dated 1 February 1523, Erasmus reported discovering the burgundy which became his lifelong favourite drink: 'Its bouquet was neither cloying nor harsh, but mild; neither chilly nor fiery, but moist and innocuous. By all this, so gentle to the stomach that even greater quantities did no harm'. These are precisely the qualities of a mature pinot noir wine. Finesse is the mark of true burgundy; its reputation for being 'big and booty' comes from Commonwealth burgundies grown in hotter climates, and, regrettably, the past habit of some shippers of 'reinforcing' their burgundy to suit a supposed 'English taste'. There should be no question of 'I like burgundy, but burgundy doesn't like me'.

The pinot's junior partner is the *gamay*. It takes its name from a hamlet in the hills behind Meursault, but the legend runs that it was brought back from the Middle East by a knight returning from the Second Crusade. It became extremely popular among growers in the mid-fourteenth century; some say because it suffered less than the pinot from the neglect due to the ravages of the Black Death, others, that the *maladie noire* referred to in old texts was not the plague but a vine blight to which the gamay alone was resistant. But it was a highly productive variety, with a yield three times that of the pinot, and consequently inferior in quality. Get-rich-quick *vignerons* turned over land which was suitable for the pinot to the gamay, with the result that in 1395 Philip the Bold had to issue an edict ordering the extirpation of the *'très mauvais et très déloyaul plant, nommé gaamez'*. According to P. Morton Shand, the objectionable plant was not the *gamay noir à jus blanc* in general use today, but the *gros gamay* or *gamay teinturier*, which does indeed give a dark, coarse wine.

Whatever the truth of that, the edict seems not to have had any lasting success, since the prohibition had to be renewed by Philip the Good, and again by Charles VIII, Charles IX, Louis XIII and Louis XV. Only the phylloxera crisis brought the pinot back into preponderance, as by the time the vineyards were replanted, quality had become a more paying proposition than quantity. On the other hand, whereas the gamay produces an unremarkable or even disappointing wine on the limestone soil of the Côte d'Or, on the granite soils of the Beaujolais, where the pinot does not flourish, it produces the light, fruity wine that we associate with the name of the region.

In the Côte d'Or, a recognised practice is to ferment pinot and gamay grapes together in the proportion of a third to two thirds respectively, the resulting wine being known as *Bourgogne Passetout-grains*. As restaurants generally mark wine up 100%, putting pinot wines beyond the reach of most pockets for everyday drinking, a passetoutgrains is excellent value as a table wine, and can be recommended to travellers who are tired of ordering beaujolais simply because it is the only name they know.

The noble plant for white wine is the *chardonnay*, which takes its name from a village in the Mâconnais. It is often called, even by the *vignerons* themselves, though inexactly, the *pinot blanc* (a related but distinct species now extremely rare in Burgundy). In Chablis, the chardonnay is known as the *beaunois*. It can fairly claim to produce the finest white wines in the world—dry, and with a taste of what the French call 'gunflint'. It is the ideal wine for all seafood. As the chardonnay (along with the pinot noir, lightly pressed so as not to release the colouring matter in the skin) is also the plant which produces champagne, it holds the palm for sparkling as well as for still wine.

The white counterpart of the gamay is the *aligoté*, a high-yield plant grown on soils unsuitable for the chardonnay. Wines produced from it are not allowed to call themselves anything more specific than *Bourgogne Aligoté*. It is an obvious choice for the cost-conscious diner (what a pity that aligoté and passetoutgrains are never seen on English wine-lists!). A good aligoté can possess character, but should invariably be drunk young.

The next determining factor is the soil. The vine prefers stony, well-drained soils which warm easily. The soils of Chablis, the Côte d'Or, the Côte Chalonnaise and most of the Mâconnais are composed of limestone, silica and marl, while the Beaujolais is a territory of schists and granite. The actual proportions of limestone, clay, silica, ferrous oxide and trace elements vary at every step, and it is this which creates the individuality of each *cru* or growth. This is why, for the very best wines, the actual vineyard in which they are grown is of such importance. In Bordeaux the best wines are identified by their château names, because each château produces a wine of homogeneous quality from the ensemble of soils within its boundaries (also, a mixture of grape varieties is employed). In Burgundy, the very best are identified only by the name of the field in which they are grown, known confusingly as the *climat*. These are the *grands crus*, and their labels bear only the word e.g. 'Chambertin', 'Musigny', 'Romanée-Conti', 'Montrachet', followed by the words *appellation contrôlée*. Wines from less favoured ground are known simply by the name of the village where they are harvested, e.g. 'Volnay', 'Pommard'. If a village wine comes from a single vineyard, the name of the vineyard may be inserted after the name of the village; in the case of a *premier cru* (one step below the *grands crus*), the vineyard name may be printed in the same size letters as the village name, and sometimes the words *'Premier Cru'* are added.

So far, so simple. The complication is that all the Côte d'Or villages which possess a *grand cru* have, over the last 150 years, added its name to their own. Gevrey has become Gevrey-Chambertin, Morey, Morey-Saint-Denis, Chambolle, Chambolle-Musigny etc. It would be easy to say that any hyphenated name indicated a village wine, hence a wine of lesser quality. However, the villages of Gevrey and Aloxe are awkward exceptions. In Gevrey, the *grand cru* vineyards of Charmes, Mazoyères, Mazis, Griotte, Chapelle, Ruchottes and Latricières have all suffixed 'Chambertin' to their own names. This usage is quite legitimate, since they all border on the Chambertin or the Clos de Bèze and, at their best, are only slightly inferior to them. Aloxe has the only red *grand cru* of the Côte de Beaune, the Corton. The village has rechristened itself Aloxe-Corton, which is thus the name of its village wine. But the vineyards surrounding the Corton, which produce wine no whit inferior, have hyphenated their own names with that of Corton, thus: Corton-Clos du Roi, -Perrières, -Bressandes, -Renardes, Languettes, -Pougets, -Vigne au Saint. Corton-Charlemagne is likewise an exception, being one of the five white *grands crus* of the Côte d'Or (the others are the Montrachet and the adjoining *climats*). Unless the wine-drinker can familiarise himself with all these names, his only hope is to learn the above exceptions by heart, plus the, original names of all the hyphenated villages between Fixin and Santenay. One last note: Ladoix-Serrigny and Prémeaux-Prissey are the names of communes each formed by the amalgamation of two villages. Neither sells wine under its own name, though plain 'Ladoix' is ocassionally found.

Côte de Nuits-Villages comes from those villages of the Côte de Nuits which do not have the right to their own appellation (the exception is Fixin, which does sell some wine under its own name). *Côte de Beaune,* without other qualification, comes from the immediate environs of Beaune. However, many lesser-known villages of the region may add the name to their own by way of clearer identification, e.g. *Saint-Aubin-Côte de Beaune. Côte de Beaune-Villages* is simply a 'declassification' at the disposal of any village of the Côte de Beaune except Beaune itself, Pommard, Volnay and Aloxe-Corton.

Chablis and *Mâcon* are regional appellations, and are thus much less specific than the village names of the Côte d'Or and the Côte Chalonnaise. The system of Beaujolais appellations runs to a slightly different pattern, and is explained in the last chapter. At the bottom of the heap, but by no means necessarily to be despised, is the catch-all appellation *Bourgogne,* which can be applied to all pinot noir and chardonnay wines grown in Burgundy, and to a few gamay wines from the Beaujolais.

If a wine is blended, its appellation must be reduced to the appropriate classification. For example, a blend of Savigny and Pernand becomes *Côte de Beaune-Villages;* but a blend of Pommard and Volnay would become only *Bourgogne,* as would a blend of Gevrey and Vosne; a blend of Chambertin and Charmes-Chambertin would, however, become *Gevrey-Chambertin.* Sometimes a *vigneron* may be forced to declassify simply because he has exceeded his production quota for a particular appellation—and here some bargains are to be had if the source is trustworthy.

The climate (and not the *climat*) creates the variations between diffferent vintages or *millésimes.* Burgundy is the northernmost of great red wines, grown in a climate which is continental rather than Mediterranean; the most critical moments are in April and May, when the sap has begun to rise and late frosts can wreak havoc; in early June, when the vine is in bloom and when rain can wash the pollen off the flower, causing the berries to develop imperfectly (*millerandage*) or even to abort (*coulure*); in August, when insufficient rainfall can affect the balance of acid and sugar and produce too hard a wine; and in September, when heavy rain during the vintage can wash the yeasts off the grape-skins, or worse, cause the grape to rot on the vine. A constant danger throughout the summer is that of hail-bearing thunderstorms, which can ruin an entire year's work in minutes. Today this risk is minimised by modern weather-reporting, which enables light aircraft on standby at Beaune aerodrome to take off and 'treat' thunder-clouds with chemicals to prevent the formation of hailstones.

In the last event all natural advantages are vain without the skill and guiding hand of the *vigneron*. Wits have declared that the *vigneron* weeps only three times a year: in spring when the frost has struck, in summer when everything is parched, and in autumn when he hasn't room enough to store the vintage. In fact, the *vigneron*'s year is a cycle of constant labour and vigilance, with two brief respites: in mid-winter, when the ground is too hard to work, and the last few weeks before the vintage, while the grapes are ripening. Apart from the obvious ploughing, hoeing, manuring and chemical treatments, there are the delicate tasks of pruning and tying up to the supporting wires. In the old days, the right date for picking was fixed by rule of thumb, and the declaration of the *ban de vendange* was the privilege of the lord of the manor. Today the ratio of sugar to acid can be measured scientifically, and the vintage begins when the sugar content of the grape has reached its maximum. Even so, local variations are such that, in the last resort, the individual *vigneron*'s decision must be based on his own experience and flair.

When the grapes have been picked and brought back to the vat-house or *cuverie*, red and white grapes follow different careers. The white are set immediately under the press, stalks and all (to prevent the pulp from turning into a jelly from which the liquid could not escape), and the juice is run off into barrels three-quarters full, in which all stages of the fermentation take place. The yeasts which ferment the wine are natural, and grow on the skins of the grapes during the last few weeks of ripening. A certain amount of humidity, though not torrential rain, is thus essential during that period. It is the breaking of the skins, by pressing in the case of white wine or by *foulage* in the case of red, that brings the yeasts into contact with the sugar-charged liquid and begins the breakdown of sugar into alcohol and carbon dioxide.

Red grapes have their own special treatment. After *foulage* (splitting of skins) and usually *égrappage* (removal of stalks), both of which processes are now performed by machines, the grapes are emptied into enormous open vats. The juice is always white, and acquires its colour only from maceration with the skins. In a few days, the vat becomes a foaming cauldron; the fermenting must, released from the grapes, sinks to the bottom while the less dense *marc* (pulp and skins) and stalks, if any, float on top—hence the term *cuvaison à chapeau flottant*. Periodically, liquid is drawn off at the bottom and poured over the floating *marc*, to get as much colour as possible and to aerate the must. When the first or alcoholic fermentation has died down, the wine is run into barrels to undergo the secondary or malolactic fermentation, during which the acid content of the wine is gradually transformed into those elements which contribute to the subtleties of flavour and render the wine drinkable.

The nature of the finished wine depends a great deal on the length of the vatting. Until the end of the eighteenth century, wine was generally drunk up in the year after the vintage. Glass was a rare luxury, and 'laying down' cellars unheard of. Wine was stored in barrels and drawn off into stone or leather flagons as required. The earliest glass bottles reflect this by imitating the pot-bellied, long-necked shape of their predecessors. For a wine to be ready for drinking as soon as this, it had to be vatted for a very short time or not at all (as seems to have been the case in the Middle Ages, when all the necessary colour would have been extracted by pressing). In the eighteenth century, the pinot was generally vatted for about ten to 15 hours in years when the grapes were well ripened. This system produced wines not much darker than what we should call rosé. They were fragrant, mellow and clean-tasting, but apt to turn acid if kept too long. In the exceptional year of 1795, this method produced dark, full-bodied wines which won instant popularity. Ever eager to please, the *vignerons* organised themselves to produce wine of this character every year. About this time, burgundy and bordeaux bottles assumed their definitive shapes, suitable for cellar storage (since the wine was now no longer drinkable during its first year). The first great vintage to be laid down generally was the famous 'Comet Wine' of 1811.

By the middle of the last century, the vatting lasted anything up to 20 days, and *égrappage* was only practised by the best *vignerons* when the vintage was not perfectly ripe. This wine was hard, tannic (the tannin came from the skins, stalks and pips), and indeed so astringent as to be undrinkable for the first ten years of its life. But it was the tannin that enabled it to live for 30 years or more. Nowadays, constantly increasing demand has encouraged the *vigneron* to produce a supple wine which will be drinkable in three or four years. This he does by practising *égrappage* systematically, and by vatting for four to six days, depending on the ripeness of the vintage. These wines evolve more rapidly, but 'he who spurs betimes, tires betimes'. Wines which are quick to mature are quick to decline. Too much must not be expected of them. By practising long vattings (up to 12 days) and avoiding *égrappage* in good years, a few stalwarts still produce the kind of burgundy our grandfathers drank; but they have to be sought out, as their wines are not generally acceptable to the merchants in their unblended form.

After the alcoholic fermentation, the free liquid (*vin de goutte*) is the first drawn off into tuns where it is mixed with the *vin de presse*, obtained by lightly pressing the *marc* which is still saturated with wine. For the malolactic fermentation and subsequent fining and racking, the wine is then transferred to barrels or *pièces* of 228 litres in the Côte d'Or or 215 litres in the Mâconnais and Beaujolais. The wine is ready for bottling during its second or third year. Aging in bottle occurs with both white and red wines, but is more noticeable in the latter. Despite all our knowledge and all the equipment at our disposal, no-one has succeeded in analysing or imitating this phenomenon. It remains mysterious, inspiring comparisons with the ages of man. 'Wine is a sea of organisms,' said Pasteur, 'by some it lives, by others it dies.'

Nothing is wasted. The *marc* (pronounced 'mar') is put into sacks, taken to an authorised distiller, and turned into a spirit also known as *marc*, the traditional brandy of Burgundy. One of the sights of the Côte in October is the great mobile still that travels from village to village. Constructed in 1870, it has been repaired piecemeal so often that hardly any of the original parts remain. *Fine* is the name given to brandy produced like cognac by distilling wine (rather than *marc*). The *vignerons* also have their own apéritif called *ratafia*, made of two-thirds *verjus* (unfermented grape juice) stabilised by one-third *marc*.

3 Cuisine

The Renaissance chronicler Paladin noted that 'the Burgundians dress most modestly, and with little show, and yet their bellies are said to be "lined with velvet" because of their good food'. A local proverb runs 'Better a good meal than fine clothes', and in the fifteenth and sixteenth centuries the Burgundians were reputed the best trenchermen in France. But descriptions of Burgundy as a 'gastronomic paradise' are apt to leave us looking for the wrong thing. Simplicity and naturalness are the watchwords. 'Cooking,' said Curnonsky, 'is when things taste of what they are.' And the greatest of all Lyonnais cooks, La Mère Fillioux, declared, 'I only do five dishes, but I think I do them well.' If we keep those statements in mind, we shall understand Elizabeth David when she says of Burgundian dishes that they represent the most sumptuous kind of country cooking brought to a point of finesse beyond which it would lose its character. The French at home do not 'mess their food about'. They simply present it better, give it more thought, and have an eye for variety. The plainest French dinner will consist of hors d'oeuvre, meat, vegetables, cheese and dessert or fruit; the French spend a greater proportion of their income on food than the English. Why is this?

Whereas the revolutions of the seventeenth century condemned the peasant to extinction in England, the Revolution of 1789 guaranteed his survival on the other side of the Channel. The smallholder and the 'peasant mentality' still exist in rural France. 15% of the population are on the land—five times as many as in England—often operating in ways which would be the despair of an accountant. Outside Dijon, 25% of all Burgundians are engaged in agriculture. Things are changing now; rural depopulation is causing concern, and the co-operative idea is gaining ground. But France has resisted the temptation to rationalise eating more successfully than any other advanced country, and the special relationship of the Frenchman with his table is bearing up well against the pressures of modern life.

What has been preserved above all is the variety of foodstuffs, of which the 300 different cheeses are just the most famous instance.

True country cooking is solidly based on local ingredients with centuries of tradition behind their production and preparation, and this is where the best Burgundian cooking excels. It is, according to Elizabeth David again, 'meat and poultry, game and fish in copious helpings served on fine large dishes and surrounded by the wine-dark sauces which look so effortless, and in practice are so difficult to get precisely right.'

The beef comes from the Charollais cattle, first raised in the corner of southern Burgundy from which they take their name Their white hides are a distinctive feature of the Burgundian countryside. Poultry is a speciality of Bresse. At Louhans there is a *Confrérie des Poulardiers de Bresse,* to become a member of which aspirants must bite deep into a drumstick and swear never to eat any other poultry than that of Bresse. The typical Bressan dish is chicken in a sauce of cream and white wine, with or without morels.

The two great Burgundian wine-sauce dishes, *coq au vin* and *boeuf bourguignon,* need no introduction. Unfortunately, the temptation for restaurants to cut corners is almost irresistible even in France, and it is these two dishes, the province's culinary standard-bearers, which cause the most disappointments. Firstly, there is a tendency to think that stewing meat need not be of the best quality. Secondly, correct preparation is a long business which involves marinating overnight and very slow simmering. Without a guaranteed sale, this represents a risky investment in time, space and materials. The result is that the meat is sometimes tough or, one occasionally suspects, boiled and then covered with the sauce. The sauce itself is frequently too thick and rich. A winey taste is actually a bad sign. It means that the wine has not been cooked long enough with the meat, as the aim is to obtain a fusion of their respective flavours in a new one. It is worthwhile going to a restaurant which has a reputation to protect, or seeking out a little family restaurant where the *patronne* tells *you* what you're going to eat.

Dairying is less important for Burgundy than stock-rearing, so there are few varieties of local cheese. Only Epoisses is in the same league as Brie and Camembert, though Bleu de Bresse is a nationally popular blue cheese, and Cîteaux and Saint-Florentin are worth trying when they make one of their rare appearances on a cheese-board. Chaource and Soumaintrain are much more common, but strictly speaking they come from just the wrong side of the border with Champagne. Chaource is a creamy cheese with a taste reminiscent of white Cheshire. Soumaintrain has affinities with the pungent Petit Munster of Alsace. Traditional links provide Franche-Comté with a ready market for its excellent Gruyère de

Comté (true Gruyère, however, is a Swiss cheese) and Vacherin Mont d'Or (not to be confused with the Lyonnais Mont d'Or). Perhaps better than any of Burgundy's cow cheeses are the miniature goat cheeses of the Morvan and the Mâconnais.

The pig has an honoured place in the history of Burgundian cuisine. In the thick oak forests of the Saône valley, graziers once bought pasturage rights and drove their swine down every autumn from the Morvan (or even from as far afield as Lorraine) to consume the acorns where they lay. The Morvan is still noted for pig-rearing, for its mild cured hams (*jambon cru*), its *saupiquet,* and its *jambon à la crème.* Formerly, the custom among the thrifty *vignerons* of the Côte was for a family or group of families to buy a piglet every year and rear it. When it was slaughtered, it became a miniature food factory. The flesh was salted and spiced (cubes of salt pork, or *lardons,* are still a recognised sign of a Burgundian dish), the intestines transformed into sausages (as was also the blood, the *boudin noir*), and the offal consumed fresh. *Andouillettes* are still a staple food in eastern France, though the *potée bourguignonne,* a stew of cabbages, leeks, potatoes and salt pork, is rarely seen in restaurants today. Whole sucking pig in its jelly is another rarity, usually only served, for obvious reasons, by special arrangement. On the other hand, the Burgundian ham galantine known as *jambon persillé* can be found anywhere in the province. For this, a whole uncooked ham is simmered with pig's trotters and white wine, then crushed with a fork to mix the fat with the lean. Successive layers of ham and chopped parsley (hence *persillé*) are arranged in a salad-bowl, and the jelly is poured over them and left to set.

The most common game dish is *civet de lièvre* (jugged hare, stewed in red wine mixed with the hare's own pounded liver), though the most sumptuous is certainly saddle of hare *à la Piron,* named after the Dijonnais satirist and *bon vivant* of the age of Louis XIV. After marinating in *marc,* shallots, celery, bay, thyme and pepper, the saddle is cooked first without and then with its marinade, and finally served with cream. The fortunate few who pass through Burgundy in the winter may be treated to venison and even wild boar, which can still be found in the forests around Châtillon.

Fish abound in the river Saône, and fishmongers stock plenty of coarse fish (carp, tench, perch and pike) in season. However, these rarely come in the same handy individual size as hatchery trout, nor in the same predictable quantities. This is a pity, because there are some fine traditional recipies for them, like tench *au bleu,* stuffed carp, carp *en meurette* (red wine sauce), and the celebrate *pochouse.* Freshwater crayfish, from the mountain streams of the Morvan and the Beaujolais, are a surprisingly frequent delicacy. They are served either in the form of a *gratinée* of their tails, or *à la nage* (in *court-bouillon*).

The snail is as much an emblem of Burgundy as vine-leaves and bunches of grapes. Prehistoric hunters and gatherers probably eked out their diet with snails, though Pliny informs us that the Romans had a low opinion of them. The invasion of Gaul presumably helped to change this attitude, for soon afterwards one Fulvius Hirpinus had the idea of keeping snails alive in special reserves after capture. Several years ago, a blue ceramic plate was unearthed at Sens together with a large number of snail-shells, and dated to the 3rd century—the earliest physical evidence of Burgundy's long asssociation with the snail. In the Middle Ages every monastery had its snail park, and carvings of the time portray the snail as often as the labours of the vine. Indeed, the two went together; the snails that swarmed in the vineyards were the most highly prized of all. Today, the *escargot des vignes* has fallen victim to the chemicals used to treat the vines, and demand is so great that most snails are reared in batteries or imported from eastern Europe to meet the requirements of the canneries.

On a wet day in spring or summer Burgundians still comb the hedgerows in search of the yellowish, dark-banded shells of *helix pomatica*. Anyone tempted to follow their example should remember that it is vital to 'park' the snails for several days, feeding them only lettuce, thyme and water. This is to allow them to rid their digestive systems of herbs that might cause food poisoning. Then they have to be boiled to detach them from their shells, and cooked in a *court-bouillon* of white wine. When ready, they are replaced in their shells between two packings of stuffing. The Burgundian stuffing, consisting of garlic butter, shallots and parsley, is probably the best-known of all. It is supposed to have been invented about 1750 by an innkeeper of Bassou, on the Yonne between Auxerre and Joigny, and popularised by the stagecoach travellers who patronised his posting-house. In fact, the recipe is almost certainly traditional. The snails are finally put in the oven, and served when the butter is sizzling.

4 Dijon

Two and a half hours out of the Gare de Lyon, on emerging from a three-mile-long tunnel, the traveller by rail has his first indication of the approach of Dijon. The train descends through cuttings and over viaducts into the valley of the Ouche, skirts Lake Kir (across whose waters the high-rise blocks of Fontaine d'Ouche brashly advertise the new Dijon), and draws to a halt at the platforms of Dijon-Ville.

The railway has a special importance for the town. Without it Dijon would have become a backwater, instead of the thriving city of nearly a quarter of a million inhabitants that it is today. Dijon is an embarrassment to determinists: there is simply no compelling economic or geographical reason why the province should have its capital there. Admittedly, the town commands the gap through which the Ouche flows out on to the plain of the Saône—but the valley's north-east/south-west orientation cuts diagonally across the natural line of communications. Hopeful local historians have spoken of the tin-route and the Roman road from Lyon to Trier; but the tin traders almost certainly crossed the watershed between the Seine and Saône basins by way of the hilltops well to the west of the town (this route avoids the forests and marshes of the valleys, and was in use right up until the end of the Middle Ages), while the Romans marched to the Rhineland along the ridge to the east.

The name *Divio* does not occur until the 6th century, but all the indications are that at the time of the Roman Empire's first difficulties, 300 years earlier, the inhabitants of several scattered hamlets joined forces and withdrew to the most easily defensible site. It was the existence of this fortified position and the concentration of the local population that created the 'crossroads', and not vice versa.

The next turning-point was the strategic withdrawal to Dijon of the bishops of Langres in the 5th century. One of these refugee bishops capitalised on the discovery of the supposed relics of St Benignus, the legendary evangeliser of Burgundy, and founded a basilica served by a community of monks. This monastery was to become a centre of the cultural revival that followed the end of the great invasions. Duke Robert I made Dijon his capital in 1032, but his reasons seem to have been purely political. Eager to take issue with the church over jurisdiction and privileges, the duke must have wanted to be well outside the orbit of his chief ecclesiastical rival, the bishop of Autun. Dijon was the only sizable town that he could call his own (the bishops of Langres had long since returned to their see). Yet neither Robert nor his successors made any attempt to create in Dijon itself a background worthy of a ducal court, preferring their nearby castles at Rouvres or Talant. What made Dijon's fortune was the advent of the Valois dynasty of dukes in 1364. The empty title of 'capital' acquired substance as Philip the Bold built himself a palace worthy of his status, established a modern administration in the town, and began work on a family mausoleum. The reversion of Burgundy to the crown in 1477 actually enhanced the position of Dijon, since it became the seat of a provincial Parlement, or High Court; the town's constant growth as an administrative centre bent the lines of communication by a sort of magnetic attraction.

When the Revolution of 1789 carved up the provinces into departments and centralised power in Paris, Dijon lost its raison d'être. Only the railway could save it from stagnation, but the planners' original intention was for the Paris-Lyon line to proceed by the most direct route, via Auxerre and Beaune. The corporation voted a huge subsidy for the promotion of Dijon's case, and the city engineer, Henry Darcy, drew up an alternative plan by which the line would pass via Montbard and the long tunnel at Blaisy-Bas. His report carried the day, and on 1 June 1851 the first train passed through on its way south. Dijon was soon established as the principal junction in eastern France, and its modern development had begun. In less than 50 years, its population doubled. Darcy also endowed Dijon with its first modern water-supply, and although he refused any exceptional payment, his grateful fellow-citizens gave his name to the great open square which is now the hub of Dijon's traffic system. It is a gratifying thought that in a country where street names change at the drop of a hat, at least one town has remained faithful to its true benefactor.

Dijon's gastronomic reputation was well established in the four-teenth century, when it was commended by the young Charles VI during a visit to his uncle's duchy. Today, Dijon is the seat of the Etats Généraux de la Gastronomie Française, and holds an international gastronomic fair every year during the first fortnight in November.

The town's best-known product is mustard. Relatively few people are employed in its manufacture (there are no giant concerns in Dijon; the biggest single employer is the Ministry of Education, followed by the railways), but they produce half France's output. What passes for French mustard abroad is closer to the mild 'condiment' mustards than to the standard article, which is hot and yellow. It was introduced into Gaul by the Romans, but did not become the smooth paste we know today until the eighteenth century. The grains were crushed sufficiently to release the flavour, but not ground fine; this preparation is still sold as *moutarde à l'ancienne,* and is more piquant than the modern variety. Slightly different characteristics can be obtained by using either vinegar, verjuice (the very acid juice of unripe grapes), or wine. Amateur etymologists have tried to derive the word *moutarde* from Philip the Bold's motto *'Il me tarde'* ('I am impatient'), and have even reported the phrase as *'Moult tarde'* to make the idea seem a little less fanciful. *Dijonnais* or *à la dijonnaise* after a meat dish means in a mustard sauce, and the Dijonnais have a weakness for adding mustard to their salad sauces, making mere *vinaigrette* seem insipid by comparison.

Dijon is also noted for its gingerbread. It was the Chinese who first had the idea of mixing honey and spices into dough before baking, and Genghis Khan's warriors ate it as part of their staple diet. Gingerbread reached Europe from the middle east in the fourteenth century, and for many years Rheims was the centre of production in France. After the Revolution, many gingerbread bakers left their native Champagne and settled in Dijon, enabling it to supplant Rheims.

Dijon is only on the fringes of the wine trade, whose true headquarters is Beaune. In 1840, however, two gentlemen named Lagoutte and Joly went to Paris on business and were impressed by the popularity of blackcurrant liqueur there. Burgundian peasants had long been making this liqueur (*crème de cassis,* or simply *cassis*) for their own private consumption. Lagoutte and Joly decided to go into commercial production. After a shaky start, they succeeded so well that Dijon now produces 85% of all France's *cassis.* The blackcurrants themselves are grown along the Côte or up in the Arrière-Côte, and in summer it often needs a second glance to distinguish the blackcurrant shrubs from the vines (which acquire thick gnarled stocks over the years). A favourite Burgundian apéritif is made from *cassis* and ice-cold white wine, and is known as *Kir.* Canon Kir, priest, parliamentary deputy and mayor of Dijon for many years after the last war, has become so much a legend that a book about him is entitled 'Did Canon Kir really exist?' The large artificial lake formed by damming the Ouche (its function is purely recreational) was his brainchild, and on his insistence the only apéritif served at mayoral receptions was *blanc-cassis*, now renamed after him.

From all points of the compass, Dijon's most striking landmark is the cathedral of Saint-Bénigne. From the railway bridge over the Paris road rises a broad, straight avenue, a perfect perspective culminating in the massive twin towers and octagonal belfries of the west front. To the visitor's surprise, when he arrives on the parvis, two other churches stand in echelon behind the cathedral. This whole quarter was once known as 'Christendom'; it stood on the site of Dijon's earliest Christian cemetery, and it was among the old tombs that the cult of the obscure martyr Benignus grew up in the 6th century. The monastery which bore his name knew its finest hour under Abbot William of Volpiano, godson of the Holy Roman Empress Adelaïde and special protégé of St Mayeul of Cluny, who sent him to reform Saint-Bénigne at the request of the bishop of Langres, Brun de Roucy. So revered was the abbot by the people of Dijon that they christened the west gate 'La Porte Guillaume' after him; the name remains, though the gate was demolished shortly before the Revolution and replaced by an elegant little triumphal arch.

Abbot William determined to crown his reform with the rebuilding of the abbey church, which he began in 1001. He traced the designs himself, and entrusted much of the work to compatriots from Lombardy. Of this splendid structure, nothing has survived except the crypt of its most bizarre feature, a vast two-storeyed domed rotunda inspired ultimately by the Holy Sepulchre in Jerusalem. The rotunda escaped the general reconstruction in the late thirteenth century, but succumbed to revolutionary philistinism in 1793. Everything above ground level was demolished, the roof of the crypt was stove in, and the rubble of the upper floors tipped into the gaping hole. 50 years later, during the building of the cathedral sacristy, the crypt was rediscovered when a horse put its hoof through some vault-masonry. Although freely restored, the crypt with its forest of columns retains its air of primitive mystery. The crudely carved capitals, depicting barbaric figures whose arms are raised in prayer, are relics of the earlier Carolingian sanctuary.

The present church embodies a very staid version of Burgundian Gothic, if such a style can be said to exist. The interior is well-proportioned, but outside the effect is ponderous, even a little dull. Dijon never acquired a cathedral of the first rank, for the simple reason that it did not become an episcopal see until 1731.

Even then, the first cathedral was established for reasons of economy in the secularised abbey of Saint-Etienne. Saint-Bénigne is an abbey church rebuilt at a period when the monasteries were in spiritual and financial decline. It fell vacant as a result of the suppression of religious communities during the Revolution, and as it was far grander than Saint-Etienne, the bishop took the opportunity to transfer there in 1805. Part of the building's charm is that it seems to have been furnished from a jumble sale. Nothing except the bare walls really belongs there. The tombs and sculptures come from Dijon churches that disappeared in the holocaust, the chancel panelling comes all the way from La Charité-sur-Loire, and even the tympanum over the west door, portraying the stoning of St Stephen, was commandeered from the original cathedral of Saint-Etienne (hence the subject). Only one wing of the conventual buildings survives, containing the monks' dormitory; it now houses the Archaeological Museum.

In the shadow of Saint-Bénigne stands the little Romanesque church of Saint-Philibert. In the days when vines grew beneath the city wall, Saint-Philibert was the parish of the *vignerons,* and a troublesome lot they were, always organising 'conspiracies and monopolies' to obtain better wages. The church's outline has been much altered over the centuries. If the Gothic porch and the elaborate stone spire (completed in 1512) have been happy additions, the eighteenth-century side-chapels are just ugly. The demolition of the apses in 1825 can hardly be called an improvement, either. Still, the church has been handsomely restored, and now makes an ideal setting for exhibitions and concerts.

Last of the group, a little further to the east, is the decaying church of Saint-Jean. It is one of Dijon's few surviving monuments of the age of the Valois dukes, all the others having been either rebuilt in later styles or demolished. Begun in 1448, Saint-Jean must have been a splendid example of the Flamboyant style. The spire over the crossing was complemented by those that rose from the two great towers at the east end of the nave, and the apse was flanked by a pair of turrets. A stained-glass window, reputedly the finest in the duchy, featured Philip the Good and his entourage (the duke had authorised the public lottery which raised the rebuilding funds). All this was lost in the Revolution; the spires were pulled down as symbols of ecclesiastical pride, and the stained glass was shattered. The church was converted into a market, and as a final insult, the apse and turrets were demolished as part of a road-widening scheme in 1811. At least that was the ostensible motive. The rumour was, however, that the mayor, who lived opposite, wanted more daylight in his dining-room.

The statue of Bossuet is not much of a compensation. Born in 1627 in a house near the church, Bossuet became the greatest religious orator of the age of Louis XIV, but is as unread now as he was lionised in his own day. For centuries, the Place Saint-Jean (today Place Bossuet) was the centre of Dijon's community life. Fairs and markets were held among the tombstones of 'Christendom', and on Midsummer's Eve a bonfire was lit in the square and the townsfolk danced around it. In 1595 the festivities were inaugurated by Henri IV, fresh from his victory over the Spaniards at Fontaine-Française.

At the opposite end of the old town, the view down the Rue de la Liberté is closed off by one of the finest Renaissance façades in France. Saint-Michel was begun in 1497 as a sober example of late Gothic, with lavish carved decoration restricted to the north and south doors. This was a crucial period of transition, the age of the wars in Italy, from which the French invaders brought back an enthusiasm for all things Italian. By the time the builders were ready to begin the west front in 1529, the French Renaissance was in full flood. Gothic elements persisted—recessed orders, tympana, statue-niches—but they were overlaid by classical motifs—round arches, pilasters, medallions of the prophets, and an entablature with a richly-carved frieze. The console of the statue of St Michael shows figures from classical mythology side by side with subjects from the Old and New Testaments. Over the central door rises a small cupola, which formerly housed a figure of God the Father, visible through the oculus pierced in the crown of the arch. The towers, whose upper storeys were not in place until 1659, were completed eight years later by the addition of lantern-domes. The warm ochre of the stonework, and the play of light and shade on the surfaces, produce a sumptuous effect. Rodin always went to admire it whenever he had the opportunity of stopping at Dijon.

But half-hidden behind the Palace of the Dukes is something even more spectacular, of which Vauban said that it was 'a jewel without a jewel-case'. The church of Notre-Dame is built on a site so restricted that the surrounding houses threaten to stifle it; the solution adopted by the architect is ingenious. His major technical problem was how to support a lofty ribbed vault, given that the abutment piers (which received the thrust of the vault through the flying buttresses) had to stand very close to the nave, for reasons of space. His answer was to load the head of the flying buttress and prolong it through the wall by means of a sort of interior buttress. To compensate for the necessary lightness of the abutment pier, he designed the pinnacles of the pier to overhang the haunches of the arch of the flying buttress so as to prevent it from rupturing. In this way, the lateral thrust of the vault was counteracted by two sets of vertical thrusts.

There was also an aesthetic problem—to ensure that the church dominated its cramped surroundings. For this purpose, the architect came up with something completely original: a monumental façade consisting of a vast, flat expanse of wall stretched like a parchment scroll between two angle-turrets. Barely detached from the surface, a pair of superimposed arcades rest on slender columns; above, below and between them run three friezes of false gargoyles, representing the demons and lost souls condemned to wait forever at the gates of Paradise. These, however, are a conjectural restoration by a nineteenth-century sculptor. The originals, surprisingly, were not victims of religious or revolutionary fanaticism. It would appear that not very long after the completion of the façade (around the middle of the thirteenth century), a money-lender and his bride presented themselves at the church and stopped before the porch to declare their consent. At that precise moment, a gargoyle in the form of a usurer, clutching a bag of gold, fell from one of the friezes and killed the happy couple instantly. The many other money-lenders of the parish persuaded the corporation to demolish all the other gargoyles—at a price. Whatever the truth behind this cautionary tale, it is fairly certain that the gargoyles were indeed removed as a measure of public safety within a few years of being put up. Their replacement in 1881 is one of the better examples of imaginative restoration.

As the towers which should have flanked the west end of the nave were never built, Notre-Dame's personality depends almost entirely on the dramatic profile of the façade. The same building shows the restorers at their worst. Pleading the justification of the architect's 'original intentions', they erected a lantern tower and spire of quite absurd proportions over the crossing. Originally, the crossing was vaulted over at the same height as the nave, and the tower carried a belfry.

The luxuriant sculpture of the portals disappeared in the year 2 of the Revolution. The good apothecary Bernard, in an access of public-spiritedness, ran up his ladder whenever he had a spare moment and chiselled away until not a fragment remained of the 'signs of bigotry'. Apart from a few gargoyles (those on the sides of the west front), only the miniatures—grotesques, masks and human figures—have come down to us from the thirteenth century. The best-loved of them all is the sly, knowing grin of the 'old Dijonnais', tucked away in the south transept above an unsightly mass of ex-votos and a garish modern tapestry which bears the appropriate legend *Terribilis.*

The ancient wooden statue of the Virgin, 'Notre Dame de Bon Espoir', has been the object of special veneration since 1513. In that year, a Swiss army laid siege to Dijon and the defenders were outnumbered five to one. The besiegers rejected all offers of negotiation, and had already breached the walls in several places when the provincial governor, Louis de la Trémouille, played his trump card. A delegation was sent out at the head of a train of wagons laden with wine; the Swiss drank, mellowed, and relented. In return for a massive indemnity and a promise that Milan would be evacuated, they raised the siege. The devout credit this deliverance to the intervention of Our Lady.

The Dijonnais have always had a special affection for their town clock and its pipe-smoking automaton, the Jacquemart, which stands on the south corner of the façade of Notre-Dame. In 1382, Philip the Bold went to aid his father-in-law in suppressing the revolt of Ghent. He defeated the rebels at Roosebeke, and the survivors took refuge in Courtrai. When this stronghold fell, the duke decapitated its clock-tower (the symbol of its civic freedom) and presented the clock to the town of Dijon, which had provided 1000 men-at-arms for the campaign. The trophy was brought back from Flanders to Burgundy, not without mishap, on an ox-cart. Jacquemart tolled the hours in his new home without complaint until, one day in 1610, he suffered a fit of absent-mindedness. A wit suggested that perhaps he was lonely, and so the good people of Dijon gave him a bride. A century later, another humorist lamented the couple's sterility, and shortly afterwards their union was blessed with a son to strike the halves. The family was completed in 1881 by a little girl who strikes the quarters. One last curiosity: carved on the outside north wall of Notre-Dame, at eye level, is a little owl whose true significance no-one knows, but which has been worn smooth by the generations of Dijonnais who have touched it for luck.

In the letters patent by which he founded the Order of the Golden Fleece, Philip the Good referred to Dijon as 'the capital of his duchy of Burgundy, his principal seigniory, by virtue of which he is the first peer of France', so it is only natural that we should look for a great ducal palace. But it is a surprise to discover, instead of a medieval building, a grand classical composition in the manner of Versailles. In fact, 'Palais des Ducs' is a misnomer sanctioned by popular usage—the more accurate term is 'Palais des Etats'. After its absorption into the royal domain in 1477, Burgundy retained the privileges of taxing and, to a certain extent, governing itself. The States were the assembly of provincial notables which was responsible for this. In 1668 it was regularised to meet every three years; the meeting-place was fixed in Dijon, and a permanent bureaucracy (known as the *Elus*) was established to deal with the day-to-day administration between sessions. With the king's permission, the States took over the former ducal palace and, between 1681 and 1787, built themselves a home consistent with their dignity. Despite the apparent unity of the design, the palace represents all stages in the development of French classical architecture, from the baroque of the late seventeenth century through rococo to neo-classical.

The overall conception is due to Jules Hardouin-Mansart, the designer of the vast enlargements to Versailles then in progress. The executant architect was Martin de Noinville, who settled in Dijon and made his entire career there. Hardouin-Mansart's commission coincided with one from the city corporation which envisaged a large square in front of the palace, with a new access street from the west. This offered an opportunity for some town planning, and Hardouin-Mansart devised a semi-circular *place*, surrounded by a rusticated arcade. The arches were originally open, but were filled in by shops at a later date. This was stipulated in the building contract, because the corporation's intention was to create a lively commercial centre. The two central arcades were demolished in 1768 to give the Rue Vauban a dignified opening on to the *place*.

And yet the *place* lacks a focal point. The centrepiece was to have been a giant equestrian bronze of Louis XIV, by Lehongre. It was duly cast in 1690, and weighed 26 tons. But its transport from Paris raised so many difficulties that the haulier abandoned it in disgust near Auxerre, 100 miles from its destination. In 1720 an engineer from Beaune undertook to complete the journey; he did so with a transporter of his own design (drawn by 20 yoke of oxen), and for a fee which made his fortune. In 1792, it was demolished (gratis) by the revolutionaries and melted down to make cannon and base coinage. Since then, the Place Royale has been Place de la Révolution, Place Impériale, and Place Royale again with the Bourbon restoration. During the revolution of 1830 it acquired the uncontentious name of Place d'Armes, only to be rechristened Place de la Libération in 1944. The central area has been put to unworthy use as a car park.

In 1731 the palace was barely half finished. In that year the inconvenient external staircase leading to the Salle des Etats was replaced by a covered grand staircase built into a new west wing, perpendicular to that containing the Salle des Etats. The designer was Jacques Gabriel, father of the architect of the Petit Trianon at Versailles. He probably also designed the décor of the rococo Chapelle des Elus. The site of the chapel is constricted, and as the interior could originally only be lit from first-floor level, the vault is disproportionately high. This disparity was disguised by fluted Corinthian pilasters framing blind arches, and supporting wide entablatures with prominent cornices. The arches are filled with carved panels and medallions. The chapel stands in a corner of the Cour de Flore, whose quadrangle was completed in 1780, in the neo-classical style in favour under Louis XVI. Not until 1787 did the forecourt and east quadrangle (Cour de Bar) acquire their present appearance; these last buildings conform closely to those by Hardouin-Mansart and Gabriel.

Of the original palace only a few fragments remain, embedded in the later structures. The Capetian dukes had preferred their castles at Talant, Rouvres, Argilly and Brazey, but Philip the Bold transformed their inhospitable Dijon residence into something more commodious. He built the New Tower, known since his grandson's reign as the Tour de Bar after that incorrigible knight errant René of Anjou, count of Provence and titular king of Sicily and Jerusalem. In 1431, when still only duke of Bar, René was captured by the Burgundians at the battle of Bulgnéville and held prisoner in the tower for several years. Adjoining the tower is a roofed, arcaded staircase, originally one of a pair, leading to an enclosed gallery. This dates from 1615 and is the work of Roger de Bellegarde, governor of the province and Master of Horse; the sword carved on the uprights of the arch is the emblem of this latter office. Bellegarde was disgraced for joining the revolt of Gaston d'Orléans in 1631, and was succeeded by the Prince of Condé. Apart from interruptions during the Fronde, the Condés remained hereditary governors of Burgundy until the Revolution.

In the opposite corner of the same courtyard stands all that is left of the palace kitchens; the well originally stood in a tiny space, open only to the sky, which separated the Great Kitchen from the vanished Bakery. One of the highlights of any visit to the Musée des Beaux-Arts is the interior of the Great Kitchen. Its dimensions are what one would expect in a land of Burgundy's gastronomic pretensions, but even more remarkable is the ingenious principle of its construction—a true example of function dictating form. Instead of the fireplace being to the side of the building, the building is sketched in round the fireplace. A central work-space is surrounded on three sides by a vast hearth served by a chimney on each side. The work-space is vaulted by a dome in the centre of which is a fourth vital aperture, a ventilation shaft to ensure a good draught and prevent the heat and humidity from becoming unbearable. Here, in conditions that would have warmed the heart of Pantagruel, the dukes' banquets were prepared. Olivier de la Marche has given us a minute account of the organisation of the kitchen. The chief cook sat in the middle on a raised chair, and 'he must hold in his hand a big wooden ladle which serves him for a double purpose: on the one hand to taste soup and broth, and on the other to chase the scullions from the kitchen to their work, and to strike them, if need be.'

Philip the Good's Tower erupts from the roof-line of Hardouin-Mansart's urbane seventeenth-century façade. Begun by the first two Valois dukes, it was raised to its present height by its eponym to serve as a look-out post during the *Ecorcherie* (1435-44). Local sentiment gave Hardouin-Mansart no choice but to preserve the tower, though he turned necessity to advantage by putting it on the central axis of his own plan. The principle of symmetry thus prevailed. To the east of the tower is the main building of Philip the Good's palace, completed in 1455. Its south front is masked by the classical façade, but the distinctive ogee arches still dominate what remains, on the north side, of the garden laid out for the first Valois duchess, Margaret of Flanders. In her time, live game was parked there whenever a banquet was in the offing. The high roof with its ornate dormers is a reconstruction dating from 1895. Hardouin-Mansart had had the original roof demolished for the practical reason that it projected above the line of the new one.

Under Napoleon III, the Palais des Etats received its last addition when the growing museum collections were housed in a new wing. This stands partially on the site of the Sainte-Chapelle of the dukes of Burgundy, sold for demolition in 1802. The architectural loss is less than that of the dazzling collection of bric-à-brac which cluttered the interior. As the dukes' parish church, it was the official chapel of the Order of the Golden Fleece, and a repository for relics, works of sacred art, and all manner of precious gifts from popes and princes. This treasure-house was looted and vandalised by revolutionary fanatics, but the Dijon Musée des Beaux-Arts has happily kept a more civilised tradition alive.

The ground floor houses an important collection of sculpture, principally funerary monuments of the fifteenth, sixteenth and seventeenth centuries. For this later period, there are several examples of the work of the Dijonnais Jean Dubois, one of the greatest sculptors of Louis XIV's time. An even more famous native son, François Rude (1784-1855), composed the most effective of the monumental groups of the piers of the Arc de Triomphe in Paris, the Departure on the Volunteers in 1792 (better known simply as the 'Marseillaise'). He has a museum of his own at Dijon, containing casts of his more famous work, in the transept of the former church of Saint-Etienne, though he is also represented by a few small sculptures in the Musée des Beaux-Arts. There is also a room devoted to a more recent Burgundian, François Pompon (1855-1933), whose sculptures of animals have a great local popularity.

The paintings in the Museum's collection are displayed according to national schools on the first floor. As a result of the Dard gift in 1916, Dijon has a collection of Swiss and German primitives unrivalled elsewhere in France. Particularly outstanding is 'The Tiburtine Sibyl announcing the birth of Christ to the Emperor Augustus' (who is wearing a curious sort of jester's cap) by Conrad Witz, part of an altarpiece painted about 1430 and now in Basle. There is also an altarpiece commissioned by Pierre Rup, a merchant of Geneva, one of the few pictures from that town to have escaped Calvinist iconoclasm. Notable Italian pictures include a 'Portrait of a Woman' by Lorenzo Lotto, an 'Assumption' by Veronese, a male portrait by Tintoretto and Guido Reni's 'Adam and Eve'. The Dutch and Flemish schools are well represented as a result of purchases made in the seventeenth century by the bourgeoisie of Dijon. Rubins' 'The Virgin presenting the Child to St Francis of Assisi', dated 1618, is a florid baroque composition from early in the artist's career. Naturally enough, the French school predominates. In the principal French gallery the Dijonnais Quantin hangs beside Philippe de Champaigne, Claude Vignon, and Mignard. There are fine eighteenth-century portraits by Nattier (of Marie Lesczyńska, wife of Louis XV), Rigaud, Largillière and the van Loos. Interesting but little-known artists represented include Jean Tassel of Langres (seventeenth century) and the young Dijonnais Romantic Félix Trutat, whose promising career was cut short at the age of 24.

In 1766, Dijon acquired an Ecole de Dessin, founded by François Devosge and typical of the academies of painting and sculpture then springing up all over Europe. In 1781 the States set aside the first floor of the proposed east wing for the use of the Ecole, and this was the beginning of the Museum. The Salle des Statues, which overlooks the Place de la Libération, is the finest neo-classical interior in Dijon. It houses copies of antique busts and statues carved by pupils of the Ecole as a condition of having their studies in Rome financed by the States. The coved ceiling contains an 'Apotheosis of Burgundy', based on Cortona's 'Triumph of Religion' in the Palazzo Barberini, by Devosge's most illustrious pupil, Pierre-Paul Prud'hon.

The size and scope of these collections (there are also important exhibits of medieval ivories and enamels, and of Renaissance furniture) would be the envy of any provincial museum, but here they seem hardly more than accessories. The Dijon museum's greatest treasures are associated, appropriately, with the Valois dukes.

When he became duke in 1364, Philip the Bold determined not only to embellish his residence, but also to build for himself and his posterity a mausoleum, a Valois Saint-Denis. The Capetian dukes had used the abbey of Cîteaux for their burial-place, but Philip decided on a new foundation closer to the capital, dedicated solely to the glorification of his dynasty and to intercession for their souls. He purchased the manor of Champmol on the river Ouche, outside the west gate, and by a charter of 1385 he founded a Carthusian monastery or *Chartreuse,* consisting of a prior, 24 monks and five lay brothers, of whom he himself was one by way of recreation.

The Chatreuse of Champmol became a vast workshop where an army of masons, carpenters, painters and other craftsmen worked under the supervision of the most distinguished artists of the age. The architect was Drouet de Dammartin, and the decoration was almost entirely in the hands of Netherlanders, recruited from the duke's northern dominions. The Low Countries were a powerhouse of the 'international Gothic' style, and Philip's Flemish marriage was to revitalise Burgundian art and regenerate some of the spirit of Cluny and Cîteaux. Genius is a word to be used cautiously, but among the artists who worked at Champmol there was one indisputable genius—Claus Sluter.

Born at Haarlem, in Holland, Sluter became *varlet de chambre* and principal *imaigier* to the duke on the death of Jean de Marville in 1389. His sculpture is characterised by a combination of naturalism and monumentality which immediately set it apart from that of his contemporaries. His influence dominated Burgundian carving for over a century. All Sluter's surviving work was for Champmol, and as the larger pieces are still *in situ,* we must make an imaginary leap of a mile, to where a ruined gateway stands beside the road to Auxerre and Paris. The monastery was pulled down during the Revolution, and a lunatic asylum erected on the site. It is, however, not only safe to go in but free, a rare thing in France.

In the grounds stands a strange, solitary tower, a last vestige of the original building. It encloses the staircase by which the dukes reached their private gallery in the chapel. Incorporated into the nineteenth-century hospital chapel is the old west door, complete with its superb group of five statues; each stands on a sculptured console and is sheltered by an ornate canopy. This architectural arrangement is due to Marville and Drouet de Dammartin, who had imagined a conventional display of a Virgin and Child against the central pier, flanked by two upright figures in each jamb. Sluter amplified this into a full-scale dramatic tableau of the donors being presented by their patron saints, the duke by St John the Baptist, the duchess by St Catherine. The saints bend the knee, both by way of reverence and so as to fit better into frames which had not been designed for them. Sluter seems not to have had an opportunity of altering the finished work to suit his new conception. He did replace the consoles, but the bases of the statues still project.

Dynamism is the keyword in understanding the advance Sluter had made. His figures have ceased to be static. The least restrained member of the group is the Virgin; but for an over-riding impression of robustness, the graceful curve of her body and the elaborate fall of her mantle might seem mannered. The swing of her hips—a feature of earlier Burgundian Madonnas, but hitherto always an attitude of relaxation—is emphasised by the swirls of her drapery and focuses her movement and our gaze on the Christ-child. The images of Philip and Margaret are credible portraits, the best likenesses of them that exist. Despite subsequent mutilations, one can see that Sluter did not trouble to flatter the 'ugly and shrewish' duchess.

Around the corner from the chapel, protected from the weather by a kind of glassed-in bandstand, is the 'Puits de Moïse' (Well of Moses), Sluter's masterpiece and one of the most important sculptural groups of the late Middle Ages. Had the sculptor been French rather than Dutch, the group would surely be exhibited somewhere more accessible! What we see today is only the pedestal of the original structure. We must picture it as it was in 1418, when the papal legate offered an indulgence to anyone who came to visit it in a pious spirit. The monument stood 30 feet high and was dominated by a crucified Christ, surrounded by the traditional figures of the Virgin, Mary Magdalene and St John. The Calvary rose from a cistern which occupied the centre of the great cloister. The theme was the Fountain of Life, collecting the blood shed for man's redemption as it gushed from Christ's wounds. The extant base is surrounded by the six prophets who were thought to have foretold the Passion, symbolising the links between the Old and New Testaments.

The prophets hold scrolls containing the texts of their predictions. Each figure is sharply characterised, giving rise to the story that Sluter took his models from the Dijon ghetto. Moses, the giver of the

Elder Law, overshadows his companions by his massive authority. On his head he bears the two horns of medieval legend, a curious attribute which arose from a misreading of the Old Testament Hebrew. King David, his face calm, rests his right hand on the harp with which he soothed Saul's sleeplessness. Jeremiah screws up his tired old eyes as he meditates on a passage from the *Lamentations*. Zechariah bends under the burden of his foreknowledge that the price of Christ's life shall be 30 pieces of silver. All the costumes were designed to lend their wearers an aura of antique mystery, but Zechariah's is the most theatrical, with its weird oriental cap. Daniel points imperiously to his text, and Isaiah, his mission accomplished, takes his book under his arm and turns away with an air of resignation. Between these commanding figures are slender columns supporting pedestals on which stand the angels of the Passion, in realistic attitudes of grief. In a bold innovation, their outspread wings seem to hold up the overhanging entablature.

The Calvary was consciously devised as a spectacle. To enhance its popular appeal, the plain stone was transformed into a blaze of azure, scarlet and cloth of gold by the gilder Hermann of Cologne and Jan Malouel, the duke's chief painter. Traces of the polychromy are still visible, and a full reconstruction has been attempted on plaster casts at the Museum. As a final bizarre touch, a pair of gilt spectacles, the work of Hannequin de Hacht, were placed on Jeremiah's nose. The Well of Moses is a crucial turning-point in the history of sculpture. It is the heir to the stylised Gothic statuary of Chartres, yet it looks forward to the achievements of the Italian Renaissance, and in particular to Ghiberti and Donatello.

In the Musée des Beaux-Arts, other treasures from the Chartreuse have been assembled in the Salle des Gardes. The room is particularly appropriate. The elaborate chimneypiece and the minstrels' gallery date from the sixteenth century, but this is the same banqueting hall in which Charles the Rash, on the occasion of his 'joyous entry' in February 1474, proclaimed his intention of re-creating the ancient kingdom of Burgundy, 'of which the French have made a duchy'. Three years later his grandiose plans had destroyed him and his empire.

In the centre stands the Museum's chief glory, the tombs of Philip the Bold and John the Fearless. Philip lies on a huge slab of black marble, his feet resting on a lion's back, his head on a cushion beside which kneel two angels supporting his helm. Beneath the slab runs a complex of lacy Gothic arches, in and out of which parades the cortège that accompanied the duke on his last journey from Flanders to Dijon. This 'funeral march in stone' was conceived by

Clause Sluter. The general layout was designed by Marville in 1384, and the architectural detail executed by Claus de Hane. Until then, the *pleurants* or mourners had simply been a conventional motif in sepulchral art, static portraits of those present at the funeral. Sluter took the formula and revolutionised it. The grief of each small figure has its own personality. In some, whose faces and bodies are shrouded by their heavy mourning robes, the expressive power is entirely abstract. The smallness of the scale adds to the poignancy of the scene; perhaps nothing Sluter ever did succeeds as completely as these miniatures, so movingly human. They were his last work.

In 1404, shortly after completing the Well of Moses and three months before the death of his ducal patron, Sluter retired to the abbey of Saint-Etienne as a lay-brother. There he worked on the *pleurants* until his death two years later. He must have left drawings or models from which his nephew, Claus de Werve, could complete the bulk of the commission. De Werve finished the *pleurants* and the effigy in 1411, faithfully reproducing his uncle's style. His own work (the angels supporting the helm) has a softness verging on sentimentality. One only has to go to the Archaeological Museum at Saint-Bénigne to compare the sweet resignation on the face of de Werve's crucified Christ with the true serenity in Sluter's treatment of the same subject (the bust of the Champmol Calvary, exhibited nearby).

De Werve was kept back in Dijon specifically to execute a tomb for Philip the Bold's successor, John the Fearless. But the finance was not forthcoming until 1443, by which time both duke and sculptor were dead. De Werve's career, so promisingly begun, was ruined by fruitless waiting. The coveted commission for the tomb of John the Fearless and Margaret of Bavaria went to an Aragonese, Juan de la Huerta. With that disregard for originality typical of the age, Philip the Good ordered a virtual copy of his grandfather's tomb, stipulating only that it was to be 'as good or better'. 'Better', in these cirumstances, could only mean more elaborate. De la Huerta did not let his patron down; although the procession was manifestly hampered by the arcades, he made the architecture even more exuberant, to match the greater complexity of his draperies and the more contrived gestures of his *pleurants*.

De la Huerta was the Benvenuto Cellini of his day, a dabbler in big business (the duke awarded him an important mining monopoly) and prone to violent outbursts for which he paid in kind; for threatening the mayor of Dijon with his dagger, he was sentenced to sculpt a Madonna for the town. He abandoned the tomb in 1456 with a flourish of temperament, alleging that he was being asked to work with inferior alabaster. Despite his long stay in Burgundy, almost no other examples of his work exist. Amid the flat farmlands to the east of Dijon stands the village church of Rouvres, where the dukes had one of their favourite country residences. Philippe de Mâchefoing, Keeper of the Jewels and commander of the garrison, adorned his chantry chapel with a group of the Virgin and the two SS John by de la Huerta. The prominent lower eyelids and pouting mouths are hallmarks of the artist's sensual style.

The tomb was eventually finished in 1470 by Antoine Le Moiturier of Avignon. In 1790 the two dukes were exhumed and brought from Champmol to Saint-Bénigne in great pomp, as the enemies of royal absolutism. Three years later, when history had beeen re-written and they had become enemies of the people, their effigies were smashed. Souvenir-hunters rescued nearly all the *pleurants*, but only the hands of Philip the Bold and the heads and hands of John the Fearless and Margaret of Bavaria. The tombs found their present home in 1827 when the bishop of Dijon announced that there was no room for them in Saint-Bénigne. 'Miserable fellow,' said Victor Hugo, 'who expelled from his cathedral not only Philip the Bold and John the Fearless, two great princes who are dead, but also Juan de la Huerta and Claus Sluter, two great artists who live on.'

Also from the Chartreuse, and indicative of its lavish devotional furnishings, are two altarpieces by Jacques de Baërze. They are duplicates of retables that Philip the Bold had admired in Flanders. The profusion of gilded filigree ornament probably appealed to the duke more than the biblical subject-matter. One of the tabernacles has retained the wings which could be closed to protect it, and these constitute its principal interest. They were painted at Ypres by Melchior Broederlam, who accompanied the altarpieces to Dijon in 1399 and supervised their installation. Four scenes are represented, two on each panel, the Annunciation and the Visitation on the left, the Presentation of Christ in the Temple and the Flight into Egypt on the right. The artist had to overcome the technical problem of incorporating two outdoor and two indoor scenes into the awkward shape of the wings, without being able to use a unified backdrop for each wing because of the particular sequence of the four events. The result is enormously successful and unexpectedly sophisticated: though retaining some of the mannerisms of Gothic painting, it is astonishingly naturalistic for its period. There is real tenderness in Elizabeth's gesture toward Mary, and hesitancy in the Virgin's proffering of Christ to the High Priest. Joseph, a figure of coarse fun in much medieval art, is depicted sympathetically, slaking his thirst from a water-bottle. To complete the chain of ducal associations in the Salle des Gardes, there is also a small portrait of Philip the Good. This hopefully proclaims itself to be by van der Weyden, but is in fact only a copy after a lost original from Rogier's studio.

One last treasure from the Chartreuse is displayed in an adjoining room, an early Netherlandish 'Nativity' painted about 1425 by Robert Campin, the so-called Maître de Flémalle. As well as the Holy Family and the usual angels and shepherds, the artist has depicted two popular figures from the vast and now forgotten corpus of Marian legend, the midwife and her friend Salome. The latter scoffed at the story of the virgin birth until she had examined Mary for herself, whereupon her hand withered. The crisp winter landscape in which the scene is set is one of the earliest in the history of European painting, and is naturalistically handled with the precision of a miniaturist.

'Dijon is one of those provincial towns where one can still stroll agreeably,' said Huysmans at the end of the last century. It is also one of the few towns with something worth strolling to see, a compendium of domestic architecture that rivals the glamour of the great civil and religious monuments. The best place to start is the Rue des Forges, both because it is central (it is just behind the Palais des Etats) and because it has the oldest buildings. In the days of the dukes, before the Place Royale had been built and the Rue Condé (Rue de la Liberté) had been driven through a jumble of medieval buildings to link up with it, the Rue des Forges was one of the main streets of old Dijon. At the beginning of this century, one end of it was cleared to create a little square dedicated to the memory of the sculptor Rude. This square is now popularly known as the *Place du Bareuzai* (dialect for *vigneron*), after a statue of a naked grape-treader which is neither *by* Rude nor *of* him.

In the thirteenth century, when there were several different currencies circulating in Burgundy, the bankers of Dijon deposited their liquid reserves at No. 40, Rue des Forges. The pavement-level windows were the only way down into the vaults—a shrewd precaution against theft. The striking façade, with its round arches resting on clustered colonnettes and its tiny human figures grimacing as they 'hold up' the string-course, is due to the fourteenth-century banker Guillaume Aubriot who has given his name to the house. His free-thinking, priest-hating son Hugues built the Bastille and had a colourful career as Provost of Paris. The incongruous classical doorway is a relic of the building's service as a Présidial (a court of summary jurisdiction). The sculptures of Strength and Justice originally supported the royal coat of arms and a bust of

Louis XIV, mutilated during the Revolution. When the building was radically restored in 1908, these were replaced by a cartouche bearing the monogram of the owner, the poet Stéphen Liégeard. When he was *sous-préfet* of the department of Var, Liégeard fell under the spell of the Riviera and coined the term 'Côte d'Azur' on analogy with his native Côte d'Or.

Nos. 52, 54, and 56 once formed a single house, the home of the lawyer Jean Morel, who rose to become a trusted adviser of Philip the Good after his wife Simonne Sauvegrain had wet-nursed the infant Charles the Rash. But the street's showpiece is absurdly unobtrusive. A dark passage leads from the street entrance of the Syndicat d'Initiative (No 34) and opens on to the finest piece of Flamboyant architecture in Dijon, the courtyard of the Hôtel Chambellan. The Chambellan family first appear in Dijon as drapers, later as bankers, and finally involved themselves in the lucrative salt trade. Henri Chambellan crowned the family's achievements by becoming mayor, and in 1488 he rebuilt his *hôtel*. Most visitors are content to admire the double gallery and the two-storey dormer, and then leave; but right at the top of the spiral staircase in the corner, the newel becomes a pillar in the shape of a gardener, bearing on his shoulders a basket from which sprout the ribs of the vault. This can hardly be other than a visual pun on the word *corbeille* (basket), which in French doubles as a technical term for the capital of a Corinthian column.

Next door to the Hôtel Aubriot stands the house built for another major of Dijon, Jean Maillard, in 1561 (sometimes known as the Maison Milsand after a subsequent occupier). It takes us into the Renaissance with its florid decoration of broken pediments, lion-masks and festoons. These are the work of Hugues Sambin, one of the greatest of all French Mannerists, and founder of a school of gifted provincial architects whose influence was felt even in Paris. Local tradition associates him with the west front of Saint-Michel, but he would almost certainly have been too young to design it. As for actually sculpting it, he always described himself as a wood-carver and does not seem to have worked in stone. Nevertheless, he was in great demand as a designer for the homes of the new middle classes. As well as the Maison Milsand, the *échauguette* of the Hôtel Le Compasseur (No. 66, Rue Vannerie), with its leering satyr-mask bracket, has been attributed to him (the *échauguette* is a small projecting turret supported by corbelling, and is one of the hallmarks of Burgundian architecture of the period). Perhaps the most unusual work of his school is the 'Caryatid House' in the Rue Chaudronnerie, built for the Pouffiers, a family of rich coppersmiths.

Sambin's most prestigious commission came from the class which supplanted the merchant bourgeoisie as Dijon's greatest builders. The Parlement or High Court of Burgundy was established in 1480 by Louis XI, and under the Ancien Régime its judges and barristers were the élite of Dijon society. Their headquarters was the Palais de Justice, half-hidden in the maze of streets behind the arcades of the Place de la Libération. When the Parlement acquired these premises in the sixteenth century, they entrusted Sambin with the carving of the oak doors (replicas in situ, originals in the Museum) and the enclosure of the Chapel of the Holy Ghost, which occupied the far end of the vast gabled lobby. The two main court-rooms have suitably magnificent ceilings. In 1581, Odinet Godran, president of the Parlement, founded a Jesuit college (now the Municipal Library) just round the corner from the Palais de Justice. All the notables of Dijon educated their sons there; famous alumni include Buffon, Bossuet (a model pupil) and the composer Jean-Philippe Rameau (definitely a 'disruptive element', always singing and writing music in class—he never got beyond the third form).

One of the earliest of the *parlementaire* residences, and perhaps the most impressive since its restoration, is the Hôtel de Vogüé (1614) in the shadow of Notre-Dame. The luxuriant decoration recalls the style of Sambin, but apart from a certain classical restraint, there has been a major architectural change: the main body of the house has retreated from the street behind a forecourt enclosed by an ornamental portico. All the later grand town houses adopted this idea.

While the constant devaluations of the sixteenth century were ruining the *noblesse d'épée,* the lawyers of the Parlement and other office-holders were forming themselves into an hereditary *noblesse de robe.* Increasingly, it was they who upheld provincial privileges (and thus their own prerogatives) to the detriment of royal authority. With their growing wealth they bought land, and baronies whose names they added to their own—hence the indigestible length of the names of some of their *hôtels:* Bouhier de Lantenay, Perreney de Baleure, Guyton de Morveau, Richard de Ruffey. In 1659, when the young Louis XIV had come to Dijon to compel the Parlement to register an edict, President Nicolas Brulart informed him, 'I kneel only before God, Sire, your master as well as mine.' The President was exiled for his pains, but the edict was withdrawn. Louis XIV kept a tight rein on these tendencies, but under his successors the Parlements became ever more firmly identified with reaction, and succeeded in staving off effective reform until 1789.

And yet these same men were enthusiastic patrons of the

Enlightenment. They secured the foundation of a Faculty of Law, which was the nucleus of the university whose unlovely new buildings have recently risen on the hill of Montmusard; they helped to create Devosge's Ecole des Beaux-Arts where Rude and Prud'hon were trained; and they formed an Académie des Sciences, Arts et Belles-Lettres to which Rousseau gave his first address in 1750, on the theme that the advance of science was corrupting morality. The intelligentsia corresponded regularly with their counterparts in Paris, and the Place Saint-Jean (Bossuet) hummed with intellectual curiosity and fashionable table-talk. Guyton de Morveau gave public lectures on chemistry and invented fumigation, which was first tried in the crypt of Saint-Etienne (to purge it of the stench of corpses which had lain unburied during a long spell of frost). Prisiding over all this activity was the genial figure of Charles de Brosses, who dined out every evening, came home in the small hours, gambled, womanised and still found time for scholarship. His *Letters from Italy* first brought the discoveries at Herculaneum to the notice of the French public, and he enjoyed the friendship of Voltaire until they fell out over the lease of a manor near Ferney. The case came to court and Voltaire lost. It goes without saying that de Brosses was a judge in the Parlement, and that Voltaire should have known better.

On the outskirts of Dijon, at the entry to the picturesque valley of the Suzon, is the little château of Vantoux. It was built in 1704 by Jean de Berbisey, who bequeathed it as an official residence for his successors as First President of the Parlement, among whom was Charles de Brosses. Standing on a medieval site, with the moats laid out as lawns, it is a foretaste of the more relaxed age of Louis XV.

Of the many fine town houses of the era, three are outstanding. The Hôtel Bouhier de Lantenay (1759), hidden from view behind a grandiloquent forecourt enclosure, is the most stately and has been by turns Intendance of Burgundy and Prefecture of Côte d'Or. The political temperature in France can be gauged by whether the policeman outside is carrying a machine-gun or not. Next door to each other in the Rue Vannerie (Nos 39 & 41) stand the Hôtel of the Military Commandant and the Hôtel Chartraire de Montigny. The severely neo-classical façade of the former (1787), relieved by a pair of sentry-boxes surmounted by sculptures of Mars and Minerva, contrasts with its neighbour's rococo gateway. Marc-Antoine Chartraire de Montigny was Treasurer-General of the States of Burgundy in the closing years of the Ancien Régime. As well as his *hôtel*, he had come into possession of a pavilion set in gardens outside the city walls—Le Castel, built in 1707 by Martin de Noinville, executant architect of the Palais des Etats. Here the Treasurer-General gave lavish alfresco entertainments where the beau monde of Dijon competed to be seen. Poor Chartraire! The strain of constant spending was just too much. He became convinced that he was on the brink of ruin—quite incorrectly, as it turned out—and cut his own throat. Today his pleasure-dome stands forlorn in the grounds of the unromantic *lycée* which has taken its name.

The post-Revolutionary age has contributed little to the legacy of the past, except the compliment of not interfering too much with it. The Musée Magnin (Rue des Bons-Enfants, just off the Place de la Libération) provides a glimpse into a bourgeois Dijonnais house of the mid-nineteenth century. The large collection of paintings (bequeathed to the nation by Maurice Magnin) dominates most of the rooms, but all these are furnished to evoke the France of Stendhal and Flaubert. The enthusiastic attributions on the non-French old masters are largely incorrect, but the thought that Madame Bovary seethed in just such a claustrophobic provincial prison should fire the imagination of the most prosaic visitor. One could also have cited La Cloche, a hotel straight out of the late nineteenth century, but it has proved too grand for modern tastes and waits on the decision of the developers. A more worthy cause is a corner site next to the central Post Office (Place Grangier), a piece of Art Nouveau chinoiserie that no-one seems to have noticed. At least so it seems, since all the ground-floor businesses except one have chosen, and been permitted, to tear out the panelled shop-fronts that were an organic part of the design.

Opportunities have been thrown away since the war. New suburbs and industrial estates have sprouted like cancers on the periphery of the old town. By a stroke of poetic justice, however, this frenzy of development is to be rewarded by economic failure of a sort. The motorway planners have executed the sentence commuted by the railway planners of the nineteenth century: the motorway links Auxerre directly to Beaune (making the latter the great road junction of eastern France) and Dijon is served by a mere spur. The great white hope of the advocates of growth at any cost has been the high-speed turbotrain, planned to run between Paris and Lyon on a specially-constructed line. Here again, the government has decided that it should pass by the most direct route and join the existing track at Mâcon, adding another factor to the latter's rapidly growing importance.

The City Corporation have bowed to the inevitable with good grace. They have decided to make the most of the fact that Dijon is still one of the most congenial towns in France and to concentrate on the 'tertiary' sector—education, tourism, and 'paper-processing'. There has been a big cleaning and restoration campaign (one unfortunate result of which, in the Place du Bareuzai, has been to strip the ivy off a building that was better hidden), and two large pedestrian areas have been created in the old town.

Dijon is a microcosm of Burgundy; just as the whole province, despite its great churches and châteaux, remains a land of peasant villages and country roads, so its capital is a town of back-streets and courtyards. In particular, the Rue Verrerie has an array of half-timbered houses whose projecting upper storeys rest on carved beams, some portraying traditional subjects like grapes or snails, others depicting everyday scenes: drapers measuring cloth, a hunter taking aim at a hare.

Other streets have missed being singled out as tourist attractions and still feel lived in. A good example is the Rue Monge, the southward continuation of the Place Bossuet. At one end is Le Muet's elegant Hôtel Bouchu, at the other a straggle of half-timbered buildings. In between, in a niche over the door of the Bar du Midi is, of all things, a large Madonna; the tiny Hôtel du Raisin next door has been a *bistrot* for nearly 300 years; and right opposite is the Place Emile Zola, formerly Place du Morimont, the venue of Dijon's public executions. The Raisin presumably did a brisk trade with thirsty spectators. A *pissoir* now occupies the position of the stake where heretics and husband-poisoners were burnt alive.

Even if there were no other reason for coming to the Rue Monge, the Hostellerie du Sauvage would provide one. Parts of the building date back to the fifteenth century, and there has been an inn on the site for 400 years. The Sauvage is only a grill, but it fulfils the conditions of excellence better than its more ambitious rivals. The Trois Faisans, which enjoys an enviable view of the Palais des Etats and has traditionally been regarded as Dijon's premier restaurant, has mildly disappointed—spoilt, no doubt, by uncritical acceptance of its reputation. The Chapeau Rouge and the Grill of the Hôtel Central have the edge, though they too suffer from an expense-account atmosphere. Two restaurants (the Vinarium and the Vieux Métiers de France) offer grills in vaulted Gothic cellars, and have a certain expensive chic. The Piron (Rue Pasteur) operates on a more humble level, but is more satisfying as value for money. Otherwise, one has to go out of Dijon for anything to match the Sauvage. Logs are piled in its cobbled courtyard, joints are roasted over a wood fire at one end of the dining-room, and the meat is prepared on a butcher's block by the fireplace. The *jambon persillé*, snails, *andouillettes* and *saucisson* are excellent, and a litre jug of beaujolais makes agonising over the wine-list unnecessary. Good French cooking loses none of its Frenchness by being simple, and it does not need a *grand cru* to prove, in the words of the Latin inscription on the wine-jugs at the Sauvage, that 'Good wine maketh glad the heart of man'.

5 The Côte d'Or

From any vantage point in Dijon, a long and apparently unbroken ridge of high ground forms the western horizon. This is the famous 'Côte d'Or', the 'golden hillside', home of the great burgundies; the road from Dijon to Chagny reads like a wine-list. The sinking of the plain of the Saône in prehistoric times produced a series of geological faults of which the Côte d'Or is the most impressive. Running in a straight line from north-east to south-west, this fault has concentrated all the vital factors of great wine in a strip of land whose average width is less than half a mile. The essential conditions that it created are good drainage by means of the steep slope and stony soil, rich deposits of mineral salts washed down from the ridge, and an ideal exposure towards the morning sun.

Very early, a succession of hamlets grew up between the hills and marshlands, sited close to springs, or at the mouths of the *combes* or ravines carved out of the soft limestone by hillside torrents. The setting is unspectacular; the vineyards stretch almost without a break for 36 miles, a narrow swathe between the exposed, rocky upper slopes and the heavy, over-rich soil of the plain. 'Just a small, dry, ugly mountain,' said Stendhal unfairly—though he did go on to add, 'but at every step one finds an immortal name.' In his day, the Côte had a very different aspect. Instead of the neat rows of vine-stocks marching up the slope, there would have been a confused mass of shrubbery surrounding the occasional peach or cherry tree. The Burgundians had always propagated the vine by the most natural means: a new shoot was selected, allowed to grow long, and then layered—i.e. its tip was earthed over. Roots developed, and an independent plant came into being. This haphazard arrangement meant that the land could only be worked with backbreaking physical effort, unaided even by so simple a device as the horse-drawn plough. But the phylloxera put an end to the old ways. There could be no natural propagation with grafted vines, and the *vignerons* took advantage of the enforced change to lay their vineyards out in rows, as in Bordeaux. This not only made cultivation easier, but also ensured that each vine had all the light and space it needed. 'The vine likes only the shade of the *vigneron*'

Vineyards and Grands Crus of the Côte d'Or.

The names of districts and villages written in capitals are also the names of appellations contrôlées, except for Côte de Nuits (which exists only in the form of the appellation 'Côte de Nuits-Villages').

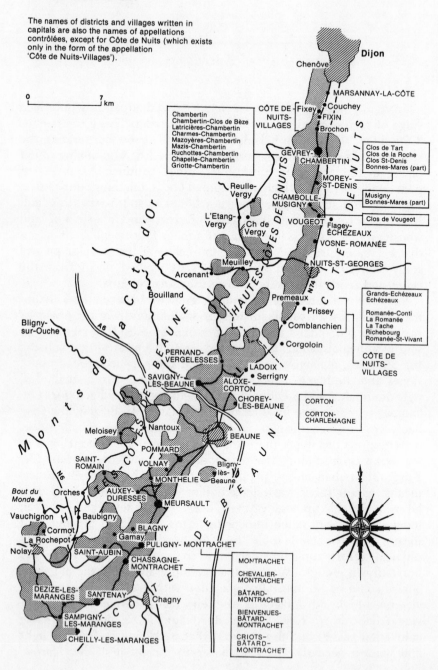

Dijon

Chenôve

0   7 km

MARSANNAY-LA-CÔTE

CÔTE DE NUITS-VILLAGES   Fixey   Couchey

FIXIN

Brochon

Chambertin
Chambertin-Clos de Bèze
Latricières-Chambertin
Charmes-Chambertin
Mazoyères-Chambertin
Mazis-Chambertin
Ruchottes-Chambertin
Chapelle-Chambertin
Griotte-Chambertin

GEVREY-CHAMBERTIN

Clos de Tart
Clos de la Roche
Clos St-Denis
Bonnes-Mares (part)

MOREY-ST-DENIS

Reulle-Vergy

CHAMBOLLE-MUSIGNY

Musigny
Bonnes-Mares (part)

L'Etang-Vergy

Ch de Vergy

VOUGEOT   Flagey-ÉCHÉZEAUX

Clos de Vougeot

VOSNE-ROMANÉE

Meuilley

NUITS-ST-GEORGES

Arcenant

Bouilland

Premeaux

Grands-Echézeaux
Echézeaux

Romanée-Conti
La Romanée
La Tâche
Richebourg
Romanée-St-Vivant

Prissey

Comblanchien

Corgoloin

PERNAND-VERGELESSES

CÔTE DE NUITS-VILLAGES

Bligny-sur-Ouche

LADOIX

SAVIGNY-LÈS-BEAUNE

Serrigny

ALOXE-CORTON

CHOREY-LÈS-BEAUNE

CORTON

CORTON-CHARLEMAGNE

Meloisey

Nantoux

BEAUNE

POMMARD

SAINT-ROMAIN

VOLNAY

Bligny-lès-Beaune

MONTHELIE

Bout du Monde

Orches

AUXEY-DURESSES

Vauchignon

Baubigny

MEURSAULT

Cormot

BLAGNY

La Rochepot

Gamay

Nolay

SAINT-AUBIN

PULIGNY-MONTRACHET

CHASSAGNE-MONTRACHET

MONTRACHET

CHEVALIER-MONTRACHET

BÂTARD-MONTRACHET

BIENVENUES-BÂTARD-MONTRACHET

CRIOTS-BÂTARD-MONTRACHET

DEZIZE-LES-MARANGES

SANTENAY

Chagny

SAMPIGNY-LES-MARANGES

CHEILLY-LES-MARANGES

la Côte d'Or

A6

CÔTES DE BEAUNE

HAUTES-

CÔTES DE NUITS

CÔTE DE NUITS

N74

Monts de la Côte d'Or

N6

HAUTES-CÔTES DE BEAUNE

CÔTE DE BEAUNE

runs a local proverb. The modern replacement of the horse and plough is the *enjambeur,* a tractor designed to straddle (hence its name) a row of vines, carrying its engine and driver clear of the plants.

The villages of the Côte show rural France at its most prosperous and comfortable. The peasants may dress shabbily for work, but the Mercedes in the garage is no longer a legend. The spacious stone houses are usually built round a small courtayrd, with the living quarters on one side, and the *cuverie* or vat-house on the other—the whole structure underpinned by a warren of vaulted cellars. One of the oldest and finest examples (though without the typical court-yard) is at Vosne-Romanée, and dates back more than 600 years. In this case, as often elsewhere, the cellars are really a lower ground floor, while the living quarters are built over them; the covered gallery is a feature which becomes more and more common as one goes south. On a spring afternoon, when the children are at school and the villagers are in the vines, the silence is complete. The main road to Lyon passes far to the east. Houses do not have numbers; it is quite enough to ask for Monsieur X's house in these villages where nearly everyone is engaged in the two principal industries of vine-dressing and tax-evasion. (With VAT at 17.6%, what *vigneron* is not going to stretch a point with favoured customers?)

The best time to pass through the vineyards is during the vintage (early September in good years), when the roads are crowded with tractors bringing back the *balonges,* the tubs full of freshly picked grapes, to the vat-houses. In October, as the vine-leaves die, the Côte d'Or is transformed into the blaze of russet and gold from which it takes its name. But at any time of the year, the *enjambeurs* will be at work, and in the spring and summer the women too are in the vines, wearing the traditional bonnets known as *quichenottes.*

Going south out of Dijon towards Beaune and Lyon, the trick is to leave behind the ugly strip development of factories and hypermar-kets by taking the Route des Grands Crus, forking right along the D122. The vine once grew right up to the city walls, but has disappeared beneath the mushrooming suburbs of Chenôve and Fontaine d'Ouche (the former is the second largest town in the department, bigger even that Beaune). The only part of this 'Côte de Dijon' still producing wine in any quantity is Marsannay, where a fairly dark rosé is obtained by a short vatting of the pinot noir. *Bourgogne Rosé* is made elsewhere, but usually only with grapes which would not withstand too long a vatting (e.g. in a wet year). However, since the First World War, it has become a speciality of Marsannay and its neighbour Couchey—to the point where their product is allowed to bear the more specific title *Bourgogne Rosé de Marsannay*. It has all the light fragrance expected of a rosé, but the use of the pinot gives a note of distinction that most other rosés lack. A more historical claim to fame is that Marsannay was, in 1443, the scene of the 'Passage of Arms of the Tree of Charlemagne', one of those extravagant pieces of chivalrous make-believe of which Philip the Good's court was so fond. Local historians have sited the tournament ground to the east of the village, down by the *route nationale*.

At Fixin begins the Côte de Nuits, a bald ridge on whose summit the limestone outcrops and offers a foothold only to the barest scrub. Fixin sells most of its production as *Côte de Nuits-Villages*. The memory of Napoleon is particularly venerated here, thanks to the efforts of one of his fervent admirers. Claude Noisot had been a captain of grenadiers during the Napoleonic Wars, and had belonged to the Emperor's household regiment throughout the exile on Elba. After Waterloo, Noisot retired to this quiet corner of the Côte and dedicated the rest of his life to the cult of his idol. He bought some land and laid out a park, complete with a miniature replica of the fort on St Helena, which served as his own house. The setting was ready—but where was the centrepiece? A mutual friend put him in touch with a fellow-admirer, the sculptor François Rude. The artist was so moved by the old soldier's devotion that he offered his services for nothing. 'I'll do you an Emperor!' he exclaimed, and came up with his 'Napoleon awakening to Immortality'. Impressively sited at the top of the hill, the Emperor reclines on a rock, symbolising St Helena; he is shrouded in his cloak, and at his feet lies the imperial eagle, lifeless. But this is the moment of apotheosis: raising himself on one elbow, Napoleon prepares to draw aside his shroud and take his place among the immortals. Noisot himself was buried nearby, standing up, sabre in hand, mounting eternal guard.

By coincidence, just down the road is the vineyard whose European reputation was created by Napoleon's patronage—the Chambertin. South of the sprawling village of Gevrey is one of the largest concentrations of world-class red wines in the whole of Burgundy. The first known proprietors of vines at Gevrey were the monks of the abbey of Bèze, who were established there as early as 630. By the middle of the thirteenth century, most of the properties had passed into the hands of the ubiquitous abbots of Cluny, who built the old château (still on view today) to store and protect their wines. The story (almost certainly apocryphal) runs that about this time, an enterprising peasant who owned land adjoining the 'Clos de Bèze' on the south decided to copy the methods used to such effect by his neighbours, the monks of Cluny. So successful was he that his wine came to be regarded as the equal of theirs, and the vineyard has ever since borne his name, *champ de Bertin* or Chambertin. Whatever the truth of that, the two are today regarded as virtually synonymous, so much so that *Clos de Bèze* can call itself simply *Chambertin* (though not vice versa). Proverbially full-bodied, wines for game and roasts, they enjoy strong support for the title of the greatest burgundy of all.

Napoleon was no gastronome. He always expressed a preference for the plainest dishes, which he wolfed down as though eating were drudgery. His predilection for Chambertin might just have given him the reputation of a connoisseur—if he had not habitually mixed it with water. His Chambertin followed him wherever he went, even on campaign; a whole wagon-load accompanied his baggage-train to Moscow and back. At Boulogne in 1805, waiting for the chance to invade England that never came, the Emperor submitted his Chambertin to the scrutiny of his old comrade-in-arms, Marshal Augereau. 'I've tasted better,' was the disarmingly frank pronouncement. Of course, the constant vibration of the mobile 'cellar' can hardly have allowed the wine to be presented at its best!

The total area of the Chambertin, with the Clos de Bèze, is only 70 acres. Seven surrounding parcels of land are *grands crus* in their own right, and by tradition are permitted to add the name 'Chambertin' to their own. They are not quite in the same class, but are always considerably cheaper. The best is Latricières, and the best-known probably Charmes. Until an unsightly hoarding was put up a few years ago, there was nothing at all to indicate that one was skirting one of the world's most celebrated vineyards. The same is still true of the Musigny, the Romanée-Conti and others; a striking instance of Burgundy's self-effacement.

Morey-Saint-Denis has two famous vineyards, the Clos de Tart and the Clos de la Roche (there *is* a *grand cru* called Saint-Denis, but its reputation is now less than the other two). Morey used to sell its wines as Gevrey or Chambolle before the law on *appelations contrôlées*, without these two names losing anything by the arrangement. Since then, the wines of Morey have gone unjustly ignored. No one vineyard is big enough to build up and satisfy a large following, and thus help to publicise the name of the village.

Chambolle-Musigny has been more fortunate. The Musigny, on the slope overlooking the château of Clos-Vougeot, is one of the four most famous *climats* of the Côte de Nuits. 'A wine of silk and lace,' claimed one commentator effusively but uninformatively. Musigny is reputed to have a more delicate taste than Chambertin, but this is arguable. It may well have been so in the last century, when long vattings must have given Chambertin a more pronounced character than it now has.

Clos Vougeot and its château have become symbols of Burgundy for the whole world. During the Revolutionary Wars, Colonel Bisson, marching past the château on what is now the RN 74, halted his troops, drew them up in battle order, and rendered full military honours. The spontaneous homage became a tradition, though there are few opportunities for soldiers to observe it in the automobile age.

Eight miles away, amidst the forests of the Saône valley, stands the monastery of Cîteaux, mother-house of the Cistercian order. In 1098 a small band of monks left the abbey of Molesme, where they had tried unsuccessfully to enforce the strict interpretation of the Benedictine rule. They went in search of some desolate spot where they would have no contact with the outside world. They settled among the rushes or *cistels* of the Saône marshes, and devoted themselves to a life of privation, labour and prayer. The beginnings were difficult. In spite of the protection of the Holy See and the dukes of Burgundy, Cîteaux might well have withered away but for a timely intervention. In 1113, a young nobleman arrived at the head of 31 companions, and his burning enthusiasm revived the enterprise overnight. His name was Bernard of Fontaine (his birthplace is now a suburb of Dijon), better known to us as St Bernard of Clairvaux. He gave the 'Cistercians' a new lead, transforming them into the standard-bearers of militant Christianity. Within two years Cîteaux had four daughter-houses, La Ferté, Pontigny, Clairvaux and Morimont; by the end of the century, there were over 1000 Cistercian houses in Europe and Palestine. The abbots of Cîteaux had the powers and prerogatives of a bishop, and took precedence at the papal court over all other heads of orders.

Nothing remains of the original monastery at Cîteaux except the ruined fifteenth-century library. To see a Cistercian monastery built according to the original plan one must go to Fontenay in the Auxois. After the suppression of religious congregations in 1790, the abbey was put to a succession of secular uses. In 1898, exactly eight centuries after the first foundation, Cîteaux was restored to its status of mother-house of the order, and the reformed Cistercians (Trappists) returned. The routine of the monks differs hardly at all from that observed in the time of St Bernard. Visitors (men only) are welcome any afternoon except Sundays and holidays. The monks make an excellent cheese, semi-soft and mild-flavoured, which deserves to be better known than it is. It is on sale in the porter's lodge at the abbey.

Clos Vougeot was the creation of the monks of Cîteaux. Starting with a few scattered donations, they patiently rounded out their estate until by 1336 they owned all the 150 acres now enclosed by the stone wall. In 1367 a fort was built in a corner of the Clos, to protect the wines from the raids that were so frequent during the Hundred Years' War. The wine was already acquiring a European reputation. When Gregory XI became pope in 1370, Jean de Bussières, abbot of Cîteaux, sent him a gift of 30 barrels of Clos-Vougeot. The Holy Father promised to remember this act of generosity, and four years later de Bussières received a cardinal's hat.

The monks made three separate *cuvées*, from grapes harvested in three different zones of the Clos. The most likely supposition is that the zones were horizontal rather than vertical, as the wine from the flat ground near the main road is considerably inferior to that grown near the château, where the slope is more noticeable. The wine of the very finest quality was never sold, but was reserved for presents made to crowned heads and other dignitaries. When entertaining at Cîteaux, the abbot disposed of a subtle but simple contrivance for ordering wine: calling his cellarer, he would say, '*Vous m'entendez*' (know what I mean) if his guests were men of rank, to whom the finest *cuvée* could be served, and '*M'entendez-vous*' if they were ordinary folk, worthy only of the second best.

In 1790, all ecclesiastical property was confiscated and the Clos de Vougeot was auctioned off with the rest. The last cellarer, aptly named Dom Goblet, managed the estate until the day of the sale. With tears in his eyes, he surrendered his charge to the bailiffs, but smuggled out enough of the last vintage to last him the rest of his life. The Clos ceased to be a single property in 1889, though all subsequent owners are legally obliged to retain the enclosing wall built by the monks. There are now 65 different owners, which poses problems in selecting a Clos-Vougeot. Vougeot is territorially the smallest of the great wine villages, but Clos-Vougeot is the largest *grand cru* appellation. The triple division observed by the monks has not survived.

The present château was built in 1551; its plain, massive buildings are the most outstanding landmark of the Côte. In 1934, a group of merchants and growers met at Nuits-Saint-Georges and decided on a publicity venture to combat the slump in the wine trade. They came up with a piece of instant folklore which has gone from strength to strength ever since, the Confrérie des Chevaliers du Tastevin. Ten years later, they bought the château of Clos Vougeot, which became the venue of their 'chapters'. Clad in robes of scarlet and gold, the officers of the order enthrone new members at banquets designed to enhance the prestige of the gastronomy and wines of Burgundy. Such has been their success that they have found imitators in all other the other wine-growing regions of Burgundy—the Piliers Chablisiens, the Compagnons du Beaujolais, the Vignerons de Saint-Vincent in the Mâconnais, the Chevaliers des Trois Ceps at Saint-Bris, the Campagnons de la Chante Flute at Mercurey and the Cousins de Bourgogne at Savigny. Apart from their 20-odd chapters a year, held in the château's great barn, the Chevaliers du Tastevin also celebrate the feast of St Vincent on the first Saturday after the saint's day, 22 January. The honour of hosting the ceremony falls to a different village of the Côte every year. St Vincent is the patron saint of *vignerons*—either because his torturers subjected him to the *peine forte et dure* (crushing by weights), or simply because his name contains the syllable 'vin'.

The village of Flagey-Echézeaux stands out on the plain, well away from the Côte. Its territory, however, marches up the slope in a thin strip containing the *grand cru* which it has added to its true name. The Echézeaux lies just outside the wall of Clos Vougeot on the south-west side, and forms part of a continuous swathe including the Musigny and the top part of Clos Vougeot. Only its unpronounceable name has robbed it of its rightful share of fame. The other wines of Flagey are marketed as Vosne-Romanée.

'If Chambertin is the king of wines, Romanée is the queen.' Certainly, no other burgundy is more highly prized than Romanée-Conti; it is the Château Lafite of the Côte d'Or, in price as well as quality. It has a delicacy and feminine fragrance which an archbishop of Paris described as 'mingling velvet and satin in a bottle'. Its extreme rarity (the average production is 6,500 bottles a year) and exorbitant cost are even more powerful attractions for some people. For over two centuries, the greater part of the Romanée was the property of the Croonembourg family. When it came up for sale in 1760, there was a rush of buyers for the vineyard which was already reputed to produce the finest wines in Burgundy. Despite the intrigues of Madame de Pompadour, Louis XV's mistress, the property eventually went to the Prince de Conti. It was the last vineyard in the province to have ungrafted vines, but succumbed during the last war when carbon disulphide, the only known treatment against phylloxera, was unobtainable. It was replanted with grafted vines, and recommenced production in 1952. It now belongs to a limited company called Le Domaine de la Romanée-Conti, which has considerable holdings in the other vineyards of Vosne-Romanée. Romanée, Romanée-Saint-Vivant, Richebourg and La Tâche are only slightly inferior to Romanée-Conti, and some experts would not hestitate to put the latter two in the same class. Courtépée, the eighteenth-century historian of Burgundy, said flatly, '*Il n'y a point de vins communs à Vosne.*'

The little town of Nuits-Saint-Georges is second only to Beaune as a centre of the wine trade, but has retained practically nothing of the other's medieval character. Its wines are among the best-known burgundies abroad, but none of them are among the very best. The success of the name is due to the fact that the appellation *Nuits-Saint-Georges* extends for fully four miles, and that consequently there is more of it. More noteworthy, though less picturesque, are the quarries gouged out of the hillside at Comblanchien. The white limestone found there resembles marble when polished, and has been in demand for flagstones and facings since the Middle Ages. The Paris Opera House is built of Comblanchien stone.

From Nuits southward, the crest of the ridge dips until it is only a few feet above the level of the road. Then, between Corgoloin and Ladoix-Serrigny, there is a re-entrant in the line of hills and the Côte de Beaune begins. Its first great name is Aloxe-Corton, announced by the polychrome roof of its little eighteenth-century château all but submerged in a sea of vegetation. Aloxe has the unique privilege of being the home of a great red wine *and* a great white. The Corton is the only red *grand cru* of the Côte de Beaune, while the Corton-Charlemagne is the only white *grand cru* of the Côte d'Or outside Puligny-Montrachet.

The Corton itself is a narrow strip running just beneath the copse that crowns the hill, but the neighbouring vineyards are in the same class and prefix their names with 'Corton'. The history of the vines of Aloxe goes back to 775, when Charlemagne rebuilt the abbey of Saulieu after its destruction by Saracen raiders, and endowed it with some of his property at Aloxe. The story goes that as the Emperor grew old and his beard grew white, the crimson stains of his favourite beverage became more and more noticeable. His wife, finding this inconsistent with imperial dignity, nagged him until at last, in exasperation, he devised a compromise—he ordered part of his vineyards to be replanted with white vines. Corton-Charlemagne ranks with Montrachet as the very finest of white burgundies. Instead of enjoying the favoured south-easterly exposition, the Charlemagne vineyard faces the setting sun—the only *grand cru* of the Côte d'Or to do so. A more recent appreciator of Corton (the red) was Voltaire. His friend President Le Bault of the Dijon Parlement had an estate at Aloxe (he built the château) and kept

Voltaire regularly supplied. The patriarch of Ferney was moved to write, 'The older I grow, sir, the more conscious I am of the value of your kindness. Your good wine is becoming a necessity.' Typically, he kept the Corton for himself, and served beaujolais to his guests.

Corton is the only red burgundy that can withstand comparison with the great names of the Côte de Nuits, though some of the better vineyards at Beaune come very close to it. The other wines of the Côte de Beaune are less full-bodied. Their fame rests on their bouquet and their delicacy, also on their sheer quantity, which keeps their names constantly before the public eye. They are ready for drinking sooner than their cousins of the Côte de Nuits.

Tucked away on the other side of the great hill that carries the Cortons is the village of Pernand, which shares the Charlemagne with Aloxe, produces a creditable white wine under its village name, and possesses a red *premier cru* whose name it has added to its own, the Ile des Vergelesses. At the head of the next valley lies Savigny, whose wines have the enviable reputation, in this impatient age, of maturing faster than those of their neighbours. They are light and scented, like the wines of Beaune, but they succeed particularly well in hot, dry years, which is unusual. Savigny is the town of fine phrases. The motto of the Cousins de Bourgogne, the bacchic association that has its headquarters in the old wine-cellar, is *'Toujours gentilshommes sont cousins'*. Over a doorway, a Latin inscription reads: 'There are five reasons for drinking: the arrival of a guest, present thirst, thirst to come, the excellence of the wine—and any other you care to think of.' And at the entrance to the cellars of the château, putting more laboured praise to shame, there is the solemn assurance that *'Les vins de Savigny sont nourrissans, théologiques, et morbifuges.'* Following one of the oldest routes linking the Paris basin to the Saône valley, the Paris-Lyon motorway thunders through the vineyards barely half a mile from Savigny. When the road was built, the priceless topsoil was recovered and redistributed, its qualities being considered unique and irreplaceable.

Beaune is the heart of the wine trade, a town that lives by and for wine. As well as the honeycomb of cellars under the houses (many of them can be visited), the old bastions of the town ramparts make perfect storage places, and have all been taken over by the merchants. The wines of Beaune have been justly famous from the earliest times. The hills to the west and south-west of Beaune were almost certainly the *pagus Arebrignus* of late Latin texts. If greater kudos is now enjoyed by the *grands crus* of the Côte de Nuits, this is because the latter are better at producing the full-bodied wines that have been in fashion since the end of the eighteenth century. When wines were drunk young, finesse and bouquet were the sought-after qualities. The high tax levied on Beaune wine proves how much it was in demand in Paris, despite the difficulties and cost of the long overland journey to the nearest river-port. The Burgundy vineyard is at its most impressive here, a mile-wide patchwork quilt covering the Montagne de Beaune almost to its summit. The sheer availability of Beaune wine is as much a factor of its reputation as its quality.

The importance of Beaune during the Middle Ages is attested by the fact that, over 400 years after the ducal capital had been moved to Dijon, the appeal courts and the Grands Jours (the duke's council of barons, knights and lawyers sitting as a high court) still held their sessions there. For their attendance at the Grands Jours, the dukes resided at their *hôtel*, rebuilt in the fifteenth century and now housing the Musée du Vin. The chapter of Notre-Dame de Beaune was second only to the cathedral chapter itself in the diocese of Autun. The collegiate church, now a basilica, is contemporary with Saint-Lazare at Autun and is in the prevailing Cluniac style of the period. Later additions include the fourteenth-century porch and the Renaissance Bouton Chapel (first bay of the south aisle) which dates from 1530. The building's most distinctive feature, however, is the crossing tower—an unmistakable part of the landscape for miles around. The bulbous tiled roof, surmounted by a lantern, was added in 1581 to provide a platform for the watch. The chevet is a striking ensemble; the Romanesque ambulatory and apsidal chapels have sprouted flying buttresses to support the high-windowed Gothic chancel, which replaced an oven vault in the fourteenth century. Inside, the choir is hung with a resplendent series of tapestries of the life of the Virgin, from the moment of her Immaculate Conception (by the kiss in the Golden Gate) to her Assumption. The tapestries were commissioned in 1474 by Cardinal Jean Rolin, abandoned at his death, and finished in 1500 for Canon Hugues Le Coq. They were woven at Tournai from cartoons by the Beaunois Pierre Spicre, who also decorated the second chapel of the north aisle.

But Beaune's showpiece is without doubt the Hôtel-Dieu. Nicolas Rolin, Chancellor of Philip the Good from 1422 till his death in 1462, architect of the treaty of Arras, was one of the outstanding personalities of the age. Born at Autun of humble parents, he was a self-made man who rose by astute practice of the law and who amassed enormous wealth by methods which were not above suspicion. Chastellain painted this picture of him: 'He used to govern everything quite alone, and manage and bear the burden of all business by himself, be it of war, be it of peace, be it of matters of

finance. . . . He always harvested on earth, as though the earth was
to be his abode for ever.' Jacques du Clercq agreed: 'He was reputed
one of the wise men of the kingdom, to speak temporally; for as to
spiritual matters, I shall be silent.'

And yet this proud and avaricious man could write, 'I set aside all
mortal cares and consider nought but my salvation; desiring by a
happy transaction to exchange for heavenly riches those earthly ones
bestowed on me by God's favour, and so render transient bounties
eternal.' With these words he founded the Hôtel-Dieu in 1443, as a
refuge for the sick and impoverished of Beaune. 'It is only fitting,'
remarked Louis XI, 'that he who made so many destitute during his
life should build them an almshouse before he died.' But despite the
sneers of his contemporaries, there is no reason to doubt the
sincerity of Rolin's motives. It was characteristic of the age that
profound piety could co-exist with insane attachment to the delights
of this world—a sort of moral schizophrenia brought about of the
precariousness of life.

Rolin commissioned a design from the Fleming Jacques Wiscrère,
indicating the Hospital of Saint-Jacques at Valenciennes as a model.
The chapel was consecrated on New Year's Eve 1451, and on the
following day Nicolas and his wife, Guigone de Salins, welcomed the
first patient. The original staff were six nuns from Valenciennes, but
their rule proved unsuitably strict for a hospital. They were replaced
by local women who took the simple public (not solemn and
irrevocable) vows of the Beguines. Their uniform, consisting of a
blue woollen frock and white, winged wimple, was only abandoned
recently, after the Second Vatican Council.

The only relief to the severity of the Hôtel-Dieu's plain stone
street-front is the elaborate canopy over the main gate, with its
wrought-iron crest and pinnacles. A delightful detail is the door-
knocker in the form of a lizard poised to take a fly. But nothing
outside prepares us for the blaze of colour in the courtyard. Here
the architect has deployed all his ingenuity. To the conventional
Flamboyant style of the main walls (characterised by the ogee arch),
he has added a vast expanse of steep-pitched roof, covered with
glazed tiles laid in brilliant and complex lozenge patterns in the
Burgundian manner. The eaves project over the balcony, forming
an open gallery whose overhang creates a cloister around two sides
of the courtyard. A double row of gables, richly ornamented with
crockets and filigree cresting, breaks the monotony of the roof. At
the peak of each gable is fixed a sun, emblem of divine charity, from
behind which springs a finely-wrought pinnacle culminating in a
weathervane. The timbers are almost entirely plain, except for the

virtuoso carving of the most westerly gable, as though the sculptor had exhausted his fund of energy and invention in this one work—or perhaps it was just the donors' money that ran out. Access to the gallery is by two staircase towers in the corners, one square and free-standing, the other polygonal and concealed by the gallery. These subtle variations are part of the architect's technique, like the irregular alternation of two-, three- and four-bayed gables; to escape repetitiousness, he consciously rejects symmetry. In dramatic contrast is the grey mass of the Grand' Chambre des Pôvres, its austerity tempered only by its leaden spire and roof-crest, and a row of miniature dormers.

Inside, the vast hall of the Paupers' Ward has remained unchanged in its conception since the fifteenth century. A single nave, 235 feet long, is spanned by what seems like the upturned hull of a ship, a great panelled kingpost roof whose tie-beams issue from the throats of sea-monsters. The choice of this arrangement determined the use of slate for the outer covering, as the vault would have been too frail to carry the weight of glazed tiles. Whereas all the other woodwork in the building is oak, the ceiling panels are of chestnut—a common device in medieval carpentry, because spiders will not fasten their webs to chestnut.

On each side of the ward, a row of 14 four-poster beds is aligned so that the sick can see and follow the services in the chapel, situated behind the screen at the east end. It was of the essence of an Hôtel-Dieu that the founders should provide for the care of the soul as well as of the body. The original beds were twice as wide, and were designed to hold at least two patients (in times of epidemic, they accommodated up to four). The corridor between the beds and the wall permitted the nurses to make the beds and also serve the patients in privacy as occasion required. Each bed has a table and chair at its side; the tables were formerly laid with seventeenth-century pewter drinking services, but today only the large brass wash-basins remain (their size has saved them from souvenir-hunters). At first there was no separation of the sexes, but the young Louis XIV, who visited the hospital in 1658, was so shocked by this lack of propriety that he commanded the women to be moved to another wing. The Grand' Chambre des Pôvres remained in use until 1948, when the pressure of tourism and modern medical requirements put an end to its career. The main hospital has moved to up-to-date premises, though the Hôtel-Dieu still serves as an old people's home.

On a console over the west door of the Grand' Chambre (it has since been brought down to permit closer inspection) stood a superb

Flemish 'Ecce Homo', carved 500 years ago from a single block of oak. The chapel was wrecked during the great Terror of 1793. All its furnishings are nineteenth-century restorations, as are the beds in the ward. A plaque in front of the altar marks the burial-place of Guigone de Salins, who retired to the Hoıtel-Dieu after her husband's death until her own in 1470. Another plaque, on the south wall, records a donation of corn-land made by her stepson Cardinal Jean Rolin; the sisters were enjoined to express their gratitude by daily prayers for his soul. The floor-tiles, faithfully reproduced from the originals, bear the monogram of Nicolas and Guigone and the enigmatic motto *'Seulle étoile'* (the word étoile being represented by its rebus, or pictorial equivalent). If Nicolas meant to imply that Guigone was his 'only star', his reputation as a womaniser suggests that he must have intended the compliment in a purely relative sense.

The kitchens still serve the 240 residents, though the equipment has naturally been modernised. As well as the usual collection of pot-racks and firedogs in the double hearth, the utensils include an automatic turnspit, operated in reality by a rope wound round a drum and released by an escapement, but apparently by a small automaton called Maitre Bertrand. The equipment was built in 1698 by Dufresne, a clockmaker of Beaune.

However, the climax of any visit to the Hôtel-Dieu is a painting, Rogier van der Weyden's polyptych of the Last Judgment. Commissioned by Nicolas Rolin in 1443, it was intended as the altarpiece of the chapel of the Grand' Chambre des Pôvres. After Jan van Eyck's death in 1441, Rogier, who lived and worked in Tournai, was the best-known painter in Flanders and would have been Rolin's natural choice. Normally displaying only the five panels of the reverse, the polyptych was opened out to its full extent of nine panels on feast days. Then the patients in their beds could gaze on the fearful scene and turn their thoughts upon repentance. Hidden in a loft to escape revolutionary vandals, it was reinstated in 1836. Confronted with the nudity of the risen dead, the sisters of the time had the offensive figures clothed in sackcloth. Fortunately, this was only done in water-colour and was easily removed when the painting was sent to Paris for restoration in 1877. The restorers also separated front and back by sawing through the thickness of the panels; this enabled both sides to be exhibited simultaneously. Forced into hiding once again in 1940, in the cellars of the château of La Rochepot, it was brought back under the protection of a senior German officer who guaranteed it against looters. For many years it hung in the cramped surroundings of the Chambre du Roi (so called because Charles IX and Louis XIV had slept there), where the press of visitors created an unacceptable level of humidity. In 1974 it was moved to specially-built accommodation, equipped with the latest automatic temperature, humidity and light controls, at the back of the seventeenth-century Salle Saint-Louis.

Against the fiery sky of the Latter Day, a hieratic Christ sits in judgment, enthroned upon a rainbow. Four angels sound the last trump and the earth gives up its dead. The archangel Michael holds the scales that weigh the sins of the resurrected, while the Virgin Mary and St John the Baptist intercede for man. Behind the protagonists sit the 12 apostles, and behind them again four male figures on the Virgin's side, and three female on the Precursor's. There is no reason to suppose, as has been suggested, that these are portraits from life. For one thing, all the personages are haloed, and for another, all the 'identifications' are contradicted by known portraits, two of which (those of Nicolas and Guigone) were painted by Rogier himself on the reverse of the polyptych. More probably, the artist wanted to represent saints particularly venerated by the donors or the court, although there are no self-evident identifications. On the Saviour's right the just are escorted to the gates of Heaven, while on His left the damned are hurled screaming into the sulphurous pit. The two small uppermost panels show angels bearing the instruments of the Passion.

When closed, these upper panels depict the Annunciation, in grisaille. Beneath them, on the large central panels, are St Sebastian (whose protection was invoked against the plague) and St Antony the hermit (the original patron of the Hôtel-Dieu), also in grisaille. On the flanking panels, the donors kneel in prayer, attended by angels bearing their respective coats of arms: the Chancellor's three keys, and Guigone's tower impaled with her husband's emblem.

The polyptych is one of the most magnificent creations of international Gothic style, a worthy rival to the van Eycks' 'altarpiece of the Lamb' at Ghent. Rogier was modern in that he understood the problem of dynamic composition, and yet he conformed faithfully to the materialistic idiom of his time. What strikes one most is the extreme naturalism, or rather literalism, of the treatment. Obsessive care is bestowed on the minutest details of wild flowers and of the scales in the archangel's hand. Every hair and wrinkle has been painted individually; when the painting hung in the Chambre du Roi, the guides used a magnifying-glass to demonstrate the quality of the craftsmanship. Every jewel sewn on the Virgin's cuff has been depicted with painstaking accuracy. Especially remarkable, for a picture painted about 1450, are the nude figures of the wakened dead. The stimulus of classical antiquity, so crucial in Italy, was absent in the North. The empirical study of the nude was well advanced there, however—a fact which finds eloquent testimony in the Beaune 'Last Judgment'. The greatest splendour of costume is concentrated in the central panel: Christ's enveloping crimson robe with its gold-stitched hem; St Michael's stiff brocade pluvial, and his wings—surely the most extravagant touch of all—composed entirely of peacock's feathers.

Though the picture has suffered some damage during its long history, its grandeur is undiminished. Even after many viewings, the effect is overpowering. One hardly has eyes for the other exhibits in the room: a tapestry of the picturesque legend of St Eligius, and one of the Hôtel-Dieu's original counterpanes showing St Antony, the donors' monogram, Guigone's arms, turtledoves perched on dead branches (representing Guigone's widowhood), and the device '*Seulle étoile*' that runs through the Hôtel-Dieu like a leitmotiv.

By a happy coincidence, the centre of Beaune's tourist trade is also the focal point of the Burgundy wine trade. Chancellor Rolin endowed his foundation with an income drawn on the revenues of the salt-works at Salins, part of Guigone's dowry. By the time of his death this was already proving insufficient, and Rolin had been granted the duke's permission to solicit new donations. In those days most gifts and legacies were in kind, so it was natural for a charitable institution in a wine-growing area to acquire property in the form of vines. As a result of patient accumulation, the Hospices de Beaune (the collective name of the Hôtel-Dieu and the Hospice de la Charité, founded in 1645 and amalgamated with the former at the Revolution) today own 2,000 acres of land in Burgundy, 125 of which produce the greatest wines of the Côte de Beaune. The income derived from these holdings enables the hospital to remain independent and self-supporting.

Since 1851, the wines of the Hospices have been sold at a public auction held on the third Sunday in November. This has become a great international event, attracting merchants not only from France but from all over the world. It is also the excuse for the three-day festivities known as the Trois Glorieuses. On the Saturday night, the Chevaliers du Tastevin give a banquet presided over by the celebrity who will have the honour of opening the auction the following day. Saturday afternoon has already been given up to the tasting (as much as you like, after your entry fee has been paid) of the 31 *cuvées* offered for sale. These *cuvées* are not referred to by their strict *appellation contrôlée* (which must however appear on the bottle-label), but by the names of the Hospices' many benefactors.

The *dégustation* takes place in the *cuverie* of the Hôtel-Dieu, at the back of the inner courtyard. The auction, which takes place in the Market Hall on Sunday afternoon, is conducted by the traditional method: a taper is lit, and when it goes out its place is taken by another so long as the bidding continues; when a second candle has gone out without a new bid being made, the lot is knocked down. The prices fetched are of vital concern to the *vignerons* of Burgundy, as they determine the general price level for that particular year. The day ends with a candlelight dinner inside one of the wine-cellar-bastions of the town walls. On Monday the venue moves south to Meursault, the centre of the white-wine-growing district of the Côte. The Paulée was formerly the dinner given by each *vigneron* to his vintagers when the last *balonge* had been brought home. Its modern manifestation is a prestige bottle-party for 300 growers, each of whom brings two bottles of his best wine.

Beaune's most noted hotel, the Hôtel de la Poste, stands just outside the ramparts on the corner of the Chalon road. It is one of the very few places where the Burgundian egg dish *oeufs en meurette* is done to perfection, and would be worth a visit for that reason alone. The sauce presents no difficulty, provided it is freshly-made and not over-cooked. The principle is to poach the egg (either in the sauce or in water), and then lay it on a *croûton* rubbed with garlic, and finally cover with the sauce. The simplicity is deceptive. Above all, the timing has to be perfect; nothing must be kept waiting, and this does not suit restaurants. The *croûtons* must be warm and soft (those not rock-hard the French in moments of enthusiasm call *toasts*), and the egg must be poached very soft, so that at the stroke of a knife the yolk can escape to mingle with the sauce. This cannot be achieved with an English poaching-pan.

Pommard rivals Beaune and Nuits-Saint-Georges as the best-known name among burgundies. Its sheer availability has contributed largely to its popularity. Even leaving aside wines 'stretched' beyond recognition or simply mislabelled (unfortunately common outside France), Pommard is, in terms of volume of production, the biggest village name among Côte d'Or red wines after Gevrey-Chambertin. It has the reputation of being the most full-bodied wine of the Côte de Beaune, though some find it often unsubtle and dull. With such a copious output, wide variations in quality are inevitable. Pommard was (yet another) favourite of Henri IV, and also of Victor Hugo.

Nearby Volnay also has a great following, but for quite a different reason: it is the most delicate and exquisitely perfumed of all burgundies. The dukes of Burgundy had one of their most prized vineyards here, as well as one of their favourite country residences. In 1336 King Philip VI paid a visit, and was so appreciative of his host's Volnay that Eudes IV made him a present of six dozen barrels. Another royal aficionado was Louis XI, who celebrated his triumph over Charles the Rash by having the entire 1477 vintage of ducal Volnay conveyed to his château of Plessis-lès-Tours.

After Volnay, the wine route forks right and left. To the right, mounting the valley towards Saint-Romain, the reds continue with Monthelie and Auxey-Duresses, both of which formerly sold their wine as Pommard or Volnay and helped to enhance the fame of those two villages. Today they go unjustly ignored, but are excellent value now that names have inflated prices beyond measure. M. Pierre Forgeot has speculated that this sheltered *combe* might have witnessed the very first cultivation of the vine in Burgundy, over a century before the arrival of the Romans.

The left-hand fork descends steeply into Meursault and the region of the great white wines. For the next five and a half miles the subsoil contains large deposits of whitish marl, very favourable to the chardonnay. Probably no other village of the Côte is so redolent of comfort and well-being as Meursault. The whisper is that France's richest peasants live behind its houses' limestone walls. There are no *grands crus* here, but Meursault is one of the most consistent of the well-known Burgundy names. While remaining steadfastly dry, its best wines have a certain unctuousness that comes from a high glycerine content. Cardinal de Bernis, French ambassador to the Holy See under Louis XV, would celebrate mass with no other wine; 'I don't want my Creator to see me pull a face when I make my communion,' he explained. There are red vines at Meursault—to the north of the village—but the best of them, the Santenots, are sold as Volnay, whose territory they adjoin.

Puligny and Chassagne share 18 unremarkable acres which produce the greatest dry white wine in the world. Its price alone would compel respect from most people, but we are assured that one can never pay too much for it. The contemplation of it filled Alexandre Dumas with religious awe: 'Montrachet,' he said, 'should be drunk on bended knee and with head bared.' Chevalier-Montrachet (above) and Bâtard-Montrachet and Criots-Bâtard-Montrachet (below) have the same virtues, but to a less intense degree. They are all drier and paler than the Meursaults, with a delicious greenish tinge. Some commentators find their taste too overpowering for fish, and recommend them to be drunk either on their own, or with plainly cooked chicken. Of the village wines, Puligny-Montrachet is almost exclusively white, while Chassagne-

Montrachet is predominantly red.

Behind Chassagne, just off the RN6 and at the foot of the second line of hills, nestles Saint-Aubin, another of the great unknowns. The production is mainly of aligoté and of red *Côte de Beaune-Villages*, but of the small quantity of fine white wines, some have all the dry richness of the best Puligny-Montrachet, and are considerably cheaper. The possibility of making discoveries like this is one of the greatest pleasures Burgundy has to offer. The Hambledon vineyard of Sir Guy Salisbury-Jones (once featured in a French newsreel under the heading of '*Ces curieux Anglais*') was planted with seedlings raised at Saint-Aubin. Close by is the hamlet of Gamay, which has given its name to the controversial variety of grape.

The Côte d'Or—both the geographical feature and the department—comes to an end at Santenay, overlooked by the spectacular belvedere of the Montagne des Trois Croix. Santenay's red wines, like those of Chassagne, are closer to those of the Côte de Nuits than to those of nearer neighbours; full-bodied and distinctive, more tender and sometimes less finished than the wines from north of Beaune. Just across the border in Saône-et-Loire, Dezize, Sampigny and Cheilly produce a similar wine that is almost invariably marketed as *Côte de Beaune-Villages*. Santenay boasts a spring whose waters have the highest lithium content in Europe, and appropriately are recommended for liver complaints and gout. Today the casino is a bigger attraction than the spa.

Behind the densely-populated slopes of the Côte d'Or lies a whole region whose existence passes ignored by foreign tourists. Among the hills of the Arrière-Côte, there are places as wild and lonely as the remotest corners of the Morvan. In a few favoured spots one finds the vines of the Hautes-Côtes, many of which lay fallow until quite recently after the passage of the phylloxera. The altitude and exposure to frosts make this a territory for the gamay and aligoté, and what pinot there is goes mostly into the making of passetout-grains. There are no village names (except Saint-Romain, which is really a deep extension of the Côte de Beaune vineyard and produces some excellent white wine from the chardonnay), though wines made exclusively from the pinot are entitled to call themselves *Bourgogne-Hautes-Côtes de Nuits* or *de Beaune*, the latter being more common.

In the north, a ruined castle founded on the solid rock of a high ridge preserves the memory of one of Burgundy's most powerful baronial families, the *preux* or 'doughty' de Vergy. From their impregnable fortress, these troublesome vassals often defied the early dukes. The situation was skilfully exploited by King Philip

Augustus to humiliate the rebellious Hugues III in 1186. Hugues' son solved the problem once and for all by marrying the last baron's only surviving child, the celebrated Alix de Vergy. She later proved a shrewd and successful regent during the minority of her son Hugues IV. The castle of Vergy became a nest of Catholic Leaguers during the Wars of Religion, and was demolished on the orders of Henri IV.

To the south of Beaune, the scenery of the Arrière-Côte becomes more dramatic as limestone gorges and amphitheatres, their cliffs pitted and furrowed by erosion, create a sort of miniature Jura. Nolay was the birthplace of Lazare Carnot (1753-1823), the 'organiser of Victory', whose logistical genius—with a little help from mass conscription—turned the tide against France's enemies between 1794 and 1797. His nephew Sadi Carnot became President of the Republic, only to be stabbed to death at Lyon by an Italian anarchist in 1894.

Not far from Nolay, dominating the narrow valley that leads to Chagny and the plain, stands the château of La Rochepot. Régnier Pot, who bought the castle in 1403 and whose family have given it their name, came originally from Berry and was one of the 10,000 French knights who accompanied the duke of Nevers (the future John the Fearless) on the ill-fated crusade against the Ottomans in 1396. The Christians undertook their campaign in a spirit of bravado and chivalrous adventure. They were duly cut to pieces at Nicopolis. The duke and a few lucky survivors, among them Régnier Pot, were taken prisoner and held to ransom. At this point legend takes over: Sultan Bayazid, full of admiration for his captive's bravery, offered Régnier his sister's hand in marriage. The knight refused indignantly, on the grounds that he was already married, and that to accept would amount to a renunciation of his faith. Furious, the sultan sentenced him to a terrible combat the following day. That night, the Virgin Mary appeared to Pot in a dream and said simply, 'Strike low.' The next morning, he was given a scimitar and led to the arena, where he was confronted by a half-starved lion. Pausing only for a quick prayer to the Virgin, he marched up to the animal and shore off its front legs with a single blow. Bayazid graciously forgave the affront and set Régnier free.

What is sure is that Régnier returned and rose to become chamberlain to the duke of Burgundy, ambassador to Hungary, and a knight of the Golden Fleece. He bought the castle at La Roche-Nolay and made a considerable number of improvements to it. The most notable was a 300-foot well dug from the solid rock. which was reputed to have cost as much as the castle. His grandson

Philippe Pot enjoyed an even more illustrious career: godson of Philip the Good, knight of the Golden Fleece, chamberlain, Steward of the Duke's Household, governor of Lille and ambassador to England. His famous eloquence led to his being entrusted with innumerable special missions, among them the negotiations for all three of Charles the Rash's marriages. After Charles's death he rallied to Louis XI, who made him guardian of the Dauphin and revived the title of Seneschal of Burgundy especially for him. Understandably, his name was expunged from the rolls of the Golden Fleece, but as compensation he received the royal Order of St Michael.

Philippe Pot emerges as one of the most engaging personalities at the court of Burgundy. At the banquet of the Vow of the Pheasant, when the assembled nobles were called upon to make vows connected with the proposed crusade, Philippe Pot pledged not to eat sitting down on Tuesdays, and also to fight with his right arm bare. (Philip the Good rejected this latter vow, as if he thought Pot were serious). On another occasion, the duke, beside himself with rage after a quarrel with his son Charles, rode off alone into the night and lost his way in the woods. Philippe Pot, diplomat extraordinary, was assigned the task of pacifying him on his bedraggled return—and he did it with a joke, at the duke's expense: 'Good day, my liege, good day, what is this? Are we playing King Arthur now, or Sir Lancelot?' Many years later, his speech to the States General at Tours in 1484 foreshadows ideas of a constitutional monarchy. When he died in 1494, he was buried in the abbey church at Cîteaux and honoured with a tomb that would have been worthy of his former masters. The sculptor was almost certainly Le Moiturier, who completed the tomb of John the Fearless and Margaret of Bavaria. In the tomb of Philippe Pot, the artist is free of the restrictions imposed on him in the earlier work, and seizes the opportunity to create something original. The cortège is reduced to eight life-size cowled figures who bear the effigy on their shoulders. Rescued at the Revolution, the tomb remained in private hands at Dijon for 90 years, before being snapped up by the Louvre when the corporation of Dijon refused to make a reasonable offer for it. (Anyone interested in the art of Valois Burgundy should stop off in Paris to admire not only the tomb, but also van Eyck's 'Virgin and Child with Chancellor Rolin', commissioned by Rolin for his parish church at Autun).

Philippe Pot rebuilt his castle at La Rochepot extensively, and gave it its definitive character. But by the time it was gutted by fire during the Revolution, it had already suffered badly from neglect. Like so many other monuments, it was sold off for its value as building stone and the whole of one side, including the keep, was dismantled. In 1893 it was saved from utter ruin by Mme Sadi Carnot. Her programme could be described not so much as restoration as recreation, albeit surprisingly authentic, of a romantic medieval fortress. Perched on its hilltop, sprouting pepper-pot towers, La Rochepot revived has become as much an emblem of Burgundy as Clos-Vougeot or the Hôtel-Dieu at Beaune.

6   The Auxois

In 1456 Catherine de Châteauneuf was drawn on a hurdle through the streets of Paris and burnt at the stake. She had fed her husband poisoned cakes, and the murder had come to light through the death of a kitchen-maid who had helped herself. Philip the Good confiscated Catherine's fief of Châteauneuf and presented it to Philippe Pot. By extensions and alterations, the new owner created the castle whose exterior has remained virtually unchanged to the present day, a rare example of fifteenth-century military architecture and a landmark for travellers on the Paris-Lyon motorway.

Standing on one of the westernmost outposts of the *montagne* whose eastern edge is the Côte d'Or, Châteauneuf surveys the approaches to Arnay-le-Duc and looks out over the Auxois. Geographically, the Auxois can be divided into two sections. Firstly, a broad depression surrounding the north-eastern margins of the Morvan, eroded from the softer rocks by the action of mountain streams, watered by the Armançon and broken up by isolated groups of hills. This depression is flanked to the east by a series of parallel ridges which separate the narrow valleys of the Armançon's tributaries, the Brenne, the Ozerain and the Oze. On the lower ground the soil is rich and heavy; this was once Burgundy's granary, as the proliferation of hamlets, castles and manor-houses testifies. Since the Revolution, marsh-drainage, fertilisers and improved transport have made other areas competitive, and arable farming has steadily declined in favour of grazing. The draught-horses of the Auxois were famous until the coming of the internal combustion engine, but today the pastures are for fattening the herds of white Charollais cattle.

In the valley below Châteauneuf, another servant of the dukes (Jacques de Cortiamble, chamberlain to Philip the Bold and standard-bearer of John the Fearless) built the two surviving round towers of the château of Commarin. In 1622 the de Vienne family rebuilt the east wing; then 80 years later, after the collapse of one of the towers and the incredible escape of Charles de Vienne's baby daughter, a more radical reconstruction was put in hand. A comfortable Louis XIV residence was created, with a harmonious façade looking across the moat on to the park. Marie-Judith de Vienne, the heiress so miraculously preserved, married into the Damas family and was the grandmother of Talleyrand, Napoleon's foreign minister. For 600 years, even during the Revolution, Commarin has never changed hands except by marriage and inheritance.

At Pouilly-en-Auxois the Burgundy Canal crosses from the Saône to the Seine basin by means of a two-mile-long tunnel. The Semur road follows the canal northwards along the valley of the Armançon until the eye, lulled by the landscape, is brought up sharply by the sight of a grotesque monument. It is the church of Saint-Thibault, whose huge chancel rises to more than twice the height of the nave. About 1240, a small priory acquired some relics of St Theobald of Provins, and the fame of miracles attributed to these relics caused the nearby village to adopt the saint's name. The influx of pilgrims and their money had become so great by 1257 that the monks decided on a rebuilding programme. As far as we can tell, they first constructed a new, magnificently-sculptured north door to give pilgrims access to the church from outside the priory grounds, then a Chapel of Saint-Gilles to house the relics, and about 1290 a grandiose new chancel for themselves. They afterwards turned their attention to the monastery proper, but were overtaken by the economic crisis resulting from the Black Death and the Hundred Years' War. If they had any plans for rebuilding the nave on the same scale as the chancel, they never realised them.

By the early eighteenth century, the old nave was in ruins and the congregation had to stand in the churchyard in all weathers to hear mass. With major repairs indispensable, one architect saw no alternative to demolition. Fortunately, the villagers were horrified at the thought of losing their chancel and the work was entrusted to a less uncompromising contractor.

The treasure that the peasants of Saint-Thibault were so determined to save is, in its small way, reminiscent of Beauvais—which it post-dates by some 40 years, if the archaeologists who place it in the last decade of the thirteenth century are correct. Both represent the most exciting period of Gothic architecture, when walls were transformed into sheets of glass, vaults soared to vertiginous heights (Saint-Thibault is over 100 feet from floor to keystone), and no technical feat seemed impossible. Both were dreams only partially realised. There the resemblance ends. The Burgundian manner was more sober than that of northern France—there is no ambulatory, and long, unbroken vertical stretches of glass are avoided. The architect of Saint-Thibault was less ambitious than those of Beauvais;

despite its apparent boldness, his church is stable enough to do without flying buttresses.

The typanum of the north door is dedicated to the Virgin, her death, Assumption and Coronation. The carved door-panels recall episodes from the life of St Theobald, who presides on the central pier. Far more striking are the four statues standing in the jambs—a bishop, a noblewoman, a bearded man and a youth. No-one can say for sure who they are. One school of thought sees them as portraits of Duke Robert II (1272-1306), his eldest son Hugues V (1306-15), his wife Agnes of France, daughter of St Louis, and their friend and confidant Hugues d'Arcy, bishop of Autun; another sees them merely as conventional representations of Solomon, David, Aaron and the queen of Sheba. Even if we knew the exact date of the north door (and the chronology of Saint-Thibault is still a subject for dispute), it would still be possible that these statues were not the original occupants of their pedestals. Unless new evidence comes to light, the mystery of their identity seems unlikely ever to be solved.

To the east, a gap in the hills leads to the valley of the Brenne and the little market town of Vitteaux. For years, half the population have wanted to tear down their thirteenth-century market-hall, while the other half have sworn that they shall not pass. Admittedly, the hall is in a deplorable state, and is indeed a major traffic hazard if the RN5 is to pass right through the town; but the conservationists allege that by-pass plans have been blocked by their opponents, mainly small tradesmen, who would rather lose their history than the casual custom of motorists and long-distance lorry-drivers. There have been dramatic developments in the best tradition of Clochemerle: the pro-market faction succeeded in having the building listed, and the mayor and council resigned in protest. Actual restoration seems as far off as ever, the market-hall crumbles quietly, and the saga continues.

A little further north along the *nationale,* at Posanges, there is a well-preserved specimen of the type of castle erected in plains and valleys, where the lie of the land offered no strategic position: a square composed of four round towers linked by curtain walls. Most of these lowland fortresses, like Commarin and Bussy-Rabutin, were converted into hospitable residences in more peaceful times. Posanges is unusual in that it has retained its military character, despite a period from 1714 until the Revolution when it belonged to the Ursuline nuns of Vitteaux. To them we owe the unexpected inscription *Ad maiorem Dei gloriam* over the main gate. On the plain of Les Laumes, the Brenne is joined by the Oze and the Ozerain. In the centre of a ring of hills rises Mont Auxois, now accepted beyond reasonable doubt as the site of the grand finale of Caesar's Gallic Wars, the siege of Alesia.

Between 58 and 56 B.C. Caesar had overrun Gaul but not pacified it. After turning his attention briefly to Britain, he had had to spend most of 53 B.C. putting down a series of unco-ordinated revolts in northern Gaul. This was nothing to what took place in 52 B.C., when it seemed that a crisis in Rome might lead to his recall. A general rebellion broke out in central Gaul under the leadership of Vercingetorix, a chieftain of the Arverni, and Caesar was on the brink of disaster after failing to storm the Arvernian stronghold at Gergovia (near Clermont-Ferrand). The Aedui of Burgundy, hitherto faithful allies of the Romans, joined the revolt on the assumption that Caesar's defeat was now a foregone conclusion. However, with Vercingetorix at his heels, Caesar managed to slip away northwards to link forces with his lieutenant Labienus, who had been stamping out resistance in the region of Paris and Sens. The Romans regrouped in the territory of the Lingones (around Langres and Châtillon), who had not broken faith, and then headed in the direction of the river Saône as though trying to regain the comparative safety of Provence.

Seeing the Romans apparently in full retreat, Vercingetorix decided that he could afford to risk a pitched battle. He was wrong. Now it was his turn to be chased by Caesar. He took up a prepared position inside Alesia, no doubt hoping to repeat the success of Gergovia. But now he was no longer on his home ground, and Caesar was determined not to repeat the mistake of an assault. Instead, he surrounded the hill of Alesia with a double row of fortifications—one to keep Vercingetorix in, the other to keep reinforcements out. The besieged managed to send out an appeal for help before the ring was closed, and an army 250,000 strong arrived within six weeks. Despite its overwhelming superiority in numbers, it failed to break through Caesar's lines—the Roman cavalry even made a successful sortie. The Gallic commanders fell out among themselves, and the relief force melted away. In an attempt to save the lives of his men, Vercingetorix surrendered. Six years later, when Caesar celebrated his triumph, Vercingetorix was led in chains through the streets of Rome before being strangled in the dungeons of the Tullian prison. Romantics have seen this tragic adventure as the earliest expression of French patriotism, the birth of a national consciousness. Unfortunately, their ancestors the Gauls do not seem to have shared these noble sentiments. The self-seeking of the various tribes, each jealous of its autonomy, ensured their downfall. Vercingetorix is commemorated by a colossal bronze statue on the summit of Mont Auxois; ironically, by his imposition of the *pax Romana,* Caesar was undeniably France's greater benefactor.

Alise-Sainte-Reine has not been alone in claiming to be the original of Alesia; other contenders have been situated as far apart as Franche-Comté and Languedoc. But there must be some sound historical reason why this otherwise insignificant village should have given its name to the whole of the surrounding countryside, since Auxois is a corruption of (pagus) Alisiensis. The matter was settled by the excavations conducted between 1861 and 1865 on the orders of Napoleon III. The Emperor's interest stemmed from his work on a *History of Julius Caesar,* in which he drew instructive parallels between himself and the great Roman for the benefit of the French people. Weapons, bones of men and horses, and traces of fortifications were unearthed at Alise. Also, Caesar had referred to Alesia as a holy place with pan-Celtic associations—one of Vercingetorix's reasons for choosing it—and subsequent diggings indicate that the town was a religious centre at least as far back as the Roman occupation. The Roman remains are not very striking, and pre-Roman ones almost non-existent. All the same, the road from Les Laumes to Alise does cross Caesars's defensive ditch, parts of which were excavated in 1956 and found to be exactly as he described it; and with a copy of the *Gallic Wars,* one can easily follow the course of the campaign from the vantage-point at the top of the hill.

Les Laumes, at the foot of Mont Auxois, is the gift of the railway. In the days of steam, this was as far as the trains from Paris could go before the locomotives needed water, and so it was selected as the site for a large depot which electric power has made redundant. It is a good place to drive through as quickly as possible, though redeemed by M. Lesprit's Hôtel de la Gare, where crayfish and ham in wine-lees sauce are two of the specialities to look forward to after a morning at Alesia.

Such an arrangement would fit in perfectly with an afternoon visit to the château of Bussy-Rabutin. The interest of this former medieval fortress, transformed during the sixteenth and seventeenth centuries, lies in the fact that it was the home of Roger de Rabutin, comte de Bussy. To us it seems strange that the worst misfortune that could befall a French nobleman was exclusion from the insanitary halls of Versailles, where winter frosts turned wine to ice as it stood in the decanters. But Bussy could only see his pleasant provincial refuge as a gallery of nostalgia for his life at court. Vanity and indiscretion made him accident-prone. A promising military career came to an end when he let it be known that he considered himself Turenne's equal. The latter described Bussy to Louis XIV as 'the best officer in your army, for songs'. A first exile followed the notorious 'debauch of Roissy', when, during Holy Week, Bussy and other rake-hells sang obscene lyrics to hymn-tunes and a future cardinal baptised a frog. Bussy was accompanied into exile by his mistress, the Marquise de Montglat, and for her diversion he sketched out an *Amorous History of Gaul,* satirising the sexual intrigues of the court. The manuscript circulated privately without Bussy's knowledge or permission, and was eventually published at Liège in 1665. Despite the scandal, the king—who had not been attacked—was amused and even approved Bussy's election to the Académie Française. However, the Prince of Condé, who *had* been a victim, commissioned a hack to lampoon the king's association with Louise de la Vallière, and spread the word that Bussy was the author of the piece.

The luckless satirist landed in the Bastille, and was released 13 months later only to be banished from court indefinitely. This time the Marquise de Montglat stayed in Paris. Bussy settled down reluctantly to the life of a country gentleman, and devoted his exile to interior decoration. His efforts may not be the most exquisite in France or even in Burgundy, but they are certainly the most entertaining. Off the lobby opens the Salle des Devises, the Motto Room, which takes its name from its painted panels illustrating allegorical subjects. Bussy appears as the reed that bends but does not break, the fountain that owes its height to its high origin, the onion that makes the eyes smart. The Marquise is the siren who lures to destruction and the swallow that flies away at the first breath of winter. Above these are pictures of all the royal residences of the time.

On the first floor, the Salon des Grands Hommes de Guerre crowds together 65 portraits of great warriors from du Guesclin to Bussy himself, mostly French but with the pointed inclusion of Oliver Cromwell. The gallery of the adjoining wing houses pictures of all the kings of France from Hugh Capet, while the count's bedroom is hung with portraits of famous royal mistresses and of members of his own family, including his cousin Madame de Sévigné. Bussy surpassed himself in the decoration of the Tour Dorée, a circular room occupying the whole of the first storey of the west tower, and covered from floor to ceiling with paintings. The leading figures of the courts of Louis XIII and XIV—the kings themselves, Richelieu, Mazarin, the Condés—compete with mythological subjects and a series of portraits of the most beautiful women in society, caustically captioned. The inscription for the comtesse d'Olonne reads, 'The most beautiful woman of her time,

but less famous for her beauty than for the use she made of it.'
These four last rooms, according to Bussy, composed 'a résumé of
history ancient and modern which is all that I wish my children to
know on the subject'. Bussy was never received back at court, and died
at Autun in 1693.

The best approach to Flavigny is along the road that descends
from Alise to cross the Ozerain. It must have been this view from the
valley that inspired Chateaubriand to compare Flavigny to
Jerusalem, though the lush Burgundian countryside does not have
much in common with Palestine. The town stands on a rocky
promontory, almost isolated by the Ozerain and two small
tributaries, and the road climbs steeply to the Porte du Val. In the
Middle Ages, Flavigny was one of the most important fortified cities
of Burgundy. As late as 1589 it was, with Semur, a seat of the
provincial government when Dijon was controlled by the Catholic
Leaguers. Then the nobles and bourgeois drifted away and their
hôtels became workshops and cattle-stables. By the beginning of this
century, Flavigny was quite forgotten except as the home of its *anis*,
tiny sugar-drops with aniseed centres. The recipe dates back at least
to the seventeenth century, when a congregation of Ursulines
arrived from Langres and began to produce *anis* commercially. One
unsubstantiated account credits the Romans with introducing them
for medicinal purposes when Flavigny was a field-hospital during
the siege of Alesia. The manufacture of *anis* remained a cottage
industry until the 1900's, when production was centred on the
former Benedictine abbey.

In recent years, Flavigny has been 'discovered'. The old houses, all
in disrepair and some ruinous, are now making a fortune for their
restorers. The peasants are moving out, and the owners of antique
shops, arts-and-crafts studios and second homes are taking their
place. The town has been listed as an ancient monument, but the
price of its rescue will be part of its charm.

The heart of Flavigny is the church of Saint-Genès, unremarkable
on the outside, but which boasts an interesting set of choir-stalls.
Though not as fine as those at Montréal or Brou, they have the same
rich sense of caricature and earthy humour. One of the characters
blows his nose without a handkerchief, 'like an archdeacon' as the
French say, though why this should have been thought typical of
archdeacons is a mystery. The church possesses one incomparable
work of art, a late fifteenth-century statue known popularly as 'the
Smiling Angel'. It stands in a mouldering side-chapel and is in fact an
Angel of the Annunciation, though the other half of the group has
vanished. He greets Mary with a graceful reverence and a sublime

smile. We do not know the sculptor's name, only that he evidently worked in the best traditions of Sluter and Le Moiturier. The statue was found in the vaults of Saint-Genès in 1933, smashed in 30 pieces.

The Maison Lacordaire is named after the Dominican preacher and disciple of the Catholic liberal Lamennais. Lacordaire and six companions, 'riding on carts, like patriarchs', arrived in December 1848 with the absolute minimum of belongings; in the whole house there was only a chair apiece. They set up a small community whose premises, originally the residence of the bailiff of the Auxois, are now occupied by a convent of Dominican nuns.

Today, Flavigny has become a centre of Catholic traditionalism. Father Coache, head of the seminary there, is a staunch supporter of Archbishop Lefebvre and the campaign against the Vatican II reforms.

From the Porte du Bourg, the only entrance to Flavigny not guarded by a precipice, the old road strikes out across the plateau that separates the valleys of the Ozerain and the Brenne, and heads in the direction of another fortress-town—Semur, capital of the Auxois.

In the eighteenth century, Semur-en-Auxois was called 'the little Athens of Burgundy', a comparison which is not as far-fetched as that of Flavigny with Jerusalem. Swarming up the sides of a pink granite bluff surrounded by a meander of the Armançon and superbly crowned by the church of Notre-Dame, it does have the air of a northern Acropolis. In fact, the most spectacular approach is not from Flavigny, but from the Lac de Pont or from the Paris road (N80). In both these cases, one has a clear view of the town across the ravine before going down to one of the bridges. The ground-plan of the old town is shaped like an hourglass; its neck was defended by an impregnable citadel, of which only the four great towers remain. On the death of Charles the Rash, Semur declared for his daughter Mary and, after a long siege, was savagely punished for its resistance to Louis XI.

The Pont Joly crosses the river in a single bold span to the foot of the Tour de l'Orle d'Or, once one of the town's principal gates. Nowadays one has to climb past it and double back into the town centre through the barbican which precedes the massive Porte Sauvigny, the gateway of the *bourg*. A cramped medieval street leads to Notre-Dame, founded in the 9th century by the semi-legendary Girard de Roussillon, and rebuilt by Duke Robert I in 1060 in expiation for the murder of his father-in-law. The present building is pure Gothic, begun in 1225, and provided in the fifteenth century with a peculiarly Burgundian feature, a large porch.

The term 'miniature cathedral', often used of Notre-Dame de

1 DIJON—West front of the church of Saint-Michel.

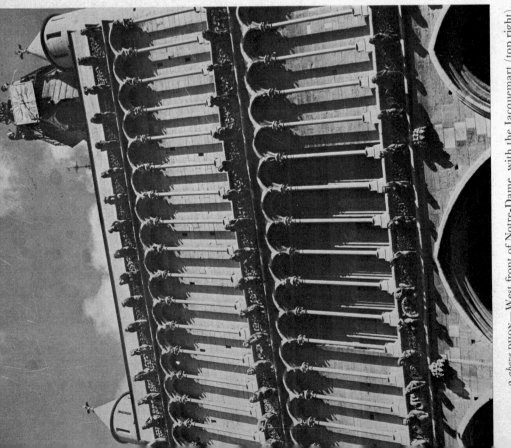

2 *above* DIJON—West front of Notre-Dame, with the Jacquemart (top right).

4 DIJON—'Moses', from the Well of Moses at the Chartreuse de Champmol, by Claus Sluter.

5 *opposite, top left* DIJON—*Pleurants* from the tomb of John the Fearless and
Margaret of Bavaria, by Juan de la Huerta. (Musée des Beaux-Arts).

6 *opposite, top right* DIJON—Newel-head at the Hôtel Chambellan,
Rue des Forges.

7 *opposite* SEMUR-EN-AUXOIS—Church of Notre-Dame, with the
Pont Pinard in the foreground.

8 *above* CHÂTILLON-SUR-SEINE—Church of Saint-Vorles; seen from
the banks of the Douix.

9 SENS — Cathedral of Saint-Etienne: rose-window of the south transept.

10 AVALLON — Church of Saint-Lazare, small portal ('Florid Romanesque' style).

11 *opposite*, *top* AUTUN—the town, with the cathedral of
Saint-Lazare, seen from the south.

12 *opposite* AUTUN—Cathedral of Saint-Lazare: tympanum of the main
portal—the 'Last Judgment' by Gislebertus.

13 *above* SULLY—the château: north wing and water-stairs.

14 *above* ANZY-LE-DUC—
crossing-tower of
the priory church.

15 *left* SEMUR-EN-
BRIONNAIS—chevet and
crossing-tower of the
church of Saint-Hilaire.

16 *opposite* PARAY-LE
MONIAL—Basilica of
the Sacred Heart,
reflected in
the River Bourbince.

17 *left* TOURNUS—entrance to the former monastery close, with the church of Saint-Philibert in the background.

19 *right* CLUNY—Clocher de l'Eau Bénite, seen from the gateway to the abbey grounds.

20 *above* CLUNY—interior of south transept.

21 SAINT-POINT—the château, Lamartine's favourite residence.

22 *opposite* SOLUTRÉ—the Rock.

23 BROU (BOURG-EN-BRESSE) — Tomb of Margaret of Austria.

Dijon, could be applied with much more justice to Notre-Dame de Semur. Apart from the astonishing impression of height, due to the extreme narrowness of the nave and the absence of a triforium, this is the only Gothic church in Côte d'Or with an ambulatory. The choir and transept, unlike the nave, have a triforium; its arches and portrait gallery of grotesques add a decorative element to the airy elegance of the east end.

The second side-chapel off the north aisle houses a fine polychrome Entombment sculpted about 1490. The burial of Christ, featuring the Virgin, St John, the Three Maries, Nicodemus and Joseph of Arimathaea, was a theme that appealed to the crude sense of compassion of the late Middle Ages. The subject, which was especially popular in north-west Europe, is treated here with great restraint. The three succeeding chapels are remarkable for their stained glass. The window of the first (c. 1536) relates the story of St Barbara, but it is the other two that steal the scene with their rare secular interest. These are guild chapels of the late fourteenth century, and their windows proudly illustrate the everyday work of their sponsors. In the Butchers' Chapel, one guild member slaughters a beast while another prepares meat at his stall. In the Drapers' Chapel next door, the window is a complete visual guide to cloth-working, though only four of the eight lights—those depicting weaving, fulling, carding and shearing—are original. The simplicity of the designs is a delight for those who tire easily of trying to decipher the more conventional 'biblical' windows.

Outside, the sculpture of the west doors has almost disappeared, but the north door (Porte des Bleds) has escaped mutilation. Framed by the Labours of the Months, the tympanum tells one of the most exotic stories in the *Golden Legend,* that of St Thomas and his journey to India. By way of light relief and local colour, the sculptor has completed the doorway with a pair of snails, which crawl up one of the pillars.

Semur is the home of the oldest horse-race in France, the Course à la Bague (run every year on 31 May from Villenotte to the Promenade du Cours at Semur) which goes back to at least 1643, when it replaced a foot-race in which the runners 'exposed themselves pointlessly to death and endangered their souls by indulging in sports reminiscent of pagan antiquity'!

Despite the defiant aspect of their towers and ramparts, we have it on the authority of Sebastian Munster, a monk writing in 1552, that 'the citizens of Semur are peaceful people, gentle, good-natured and charitable, loving and cherishing one another, and delighting in the company of strangers'. That they were at least charitable, we know from their gesture to the songwriter Béranger in 1821, when the latter was imprisoned for outrage to public morals. They sent him a hamper of Chambertin and Romanée, and 'prescribed internal shower-baths during my stay in Sainte-Pélagie'.

Eight miles to the west lies Epoisses, whose château can reasonably claim to occupy the oldest continuously fortified site in Burgundy. In 598 it became the residence of the Frankish king of Burgundy, Thierry, and his grandmother Brunnhild—the bogeywoman of French history under the name of *la reine Brunehaut*. Expelled from the court of her other grandson, the king of Austrasia, Brunnhild had taken refuge in Burgundy where, by pandering to Thierry's debauched tastes, she was able to wield supreme power. The Irish monk Columban was an outspoken critic of the young king's dissolute life. Tradition records that when he was invited to Epoisses to bless the royal bastards, he refused to touch the banquet prepared in his honour, and the vessels in which it was served shattered miraculously. The irregular layout of the present château (dating mainly from the fifteenth and sixteenth centuries) is the result of a partial demolition during the Revolution. The buildings originally formed an octagon defended by seven towers and a moat. Epoisses was acquired by marriage in 1661 by Guillaume de Guitaut, and still belongs to his descendants. Madame de Sévigné, who was a friend and near neighbour (at Bourbilly), often came to stay.

The village is known best for the cheese which bears its name, the only classic cheese of Burgundy. The surrounding pastures are an island of dairy cattle (the Eastern Pied Red) in a sea of Charollais beef. The small cylindrical cheeses, weighing about half a pound, are ripened on rye-straw and sponged at regular intervals with a mixture of white wine and *marc*. The inside remains yellow and medium-soft, while the rind turns orange-red. Epoisses can be eaten as a cream cheese in the summer, but the matured variety, available from November to May, is more characteristic and savoury. Brillat-Savarin called it 'the king of cheeses', so that the Burgundian historian Courtépée was not speaking simply from bias when he said, in 1775, that 'Epoisses has the edge on Brie'.

From Semur the Paris road, the N80, leads to the northern confines of the Auxois and its other principal town, Montbard. The rivalry between the two was once as acrimonious as that between Dijon and Beaune, but today their interests are divided, with Semur as the tourist attraction and Montbard as the industrial centre. The castle of Montbard, built on the summit of a hill overlooking the Brenne, was one of the most important in Burgundy and the dukes frequently resided there; but any traces of their rule have been overlaid by the passage of Georges-Louis Leclerc, comte de Buffon.

Born of a *parlementaire* family and educated at Dijon, Buffon was one of the great scientific figures of the eighteenth century. He was appointed Keeper of the Royal Gardens (the present-day Jardin des Plantes in Paris) at the age of 32. Between 1749 and 1767 he published the 15-volume *Histoire Naturelle* which made him one of the founders of modern naturalism. Pre-Darwinian natural history is even more neglected today than pre-Newtonian physics, and the description of the horse as 'man's noblest conquest' is the limit of most people's acquaintance with Buffon's life's work. He did have other interests: his *Discourse on Style* (in which he declared that 'the style is the man') could excite no less a philosopher than Wittgenstein nearly two centuries after it was written. The count was also a pioneer industrialist, setting up a model ironworks at the nearby village from which he derived his title. The Vallourec metal tube factory at Montbard maintains the tradition.

Honours were lavished on him, and he became, like Voltaire, a much-visited celebrity. The Emperor Joseph II arrived unannounced at the Jardin du Roi and said, 'Monsieur de Buffon, with your permission, we shall deal as equals, for at the moment I am in the territory of your empire.' Rousseau came to Montbard and knelt down to kiss the doorstep of Buffon's study. However, the most interesting of all these visitors was a young man named Hérault de Séchelles, Advocate-General at the Parlement of Paris and future member of the Convention, because he has left us an account of his *Journey to Montbard* in 1785 which is one of the unknown gems of French literature. In it, he draws a deft and witty thumbnail sketch of Buffon at home, with the emphasis on the human side of the great man.

We learn that the count rises at five and works till one or two, when he dines. Then he loves to be able to relax and tell dirty jokes, which are sometimes so coarse that the ladies are obliged to leave the table. He prefers to reduce love to the purely physical, and has a passion for young girls which he indulges freely at Montbard, claiming that grown women take up too much time. Although a freethinker, he regards it as his duty as lord of the manor to attend mass. He often strolls in the gardens while the service is in progress, putting in an appearance only at the highlights. His famous vanity is absolute, but sincere—in any case, says Hérault, it is not really vanity, because he is only doing himself justice. When his son raised a column in his honour, Buffon was moved to tears and declared, 'My boy, it does you credit.' His conversation centres on himself, a subject on which he speaks entertainingly and always with the highest praise. He recommends Hérault to read the works of the great geniuses; 'there are scarcely more than five—Newton, Bacon, Leibniz, Montesquieu and me', though he confessed to certain reservations about the first four. Buffon died suddenly three years after Hérault's visit, while at work in the Jardin du Roi. He was 81. Fate was less merciful to Hérault de Séchelles, who was guillotined in the purge of the Dantonists in 1794. Buffon's son followed him to the scaffold three months later, only a few days before the fall of Robespierre. His last words were simply, 'Citizens, my name is Buffon.'

The old count disliked Paris, which he found too distracting, and did nearly all his writing at Montbard, where he spent eight months of the year. In 1742 he demolished most of what remained of the old castle, and transferred to a new mansion in the town. All he retained were the walls and two towers: the Tour Saint-Louis, where he kept his library, and the Tour de l'Aubespin, at the foot of which he made the first scientific observation of what we now know to our cost, that deflection by high buildings increases the force of wind. His study, which can be visited, is a little pavilion erected on the site of a tower and decorated with illustrations of birds. It was here, over a period of 25 years, that he wrote most of the *Histoire Naturelle*.

The memory of Buffon is Montbard's only attraction today, but it would be a shame on this account not to make a detour to dine at the Hôtel de la Gare. M. Belin was formerly chef of the liner *Normandie,* and this is a distinction one expects to pay for. Even so, the smoked trout is well worth the supplement, and the *saupiquet montbardois,* slices of smoked ham with mushrooms in a wine and cream sauce, is a speciality of the house. Those who intend to tour Burgundy in the grand manner should note that M. Belin has the finest cellar of historic vintages in the province, including the Romanée-Conti 1928 (at over £200 a bottle).

At Marmagne, just outside Montbard, a lane leads off down a valley into the forest. In 1118, 12 monks under the direction of their abbot, St Bernard, left Clairvaux and founded a hermitage in the neighbourhood. Bernard returned to Clairvaux, but by 1130 the community had outgrown the settlement, and the monks were obliged to move down the valley to a more spacious site. These were the beginnings of the abbey of Fontenay, the only one of the great Burgundian abbeys to have come down to us virtually intact.

As the connection with St Bernard indicates, Fontenay belonged to the Cistercian reform of the Benedictine rule. The Cistercian ideals were firstly complete self-sufficiency, so that the monks could avoid corrupting contacts with the outside world, and secondly absolute austerity, to purge the innate sinfulness of man. This, it was claimed, represented a return to the true spirit of St Benedict, and was in conscious opposition to the increasing worldliness of Cluny. The Cluniac administrative system, whereby the abbot of Cluny was the abbot of every monastery of the Cluniac obedience, was abandoned as over-centralised. It was replaced by a 'pyramid' system of affiliation, by which Cîteaux established four independent daughter-houses whose abbots were responsible to the abbot of Cîteaux. These abbeys sent out offshoots in their turn, whose abbots were responsible to their immediate mother-house. Thus the abbot of Fontenay, the 'second daughter of Clairvaux', was directly responsible to the abbot of Clairvaux, and only ultimately to the abbot of Cîteaux.

This established a strong chain of command which turned the Cistercians into the most effective instrument of the church militant. Another strength of the Cistercians was that, unlike their predecessors, they based their whole economy on an army of lay-brethren. The movement was essentially aristocratic, and it was unthinkable that illiterates should be admitted to full monastic status. However, these 'rustics without learning or fitness for war' could still be formed into a disciplined labour force which required no wages, had no families to support, and could not withdraw its labour. The lay-brothers, who often outnumbered the monks by three or four to one, were the secret of Cistercian agrarian success.

Like almost all Cistercian monasteries, Fontenay adheres closely to a standard plan. The site is secluded—so much so that the abbey is quite hidden by trees until one is right on top of it—and well-watered (hence its name, 'Fountains'). As for the buildings, a Cistercian monk from another house would have felt at home within half an hour, so similar was the layout. Everything required for communal life was to be found in the abbey grounds: the monks had their own bakery, and even a forge whose hammers and bellows were driven by waterwheels (the stream was especially diverted for this purpose).

Inside the church one senses the full force of Cistercian asceticism. 'Why this excessive height of churches,' wrote St Bernard, 'this inordinate length, this superfluous width, these sumptuous ornaments, these curious paintings which draw the eye and distract the attention and disturb contemplation? We monks, who have left the ranks of the people and renounced the riches and glory of the world for the love of Christ, whose devotion do we claim to awaken by these ornaments?' The luxuriant sculpture that is the splendour of Autun and Vézelay, both contemporary, is absent from Fontenay.

Even the capitals are no more than leaf-shapes simplified to abstraction. There is no bell-tower, because these were not only considered works of pride, but attracted the eye by their silhouettes and the ear by the sound of their bells. As the avowed aim of the community was to live apart, it was satisfied with a small belfry pinnacle mounted on the north gable of the dormitory. The only concession to the senses was the pointed tunnel vault, with its acoustic properties—which reminds us that St Bernard loved music just as much as did the Cluniacs. The church was financed by the generosity of Everard, bishop of Norwich, exiled from his see during the 19-year civil war between Stephen and Matilda. It was consecrated in 1147 by Pope Eugenius III, himself a Cistercian. The very pursuit of simplicity lends the interior a kind of solemn magnificence. There is no clerestory, and the nave would be like a cavern were it not for the windows in the end walls.

From the south transept the stone night stair leads to the monks' dormitory. Here the monks slept fully-dressed on straw pallets, without heating and with a single blanket to cover themselves, summer and winter. Their day began with the bell that summoned them to the night office, between one and two in the morning. Six or seven hours a day were given over to divine service, the rest being devoted to manual or intellectual labour and the study of the scriptures. There were two meals a day, of water, coarse bread and boiled vegetables; meat and fish were forbidden, at least during the first century of the order's existence. After supper, taken at about five o'clock, the monks went to bed. Both choir-monks and lay-brothers took vows of perpetual silence, except for the purposes of worship. Self-abnegation continued even beyond death: corpses were laid, without coffin or shroud, in graves marked only by a plain wooden cross.

If the church was the spiritual heart of the community, the chapter-house, immediately beneath the dormitory, was its social centre. Here the rule of silence was relaxed so that the monks could discuss the affairs of the monastery, listen to the recital of articles of the rule, hear the latest death-notices from other houses, and receive their orders of the day. They also confessed themselves publicly and were given their penance, usually corporal punishment delivered on the spot by a fellow-monk. The chapter-house is prolonged by a small parlour and then a large room whose massive ribbed vault rests on five central pillars. This was probably where the monks' non-manual labour was done. A small door on the right opens on to the *chauffoir*, the only place in the monastery where fire was permitted outside the kitchens and forge. Every morning the monks came here to grease their sandals, and in the winter, when they were neither in church nor occupied outside, they were allowed to come and warm themselves. Another larger *chauffoir*, whose fireplace once backed on to this one, probably served as a work-room for scribes and copyists. The refectory was demolished in 1745, but two bays of its inside wall have survived as the outside end wall of the *enfermerie*, with which it formed a quadrangle. This *enfermerie*, built in 1547, was, on the ground floor at least, a lock-up for miscreant members of the community and runaway serfs from surrounding estates. A quotation from the 121st Psalm assures the inmates that: 'The Lord himself is thy keeper, the Lord is thy defence upon thy right hand; so that the sun shall not burn thee by day, neither the moon by night.'

The cliosters, where the light penetrates freely, have a charm which contrasts with the starkness of the church. Here one can almost sense the decorative instinct straining to break out of its shell. There is a definite attempt to avoid monotony. No opening is exactly opposite any other, there are subtle variations in the positioning of the fluted piers and round columns that support the arcades, and each range of the cloister has a slightly different vaulting system. The external buttresses of the north range, instead of reaching down to the ground like all the others, rest on twin or clustered colonnettes. These cloisters seem to express the other side of the Cistercian character, the spiritual warmth that animated the austere rule. St Bernard was the first to draw attention to the Virigin Mary as an ideal of beauty and a mediator between man and God, the first to stress the pathos of Christ's sufferings on the Cross: 'One drop of the precious blood would have sufficed to save the world, yet it was shed abundantly.' He was the 'honey-sweet teacher', whose declared aim in his sermons was not so much to expound the words of the scriptures as to reach people's hearts.

The Cistercians belonged to the last age which thought that it was good for all men to be monks. By the end of the twelfth century, economic development, comparative peace and the growth of towns had diminished the importance of the abbeys. The mendicant orders, the Dominicans and Franciscans, drew more and more of the genuine vocations; monastic ardour cooled, and Cistercian houses came to be like the rest. The Commende, a pernicious system whereby abbots—sometimes lay, and always absentee—were nominated by the king without even the formality of an election, reached Fontenay in 1557. Thereafter the abbey declined until it was sold as national property in 1791. Only its remoteness, and the fact that the purchaser chose to turn it into a paper-mill, saved it from wholesale destruction. In 1906 Fontenay became the property of M. Edouard

Aynard, who restored it to its pre-Revolutionary condition.

In 1830, Europe's first trout farm was set up on the Fontenay estate, using scientific methods to revive an art practised by the monks. The stream flows past the forge and down a cascade into a pond holding 4,000 fish, but the main hatcheries are further down the valley towards Marmagne. Fontenay trout were particularly appreciated by Buffon and his guests, so it is especially appropriate to eat them at M. Belin's in Montbard. One can also hire a rod and line at the hatchery and catch trout straight from the ponds.

North-east of Fontenay lies the broad plateau of the Châtillonnais, a region distinct from the Auxois. Under the Ancien Régime it formed a baileywick called the Montagne, though the Morvan and the hills of the Côte d'Or are up to 600 feet higher above sea level. Just outside Saint-Seine-l'Abbaye, the road from Dijon to Troyes climbs steeply to the summit of the Burgundian divide. On the eastern side of the road, the waters of the Ignon find their way eventually to the Mediterranean, while to the west, those of the Seine follow the gentle tilt of the land towards Paris and the English Channel. The source of the latter river is marked by a grotto erected by the city of Paris in 1865, complete with the Seine in effigy. This is not wholly ridiculous, because excavations have revealed a Roman temple, dedicated to the goddess Sequana, not far from the spot.

Those areas of the plateau nearest the Auxois, cleared by the monks of Fontenay and Saint-Seine, are agricultural and featureless. Modern fertilisers have rendered them arable, but until recently the soil was too dry and porous to support much other than rough pasture. From the fourteenth century onwards, sheep-rearing was the region's principal activity. The quality of the local merino fleece made Châtillon-sur-Seine the centre not only of Burgundy's wool trade, but of Champagne's as well. The rest of the Châtillonnais is a vast forest which was the favourite hunting ground of the Capetian dukes. Woods and forests account for 42% of the surface area of the department of Côte d'Or, and most of them are north of Dijon, on the plateaux of Langres and Châtillon.

Water percolates easily through the limestone surface rock of the Châtillonnais and, where it meets the impermeable layer, forms complete underground river systems. Some streams, like the Laignes, disappear into the bowels of the earth for miles and then re-emerge wherever the impermeable layer reaches the surface, usually at the foot of a cliff. This is the case with the most famous of all these resurgences (*douix* in the Burgundian dialect), at Châtillon itself. The Douix issues from a cavern overhung by trees and a thick shelf of rock, and they say that on dark nights a ghostly presence ruffles the face of the waters.

Well into the nineteenth century, it was customary to throw bread into the Douix and the Seine at Candlemas.

From the top of a steep hill, the church of Saint-Vorles dominates Châtillon-sur-Seine. Despite substantial later alterations, it dates from the earliest period of Romanesque (980-1000) and was probably built by Brun de Roucy, bishop of Langres—the same who secured the nomination of his relative William of Volpiano to the abbacy of Saint-Bénigne. There is a transept at each end of Saint-Vorles, a 'double-ender' plan which originated with the Christians of North Africa and had been popular in Carolingian churches, especially in Germany.

St Bernard spent much of his boyhood at Châtillon, where he was educated by the canons of Notre-Dame. One Christmas Eve, while waiting for midnight mass to begin, he had an intense religious experience which decided his vocation. Around this core of truth, the repressed eroticism of medieval Christianity built the legend of the saint's drinking the Virgin's milk. The statue associated with this event used to be displayed in the crypt of Saint-Vorles. This cult-object has long since vanished; today, the church's main artistic attraction is its Entombment group, dating from 1527. The appeal of the elegantly-posed figures is to the theatrical rather than the religious sense. The turbaned Nicodemus looks more like the Grand Turk than 'a ruler of the Jews', and Mary Magdalene, her breasts straining voluptuously at her bodice, wears an unrepentant décolle-tage. Châtillon fell more within the artistic orbit of Troyes than of Dijon, but this is less a different technique than a new outlook, the spirit of the Renaissance freshly imported from Italy.

In February and March 1814, while Napoleon tried vainiy to stem the Allied invasion of France, Caulaincourt tried with no better success to negotiate acceptable peace terms at the 'Congress of Châtillon'. In September 1914, the French G.H.Q. was briefly moved to Châtillon during the runaway German advance on Paris. Joffre, the French commander-in-chief, kept a cool head and never missed his two well-cooked meals a day. It was from the Château Marmont that he issued his famous Order of the Day No. 6: 'At a moment when we are fighting a battle on which the safety of the nation depends, everyone must be reminded that this is not the time to look behind us.' On 6 September, the French counter-attack was launched on the Marne; the Germans lost their nerve at the psychological moment and retreated to the Aisne, where they dug themselves in and began the four miserable years of deadlock. This was the last moment at which the Germans could have won the war in the West—the 'miracle of the Marne' had saved France.

A few miles below Châtillon, the Seine is commanded by Mont Lassois, an isolated hill rising 300 feet above the surrounding plain. Here the river becomes navigable, and in January 1953, striking proof of the area's prehistoric importance came to light with the discovery of an undisturbed tumulus near the village of Vix. It was the tomb of a young princess (or priestess) who died about 500 B.C., and among the treasures it contained was a huge bronze *krater* or mixing-bowl, the largest ever discovered. It stands five feet five inches high, weighs four hundredweight, and would hold 275 gallons. Its Gorgon's-head handles and frieze of charioteers mark it as Greek or Etruscan work, thus affirming the existence of far-reaching trade contacts between Burgundy and the Mediterranean world.

The Vix vase, and a complete wine service also found in the tomb, show that wine was already appreciated in central Gaul at that time, though not necessarily produced there. Among the several personal items that the princess took with her on her last journey was a solid gold diadem ; two tiny winged horses (presumably loops for a fillet) add a Scythian flavour, and this piece of jewellery may indeed have come from Central Asia or the Ukraine. The Vix treasure is on view at Châtillon in the Maison Philandrier, a Renaissance mansion with a distinctive round staircase-tower.

The tin route from Britain passed up the Seine to the end of navigation, where the cargoes were unloaded and carried overland either through the Alps and over the Brenner Pass to Italy, or simply across the watershed to the Saône at Chalon, whence they travelled down the Rhône to the sea. The first route would have been favoured by the Etruscans, the second by the Phoenicians and, after the foundation of Massilia (Marseille) in 600 B.C., by the Phocaean Greeks. Either way, the break in the journey at Mont Lassois (*Latisco*) was unavoidable, and the inhabitants grew rich on tolls, haulage dues, and the general benefits of trade. They were Celts of the 'Hallstatt' culture, and the appearance of the Gauls ('La Tène' Celts) in the 5th century B.C. seems to have put an end to their prosperity. The prestige of their princes, however, would help to justify the importance of nearby Alesia as a Celtic holy place. The Greeks had a legend that Alesia had been founded by Heracles, who married a local princess and fathered a son called Galates, the eponymous ancestor of the Gauls. This must be a distant memory of the power of the rulers of Latisco and of their earliest contacts with the Greeks.

7 Lower Burgundy

'Lower Burgundy' is a convenient term for the limestone plateaux that shelve gently north-westwards from the Auxois and the Morvan down to the Paris Basin. Historically, all of it was included in Frankish Burgundy, but in the eleventh century it passed by marriage under the sway of the powerful counts of Nevers. Philip the Good recovered the county of Auxerre in 1424, but it was not until 1964 that the counties of Auxerre, Tonnerre and Joigny—merged in the department of Yonne since the Revolution—became 'Burgundian' once more with the creation of the 'Burgundy Region'. The vine, now restricted to Chablis and a small area south of Auxerre, was planted much more extensively before the phylloxera. A royal edict of 1416 describes as 'burgundy' 'all manner of wines grown above Sens bridge', a fact which justifies the claim of Sens to be the gateway of Burgundy. The only natural barrier is the Forest of Othe, in the far north-west; on the other sides, the borders with Champagne and the Orléanais are no more than lines on a map. The life of Lower Burgundy centres on the valleys of the Yonne and its tributaries, the Armançon and the Serein. Until the motorway thrust peremptorily across the plateaux, their meandering courses marked the principal lines of communication.

The valley of the Armançon is privileged to be the site of Burgundy's most celebrated Renaissance châteaux, Ancy-le-Franc and Tanlay. Of the two, Ancy-le-Franc is the more classical and restrained, though it makes up for this with an interior that rivals Fontainebleau. In 1500, Bernardin de Clermont, a nobleman from Dauphiné, married the countess of Tonnerre. Their son, Antoine de Clermont-Tonnerre, was fortunate enough in his turn to marry the elder sister of Diane de Poitiers, mistress of the future Henri II. This opened up a career at court which led to Antoine becoming Grand Forester of France, and in 1546 he decided to rebuild his principal residence in the new Italian style.

The architect he employed was Sebastiano Serlio of Bologna, who had been advising on the construction of Fontainebleau, and had published an illustrated handbook for architects which enjoyed great popularity in France. Ancy-le-Franc is an excellent example of the quality to which Serlio owed his success—not original genius, but adaptability Starting from drawings which show something like the early Renaissance villas of the Venetian mainland, he created a building which was more French in character. For instance, he adopted the high French roof with dormers, which he praised in his treatise for its practical value in northern climates.

The exterior is severe, and seems squat and unassertive. This is because the proportions have been altered by the filling in of the moat; the recent digging out of the moat in front of the east façade of the Louvre shows what a difference this can make. The courtyard, on the other hand, has a sumptuous decoration of scalloped niches and Corinthian pilasters. On two sides, arcades give on to a ground-floor gallery. On each wall of the courtyard, the ground-floor pilasters frame four square tablets with gold lettering, each bearing one of the words 'Si omnes ego non'. This motto of the counts of Clermont is an abbreviation of St Peter's words to Jesus, 'Although all shall be offended, yet will not I.' The winner of these biblical honours was Count Sibaut of Clermont, who quoted the phrase to the Burgundian pope Calixtus II, elected at Cluny after the death in exile of Gelasius II in 1119. The count's assurances proved more reliable than the apostle's; in the following year, he helped to drive the Emperor's partisans out of Rome so that the legitimate pope could be installed. Calixtus showed his appreciation by granting the motto 'Si omnes ego non' to the Clermont family , as well as the right to wear St Peter's keys on their coat of arms, with the papal tiara as a crest.

The 18 apartments and galleries received an extravagant painted decoration in which mythological subjects alternate with biblical ones in the manner of the time. The technique is not early Italian fresco, since dry surfaces were used; the artists were Primaticcio and his pupils, another link with Fontainebleau. These rooms, which are the real reason for a visit to Ancy-le-Franc, would take too long to describe in detail. At best one can mention the chapel, with its murals of the Desert Fathers, and the two long galleries—the Galerie des Sacrifices, whose grisaille murals depict Roman sacrifices, and the Galerie de la Pharsale (attributed to Niccolo dell'Abbate), in which Caesar's victory over Pompey at Pharsalus is fought out in scenes of hectic nudity.

The château was not completed until 1622, though one chronicler declared, 'One might almost think it had been raised in a single day, such satisfaction does it give the eye.' Henri III, whose portrait hangs in the Salle des Gardes, stayed at Ancy-le-Franc on his return from a brief stint as elective king of Poland (the early death of his elder brother, the wretched Charles IX, had brought him unexpectedly to the throne of France). His three successors, Henri IV, Louis XIII and Louis XIV all paid visits. The Sun-King called in on his way back from the conquest of Franche-Comté in 1674 (a military picnic organised for his benefit by Vauban and Louvois). In 1684, massive debts forced the Clermont-Tonnerres to part with both their county and their château. The purchaser was their neighbour Louvois, Louis XIV's minister of aggression, who had coveted Ancy-le-Franc since his visit of ten years before. It seems that his duties at Versailles left him no time to enjoy the acquisition, though his wife resided there. She was a close friend of Madame de Sévigné, who visited the château and was especially fond of the intimate little Pastor Fido cabinet, so called after its series of pictures (ascribed to dell'Abbate) illustrating Guarini's idyll of that name.

Tanlay is a complete contrast. Whereas Ancy-le-Franc was the creation of a single designer in a single design, Tanlay is the product of two quite separate campaigns of construction. Ancy-le-Franc is compact, but Tanlay is rambling—it actually has two distinct sections. And whereas the moat has disappeared at Ancy-le-Franc, at Tanlay it has survived to superb effect. The whole mood is less disciplined, but more spacious and relaxed.

The estate of Tanlay was bought in 1535 by Louise de Montmorency, mother of the Coligny brothers who played such a prominent part in the Wars of Religion. She gave it to her fourth son, François d'Andelot, and in 1559 rebuilding began. It is not easy to say how much of the main château is d'Andelot's work: perhaps the arcades flanking the courtyard, and certainly the north-west tower, with its remarkable painted ceiling. Tradition has it that François and his brothers Gaspard (Admiral of France) and Odet (who, even though he had turned Protestant and had married, remained a bishop and a cardinal for many years—at court his wife was referred to as Madame la Cardinale) held meetings with other Huguenot leaders in this tower-room. Hence the theme of the painting—an allegory, possibly based on a poem by Ronsard, of the rivalry between Catholic and Protestant factions at the court of Catherine de Medici. Jupiter presides, while in the centre of the group, the Janus-headed monarchy smiles on the Catholics and glowers at the Huguenots. Gaspard and François appear as Neptune and Hercules respectively, the Queen Mother as Juno with her peacock, and François de Guise and Diane de Poitiers as Mars and Venus. Around an anvil, the Catholics forge the weapons of war. This mythological propaganda poster has earned its setting the title of 'Tour de la Ligue'—incorrectly, since the Catholic League belongs to a later phase of the Wars, when most of the principal subjects of the painting were dead. François de Guise and Gaspard de Coligny perished violently—the former assassinated by a Protestant in 1563, the latter murdered in his bed on St Bartholomew's Day 1572, as he lay recovering from an earlier attempt on his life. Odet, who has not been identified in the painting, escaped to England in 1571, only to be poisoned at Hampton Court by one of his own servants.

François d'Andelot alone was a victim of nature. Just before his death in 1569, he began the 'Little Château' as a huge gatehouse to his estate. It stands at the end of a long alley of lime-trees, though the perspective is lost to most visitors because the N59 cuts across it so close to the château. D'Andelot's gatehouse, completed by his son-in-law after 1574, is a fine example of the sort of provincial architecture whose most accomplished exponents were Ribonnier and Hugues Sambin. At Tanlay, the period's fondness for rich surface effects takes the form of rustication cut into elaborate lace-work patterns.

The main château had to wait until 1642, when it was acquired by Michel Particelli, son of a Lyonnais banker of Italian origin. Particelli was one of Mazarin's most successful tax-gatherers, so successful, in fact, that the cardinal was obliged to part with him in 1648 because of his unpopularity. The Intendant confided the completion of Tanlay to Le Muet, one of the precursors of the 'classical' Louis XIV style. The architect's passion for symmetry still left room for elements of fantasy: domes and chimney-stacks, alternating dormers and *oeils-de-boeuf*, and a lodge preceded by a pair of sentry-boxes capped by rusticated pyramids. The biggest natural advantage was the moat, which is so wide (nearly 70 feet) that the château seems to be floating in the middle of a lake. A later owner made the most of this possibility by demolishing the wall that screened the courtyard from view. Le Muet embellished the park with a canal, closed off by an ornamental water-tower, which feeds the moat with fresh spring-water. The most striking part of his interior decor is the long gallery, painted in grisaille to give an illusion of niches, statues and a coffered ceiling inlaid with bas-reliefs.

The building was finished in six years, with a work-force so large that Le Muet had two surgeons on permanent call for the sick and injured. The enormous expense broke even Particelli. When he died in 1650, his son and heir commented, 'Damn the man—Intendant of Finance twice, and he leaves debts of 200,000 écus!' His mistress, however, spoke more affectionately of him: 'This large man is pleasant company, and very clean.'

Tonnerre straggles up its hill from the banks of the Armançon to the church of Saint-Pierre, with its south-facing Renaissance façade. On the north side of the church, at the foot of a limestone cliff, the waters well up in the middle of the Fosse Dionne—a Burgundian *douix* which, before the day of the launderette, was put to practical use as a public wash-house.

Looking from the hilltop like a huge capsized boat, the Old Hospital is Tonnerre's most distinctive building. It was founded in 1293 by Margaret of Burgundy, widow of St Louis' younger brother Charles of Anjou, the titular king of Sicily. The interior arrangement was the same as that adopted 150 years later at the Hôtel-Dieu in Beaune—the beds were aligned feet towards the altar, so that the patients could follow the services which were conducted in the apse. The vast panel-vaulted chamber ceased to serve as a hospital in 1630, and became a parish church until the rebuilding of Notre-Dame (which explains the large number of tombstones let into the floor).

The Hospital's most precious possession is an Entombment presented to it in 1454 by a rich burgess of the town. We know nothing of its sculptors, Jean Michel and Georges de la Sonnette; which is a pity, because this work is one of the best to emerge from the Sluterian tradition, and the finest of all the Entombments in Burgundy. The artists avoid the temptation to display their technique with over-complicated drapery—a common pitfall among Sluter's disciples—and manage to prevent pathos subsiding into sentimentality.

Very different is the Hospital's other monument, the tomb of Louvois (who had acquired Ancy-le-Franc and the county of Tonnerre in 1684). It was originally in the Capuchin Convent in Paris, where its great weight warped the wall so badly that the side-chapel in which it stood had to be rebuilt. The Marquise, who commissioned the tomb from Girardon and Desjardins, had herself portrayed grief-stricken at her husband's feet; life-size bronze figures of Vigilance and Prudence stood either side of the base. In 1793, the tomb was transferred to the Museum of French Monuments, where the Marquise was transformed by the author of the catalogue into an allegory of History 'holding an open book and seeming to turn tearful eyes towards Louvois as she points out the passage that recounts his operations in the Palatinate' (Louvois had been responsible, in 1689, for the destruction of Worms, Speyer and Heidelberg in a 'pre-emptive strike against the Grand Alliance). When the Museum was closed in 1819, the monument was given to the town of Tonnerre, minus the green marble sarcophagus on which Louvois' effigy had lain. The story was that Napoleon had commandeered it as a bathtub.

Tonnerre's most famous son (and daughter) was born at the Hôtel d'Uzès, now the Caisse d'Epargne, in 1728. Charles Eon de Beaumont, generally known as the Chevalier d'Eon, was one of the more bizarre personalities of the eighteenth century. Even his own parents seem to have been unsure of his sex: at the age of three, he was put into girl's clothes and renamed Charlotte. Sexual ambivalence was regarded as an excellent qualification for intelligence work, and after a military education (as a man), the Chevalier was sent to St Petersburg, where he was received (as a woman) by the Tsaritsa Elizabeth. From 1762 he served as a secret agent in England, but seems to have fallen out with his superiors over his refusal to put on women's clothing again. It is just possible that, in the course of his duties, he insinuated himself into the so-called 'Hell-Fire Club' whose members included Lord Sandwich and John Wilkes (enemies in Parliament, but companions in lechery). In fact, the Chevalier's only recorded visit to the club's headquarters at Medmenham Abbey was in May 1771, when he submitted to examination by a jury of ladies of quality who were to pronounce on his sex. Bets of over £100,000 were involved—but the verdict was 'doubtful'. As a result of a lawsuit concerning the wagers, a fresh jury was called six years later. They found that the Chevalier was female, and he spent the rest of his life dressed accordingly. When he died in London in 1810, the doctor who conducted the post-mortem ruled that he was 'without any shadow of doubt a male person', and he was buried as such at St Pancras.

From their sources in the vicinity of Arnay-le-Duc to their junctions with the Yonne below Auxerre, the Serein runs roughly parallel with the Armançon. Never as important as the other two valley routes (its towns drew their prosperity from cross-country traffic), the valley of the Serein lives up to its name. North-east of Avallon, the little hill-town of Montréal surveys the Serein's passage from the Auxois into Lower Burgundy. Its dignity as 'Mount Royal' dates back to the early 7th century, when, along with nearby Epoisses, it was a favourite residence of the diabolic Queen Brunnhild and her dissolute grandson Thierry II.

Viollet-le-Duc, who was not only a great restorer but a leading light of the French nineteenth-century Gothic revival, admired the church's elegant simplicity and economy of means so much that he published an *Estimate for the construction of a church similar to that at Montréal*. People already suffering from a surfeit of churches will still want to visit this one, for the sake of the choir-stalls. They were sculpted in 1522 by the Rigoley brothers of Nuits-sous-Ravières, near Ancy-le-Franc, and are Burgundy's finest wood-carvings in the popular idiom. As well as misericords and end-panels, there are large free-standing groups at the end of each pew. Most of the subjects are from the New Testament; the most appealing is certainly the panel showing Christ in the house of His parents, with Mary sewing while Joseph works away at his carpentry. Scenes like this one—which so offended bourgeois Victorian taste when Millais painted it—found ready favour in the late Middle Ages, when easy familiarity with things divine, rather than reverence, was the rule. The group that surmounts this panel strikes a different note from all the others: two men sit at a trestle-table and pour each other a drink from a large wine-jug. The favourite explanation is that it represents the brothers Rigoley themselves in their lunch-break.

'Noyers,' said Gaston Roupnel, 'is unique in France.' Perhaps this is an overstatement, but the charm of this 'background for a historical pageant' is undeniable. Almost surrounded by a meander of the Serein, Noyers (pronounced 'Noyère') is still defended by its 16 round towers and its two gates, the Porte Peinte and the Porte Sainte-Verrotte. The Sainte Verrotte in question is a statue of the Virgin in the niche to one side of the arch. Every year on 15 August, the Feast of the Assumption, the *vignerons* of the district used to place a bunch of grapes (called *verrots* because they were still green) in the hands of the Virgin and of her child. The Rue Franche which leads up to the gate is so called because its residents were exempt from manorial dues. The most ingenious story of how the privilege was granted is that a certain baroness of Noyers took it on herself to support the townspeople's appeal for financial relief. Her husband agreed to exempt the whole length of the street as far as she could throw a bowl—on condition that, like Lady Godiva, she performed stark naked. History does not record if the inhabitants of Noyers were as well-mannered as those of Coventry.

Chablis, the first name that springs to mind when one talks of white burgundy, is one of the last remnants of a vineyard that covered 100,000 acres before the phylloxera. The first mention of vines around Auxerre comes in the 7th century, but the significant date is 1114, when the Cistercian abbey of Pontigny was founded. In accordance with their usual policy, the monks created a *clos* at Chablis as the mother-house had at Vougeot. They soon had imitators, and by 1280 the Italian Friar Salimbene could write, 'The wines of Auxerre are white and sometimes golden, aromatic, comforting and of strong and excellent flavour,' a judgment which

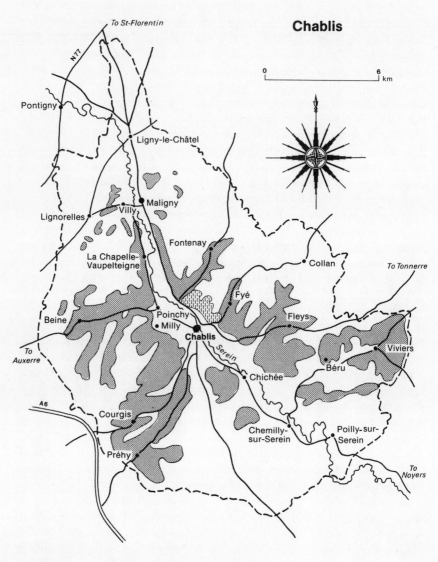

Chablis

0 _____ 6 km

To St-Florentin

N77

Pontigny

Ligny-le-Châtel

Maligny

Villy

Lignorelles

Fontenay

La Chapelle-
Vaupelteigne

Collan

To Tonnerre

Fyé

Beine

Poinchy

Milly

Chablis

Fleys

Viviers

Serein

Béru

To
Auxerre

Chichée

A6

Courgis

Chemilly-
sur-Serein

Poilly-sur-
Serein

Préhy

To
Noyers

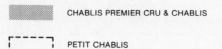

CHABLIS GRAND CRU (Blanchots, Les Clos, Valmur,
Grenouilles, Vaudésir, Les Preuses, Bougros)

CHABLIS PREMIER CRU & CHABLIS

PETIT CHABLIS

requires no alteration 700 years later—except perhaps to say that 'golden' is more applicable to Meursault than to the pale greenish tinge of Chablis. All Chablis is white, and is made from the chardonnay grape, known in this part of Burgundy as the *beaunois*. Its strong, subtle bouquet forms round about the March following the vintage, and to preserve it, the wine must be bottled in the course of the second year. The alcohol content is high (it reached a record 17% in 1959), and gives Chablis a justifiable reputation for longevity. It is one of the rare white wines which improve with age and do not discolour.

In flavour, it has a dryness which has been described variously as 'pebbly', 'stony', 'mineral', and 'flinty', which shows how awkward it is to find metaphors for impressions of taste. Perhaps the most evocative and original comment on it was Canon Gaudin's in 1759: 'When drunk, it embalms the throat and leaves behind a suave fragrance of mushroom.' These savoury qualities make Chablis the wine par excellence for seafood, especially shellfish. As early as the fourteenth century, the poet Eustache Deschamps praised it with oysters, though it goes equally well with white meat, ham and terrines.

Waterways played a major part in the development of the Auxerrois vineyards. Easy access to Paris along the Yonne and the Seine made them one of the capital's biggest suppliers. In the days of log-running from the Morvan, barrels were floated down on the log-trains. But from the seventeenth century onwards, there was an increasing tendency to plant high-yield varieties, and there were complaints from some quarters that fine plants were in danger of disappearing altogether; the proportion of red wine produced rose to three-quarters. All this came to an abrupt end when the phylloxera reached the region in 1887. When reconstitution became possible, the Paris market had been conquered by cheap wine from Provence and Languedoc, brought up by rail. This new competition reduced returns to the point where it was hardly worthwhile replanting. Only Chablis had resisted the drift towards ordinary wine, and it was precisely this insistence on quality that enabled it to survive the crisis.

The original decision not to go for quantity had been dictated by the natural advantages peculiar to Chablis and its immediate environs: ideal limestone soil, well-drained and stony, and a perfect southerly or south-westerly exposure. This does not mean that it has ever been easy to grow the vine at Chablis. On the contrary, it is quite difficult to grow the vine at all; though as so often happens, it is when the vine is stretched to the limit that it gives of its best. The particular enemy at Chablis is late frost. The vines are trained low to the ground to get the benefit of the night heat stored in the stony ground; since 1958, there have been experiments with oil heaters, though this has only proved economic for about 200 acres of the very best vines. But disasters are still possible. On the night of 28-29 May 1961, several days after the heating equipment had been removed from the protected vineyards, there were seven degrees of frost and almost the entire vintage was lost. Apart from the use of heaters, viticultural practice in the Chablis enclave is the same as elsewhere in Burgundy. Even the traditional 132-litre *feuillette* has been supplanted by the 228-litre Côte d'Or *pièce* and, more recently, by glazed tanks.

The finest vines of all, the 100 acres of *Grands Crus*, occupy a mile and a half of very steep slopes rising from the right bank of the Serein and overlooking the town. The names to remember are, going downstream, Blanchots, Les Clos, Valmur, Grenouilles, Vaudésir, Les Preuses and Bougros. The celebrated 'Moutonne' is actually a trade name used by a proprietor of parcels of Vaudésir and Les Preuses. After the *Grands Crus* comes the less restrictive appellation of plain *Chablis* (sometimes confusingly augmented to *Chablis Premier Cru* for the better plots), and finally *Petit Chablis*, which covers practically everything within a four-mile radius of the town.

The chief curiosity of Chablis itself is the church of Saint-Martin, which sheltered that saint's relics for a time during the Norse invasions in the 9th century. Rebuilt in the early Gothic style at the very end of the twelfth century, it has retained a Romanesque south door with an odd decoration of horseshoes. Theorists are agreed that they are ex-votos of some kind, but are divided over whether the protection solicited was for the animals themselves or their owners. Two of the shoes are surgical appliances for lame horses—but in defence of the second opinion, there is the fact that travellers setting out on a journey from Paris commonly nailed a horseshoe to the door of Saint-Séverin.

The abbey church of Pontigny, 'second daughter of Cîteaux', stands amidst flat cornfields on the banks of the Serein a few miles from Chablis. Its long, low mass, towerless in the classic Cistercian manner, seems to hug the earth. The arrangement of the east end—an ambulatory and apse supported by flying buttresses—has inspired comparisons with a hen huddled over her brood; 'how often would I have gathered the children together, even as a hen gathereth her chickens under her wings. . . .' Inside, the rib-vaulted nave is in an austere but handsome half-Gothic, its serenity marred only by the dark wooden rood-screen.

The first monks settled here in 1114, in what was then a clearing in the woods. The willows and poplars that line the Serein are about all that remains of the forest. The new community enjoyed the favour of no fewer than six masters, standing as it did at the junction of three counties (Auxerre, Tonnerre and Champagne) and three dioceses (Sens, Auxerre and Langres). It was a saying that three counts, three bishops and an abbot could dine together on the bridge at Pontigny without leaving their own territory. One of these benefactors, Count Thibaut the Great of Champagne, provided the money for the present church, which was begun about 1140. The original chevet was flat, as at Fontenay; between 1185 and 1210, it was replaced by the present one, clutching determinedly at the ground.

Canterbury seems to have had a special relationship with the monastery of Pontigny. In the century following the building of the new church, three archbishops took refuge there in the course of their periodic quarrels with the English monarchy. From 1164 to 1170 it was Thomas Becket, whose decision to leave the protection of Louis VII and of the pope (himself exiled at the time in northern France) cost him his life. From 1208 to 1213 it was Stephen Langton, whom King John refused to recognise. Lastly there was St Edmund Rich, who died at Pontigny in 1240 on his way to Rome to enlist papal support in his dispute with Henry III. The miracles reportedly performed by his relics gave rise to an important local cult, and to the popularity of the name 'Edme' in north-west Burgundy.

The abbey was abandoned at the Revolution, but in 1843 the church and what little remained of of the monastery buildings were brought by the archbishop of Sens and put at the disposal of the 'Missionaries to the Countryside', founded by Father Muard of La-Pierre-qui-Vire. They in their turn were expelled by the anti-clerical laws of 1905 (one of the repercussions of the Dreyfus Case), and in the following year the abbey was auctioned off to the philosopher Paul Desjardins. He felt the monastic atmosphere of Pontigny to be ideal for the 'secular retreats' he had in mind, in which literature and art, rather than religion, would be the topics of discussion. This was the beginning of the Décades of Pontigny, at which figures like Gide, Mauriac, Edmund Gosse, T. S. Eliot and Thomas Mann met for long conversations in the arbour in the gardens. After a break due to the First World War and its aftermath, the Décades were resumed in 1922 and Pontigny developed into an international scholars' retreat. Desjardins launched an 'Antibabel' to attack what he saw as the growing confusion of ideas, but the 'unique, inimitable, indefensible and indispensable' conversations of Pontigny ended with his death in 1940.

From the edge of the Morvan at Clamecy, the Yonne winds down past Châtel-Censoir and the overhanging limestone cliffs of the Saussois to the old bridge at Mailly-le-Château. The view from the terrace of the village on the hill is probably the prettiest riverscape in Burgundy, with the Yonne and its backwater, paralleled by the Nivernais Canal, executing a sweeping, lazy meander. Cravant, just below the junction with the Cure, enjoyed its greatest prosperity in the days when the wines of Beaune were embarked there en route for Paris, after their overland trek via Saulieu and Avallon.

The names of Coulanges-la-Vineuse and Saint-Bris-le-Vineux serve as a reminder that the local wine was once more important than the carrying trade for that of the Côte d'Or. Apart from Chablis, the narrow belt extending away from the river on either side from Coulanges to Chitry is the last remnant of the great vineyard of Lower Burgundy. Very few of these wines are known outside their own area, with the possible exception of the reds and rosés of Irancy. Coulanges also produces red and rosé, while Saint-Bris and Chitry produce white not only from the chardonnay and the aligoté, but also from the sauvignon of Bordeaux) which gives here a light, dry wine reminiscent of the Muscadet from Brittany).

Irancy, nestling in its valley amidst vines and cherry orchards, has a picturesqueness which is almost English—a 'fortress built by Nature for herself, against infection and the hand of war'. A less figurative fortress—the impressively solid round tower at the east end of the church at Chitry—gives the lie to any such comfortable notions. During the intervals of the Hundred Years' War, bands of armed mercenaries occupied their enforced leisure by pillaging and raping on their own account (which they tended to do anyway during official hostilities, without much regard to the political persuasion of their victims). The very practical riposte of the villagers of Chitry dates from 1364, at the height of the terror.

Seen from the Pont Paul Bert, where the N6 crosses the river, the left bank of the Yonne at Auxerre is a pageant of churches. From left to right, Saint-Pierre, Saint-Etienne and Saint-Germain recall the medieval triple division between the bishop, the monks and the people, each element of the community with its own place of worship. Joan of Arc stopped to pray at the cathedral in 1429, on her way to Chinon to present herself to Charles VII. When she returned, it was at the head of the army that accompanied the king to his coronation at Rheims. And it was at Auxerre in March 1815 that Marshal Ney, 'the bravest of the brave', who had sworn to bring Napoleon back to Paris in an iron cage, threw himself into his former master's arms and turned over his troops to the Imperial cause—a change of heart that eventually led him before a firing squad.

Auxerre's prestige goes back to the 5th century and the career of St Germanus, perhaps the most popular French saint after St Martin. Born at Auxerre of rich Gallo-Roman parents in 378, Germanus practised law at Rome before being sent back to Gaul in an important military capacity. He seems to have been converted to Christianity by Amator, bishop of his native town, who designated him as his successor. At first, Germanus was unwilling to shoulder the responsibility, but accepted when Amator's choice was confirmed by the diocesan elections. Upon taking office he drastically changed his way of life. He ceased to have sexual relations with his wife, slept on bare planks, wore a hair-shirt all the time, and ate only two or three meals of coarse bread each week. Today, the list of his mortifications carries less weight than his real achievements, which were administrative. He put Christianity on a firm footing in his own diocese, gave vital encouragement to St Genevieve, who became the patroness of Paris, and was deputed by the pope to root out the Pelagian heresy in Britain. In 448 he made the long journey to the court of the Empress Galla Placidia at Ravenna, to plead the cause of the Armoricans against the Imperial viceroy; he died at Ravenna on 31 July. The best-known of the many churches dedicated to him stands opposite the east front of the Louvre in Paris. It is called Saint-Germain-l'Auxerrois to distinguish it from Saint-Germain-des-Prés, which is dedicated to another Germanus, also Burgundian, who was bishop of Paris.

The saint's body was brought back to Auxerre and interred in the small cemetery chapel that Germanus had had built for himself. Under the auspices of Clotilde, wife of Clovis, first Christian king of the Franks, this chapel of St Maurice was refounded as the abbey of Saint-Germain. By the time of Charles the Bald, in the mid-9th century, the abbey was well established as a centre of learning, and 100 years later it is recorded as having 600 monks and 2,000 students. Those parts of Saint-Germain visible from the outside are relatively late, dating from 1277 to about 1400. The only surviving contribution of Romanesque is the west tower, oddly isolated by the demolition of the first six bays of the nave after 1811. Restoration had not yet become fashionable. More important, from the archaeological point of view, are the crypts. The sharp drop of the ground towards the Yonne enabled the Carolingian builders to create two crypts, one on top of the other, beneath an eastward extension of the chancel (the axial chapel of the Gothic church). The crypts were finished in 858, and in the following year Charles the Bald attended the solemn translation of the saint's relics to their new resting-place.

The upper crypt contains the *confessio,* or 'holy of holies', whose tunnel vault rests on the original oak beams supported by re-used Gallo-Roman columns. The sarcophagus, which was raised to its present position in 1636, is actually a sham, filled with bogus remains to fool desecrating Norsemen (who did in fact pillage the abbey in 886). The frescoes in the ambulatory, dating from about 850 but only rediscovered in 1927, are the oldest known in France. They represent the trial and stoning of St Stephen, and if an inscription has been correctly interpreted, their design is due to the 'philosophical monk' Fredilo (presumably a teacher in the abbey schools). Slightly later are the paintings of two bishops, an 'Adoration of the Magi', and a peacock spreading its tail (the peacock being taken as a symbol of Christ, because in the Middle Ages its flesh was considered incorruptible).

When the rôle of the monasteries began to decline, Auxerre's dignity was maintained by its bishops. One of them, William of Seignelay, set in motion a complete reconstruction of the cathedral in the High Gothic style of the Ile-de-France. Work began in 1215 and went on in fits and starts until 1560, which is why the upper parts of the façade and towers shimmer with Flamboyant surface effects. In 1567, Auxerre was seized by the Huguenots, who put Calvin's teachings against idolatry into grim practice. They pulled down the statues and altars, shattered as much stained glass as they could reach, burnt the choir-stalls, pitched the bells down from the tower, desecrated the tombs, stripped the cathedral of chandeliers, holy-water stoups and even organ-pipes, tore down the wrought-iron grilles, broke into the treasury and looted its contents, and left nothing behind but 'a jumbled heap of wreckage and debris'. Despite this catastrophe, the cathedral of Saint-Etienne survives as the most graceful product of mature Gothic in Burgundy, and was a special favourite of the eighteenth-century architect Soufflot (who was born at Irancy).

The richly-sculpted west doors have suffered from iconoclasts and the weather, but it is still possible to make out Hercules and a satyr mixed up with bas-reliefs of the life of Joseph in the main portal. The north portal has a particularly fine series of bas-reliefs depicting scenes from Genesis—God's undramatic, conscientious gesture as he polishes his handiwork (Adam) is very different from the same theme as treated by a Renaissance artist like Michelangelo.

The oldest and most beautiful part of the Gothic church is the chancel, built on the orders of William of Seignelay between 1215 and 1234. Miraculously, the cathedral has preserved a set of stained-glass windows that some judges have ranked above those of Chartres and the Sainte-Chapelle. The windows of the ambulatory, glazed tapestries in which azure and scarlet predominate, are thirteenth-century extracts from the Old Testament and the *Golden Legend*. The rose-window of the north transept, dedicated to the Virgin and the Trinity, was given to the cathedral in 1528 by Bishop François de Dinteville, chaplain to Louis XII and Francis I and a prelate of pomp and circumstance. Rabelais said of him, 'This noble pontiff loved good wine, like any decent man,' and went on to recount how Dinteville once proposed to transfer the festivals of the 'Ice Saints' (which fell in late April and early May, the period of the deadly late frosts) to the Christmas season, 'permitting them with all honour and reverence to hail and freeze then as much as they liked, frost being in no way harmful at that time.' This would certainly have been cheaper than the oil heaters used today by the *vignerons* of Chablis. The west window and the rose-window of the south transept were presented by Bishop Dinteville's nephew, namesake and successor.

Facing each other in the choir are monuments to two other notable personalities who were bishops of Auxerre at 100 years' interval. On the left is the praying bust of Jacques Amyot, scholar, translator of *Daphnis and Chloe* and Plutarch's *Lives,* and tutor to royalty in the person of the future Henri III; he was the incumbent of the see at the time of the sack of the cathedral by the Protestants. On the right is the medallion of Nicolas Colbert, brother of Louis XIV's finance minister.

Of the medieval eccentricities of the dean and chapter, the Feast of Fools and the Easter-Day ball game have long been forgotten; but the tomb of the Chastellux family (a post-Revolutionary reconstruction in the north ambulatory) recalls the unique privilege awarded to Claude de Beauvoir, baron of Chastellux, in 1423. After capturing the town of Cravant from the partisans of Charles VII and restoring it to the chapter, its rightful overlords, he and his descendants in perpetuity were created hereditary lay canons, with the right of attending services in full armour, booted, spurred, wearing their swords and baldrics over their surplices, and carrying their falcons on their wrists.

The crypt is a remnant of the Romanesque cathedral built after the fire of 1023 and eventually replaced by William of Seignelay and his successors. Like the crypt of Saint-Germain, its chief significance lies in its frescoes. The oldest covers the tunnel vault of the small apsidal chapel, and has been dated to the episcopate of Humbaud (1084-1114). It seems to depict *Revelation* 19 xi ff.: 'And I saw heaven opened, and behold a white horse; and he that sat upon him was called Faithful and True, and in righteousness he doth judge and make war. . . . And the armies which were in heaven followed him upon white horses, clothed in fine linen, white and clean . . . and he shall rule (the nations) with a rod of iron.' The apocalyptic interpretation is confirmed by the late thirteenth-century painting on the oven vault, which shows Christ flanked by two seven-branched candlesticks, as in the first chapter of the *Revelation*. And yet the Christ on horseback is the sole example of the subject in western wall-painting. It may be the fruit of increased contacts with the East in the years preceding and following the First Crusade, since the theme of Christ the triumphant King was better known in Byzantine art.

The people of Auxerre are commendably proud of their churches (Saint-Pierre—set in a courtyard behind a Renaissance gateway—and Sainte-Eusèbe are worth visiting) and their clock-tower with its 'astronomical' dial, showing the apparent movements of the sun and moon. On the other hand, in common with most other Frenchmen, and indeed the British of 20 years ago, they seem indifferent—if not downright hostile—to the nineteenth century. In the very centre of Auxerre stands the old Market Hall, a splendidly pompous piece of Second Empire, complete with pediments, cast-iron pillars, poly-chrome tiles and glazed plaques. The plan is either to sell it to America or knock it down.

West of Auxerre is the region known as Puisaye, once a dense, marshy forest which even now remains isolated from the currents that stir the rest of Burgundy. The great oaks that grew there made it one of the centres of druidism in pre-Roman Gaul, and as late as the twelfth century, Abbot Suger of Saint-Denis came here in search of wooden beams for the construction of his new church. When he told his carpenters what length was required, 'They smiled,' he said, 'and would have laughed if they had dared'; but Suger took them to the forests of Puisaye and found trees of the necessary height without any difficulty at all.

The spiritual centre of Puisaye is Saint-Sauveur, immortalised under the name of Montigny-en-Fresnois by Colette, in her books *La Maison de Claudine* and *Sido*. Not far from the church, in the Rue des Vignes, a rambling house with a lopsided flight of front steps bears a plaque with the simple inscription *'Ici est née Colette'*. She was born on

28 January 1873, and lived in the house she was to describe in such loving detail until it was auctioned in 1890. When she and her husband Willy made their pilgrimage to Saint-Sauveur in 1895, they were put up at the school. Colette's recollections of her corner of Burgundy are of misty landscapes, ponds and marshes which were still malarial, charcoal-burners in the woods, and the poverty of the remoter regions of France. The house and garden at Saint-Sauveur remain, but as she herself said, 'What does it matter, if the magic has left them, if the secret is lost . . .?' The countryside is tidier and more prosperous than it was then, the forest has been cut up into copses, and the men who fish the meres are there for sport rather than food.

The most crucial single event in Burgundian history took place a few miles to the east of Saint-Sauveur. In 841, Charles the Bald defeated his brother Lothair at Fontenoy-en-Puisaye. Two years later, by the treaty of Verdun, the three grandsons of Charlemagne divided the Frankish empire and effectively created the independent kingdoms of France, Germany and Italy. The relatively small portion of the Burgundian kingdom that lay west of the Saône was given to Charles, and evolved into the Burgundy we know today.

In the other direction from Saint-Sauveur, further down the Loing, the château of Saint-Fargeau was purchased in 1450 by Jacques Coeur, Charles VII's financier and builder of the unmodest mansion that bears his name at Bourges. He began work immediately on his new acquisition, but never enjoyed the benefit of it because in the following year he was arrested for embezzlement. The château subsequently became the property of Coeur's chief accuser, the *Ecorcheur* Antoine de Chabannes. Two hundred years later, by devious pathways of inheritance, it had passed into the possession of Anne-Marie-Louise d'Orléans, duchess of Montpensier and first cousin of Louis XIV.

Her rôle in the aristocratic rebellion of the Fronde—she ordered the cannon of the Bastille to be fired on the king's troops—earned her five years' banishment from court. When she arrived at Saint-Fargeau in 1652, she found 'an old house in which there were neither doors nor windows, and knee-high grass in the courtyard. . . . I was so frightened and unhappy that I began to cry'. Never one to be discouraged for long, the Grande Mademoiselle commissioned François Le Vau (the younger brother of the famous Louis Le Vau who worked at the Louvre and Versailles) to make the depressing old castle presentable. He retained the medieval pentagonal plan and the six round towers, but brought the latter up to date with domed roofs, capped by lanterns so tall that they might seem more in place on a Hindu temple. He also modernised the apartments, but his tour-de-force is the courtyard. Opposite the main entrace, two elegant façades of white stone and warm pink brick converge on a semi-circular staircase leading to a round, domed vestibule. Between the square upper windows, the Grande Mademoiselle's monogram AMLO alternates with lozenges bearing her coat of arms (defaced at the Revolution). The other wings of the château were badly damaged by fire in 1752, and have been restored in a simpler style.

The installation of 70 fireplaces showed that the duchess did not intend her exile to be lonely. Her many guests included her father Gaston d'Orléans, Turenne, the Prince of Condé and Madame de Sévigné; she regaled her little court with theatre and music, and discovered the talent of Giambattista Lulli among her scullions. She returned to favour in 1657, only to be exiled again in 1662 for refusing to marry the king of Portugal (a wise decision on her part, as he turned out to be both impotent and mad). She later gave Saint-Fargeau as a wedding present to a dubious character called Lauzun, whom she married secretly in 1681. He disposed of it in 1714, and in the following year it was acquired by the Le Peletiers, a legal family with an hereditary position in the Paris Parlement. Louis-Michel Le Peletier, deputy of the nobility at the States General of 1789, rose to be President of the National Assembly in 1790 and was later an important member of the Convention. He was assassinated at the Palais-Royal on 20 January 1793 by a former bodyguard of Louis XVI, shortly after voting in favour of the king's immediate execution. He became the Republic's first official martyr, and was buried in the Panthéon with due solemnity. His only daughter became the first ward of the Nation and grew up to be a staunch royalist. When regicides became unfashionable, Le Peletier's body was brought back to Saint-Fargeau and re-interred in the chapel, which occupies the round tower whose entrance leads off the domed vestibule.

On the road leading back to the Yonne, one might pause for a moment at Toucy to remember a man whose writings were very different from Colette's romantic effusions—the harmless drudge Pierre Larousse, whose dedication to facts would have gladdened Mr Gradgrind's heart and who was born at Toucy in 1817. One should certainly make a detour for La Ferté-Loupière to see the murals in the parish church. Executed around the turn of the sixteenth century, the long frieze over the north arcades reflects the late medieval preoccupation with Death the leveller and the vanity of life. There are two separate themes shown, the first being the *Dict des Trois Morts et des Trois Vifs*, which occurs in French literature from the thirteenth century onward: three gallants are met by three walking corpses, who tell of their past grandeur and warn the young men of their own near end. The other subject is a *Danse Macabre* of 42 figures, representing all the stations of life. Popes, cardinals, archbishops, kings, emperors, courtiers—all are confronted by themselves as they will presently be, worms' meat. The epoch's materialistic horror of death was frequently turned to good account by moralisers in this way. Later ages found the message crude and the treatment vulgar; the paintings suffered the usual fate of being whitewashed over, and were only rediscovered in 1910.

By the time it reaches Joigny, the Yonne has already been joined by the Serein, the Armançon, the Burgundy Canal and the Paris-Lyon-Marseille railway. The *vignerons* of Auxerre had taken successful direct action against their employers in 1393, but at least the dispute had been purely industrial and resolved without bloodshed. At Joigny in 1438—when politics were involved—the *vignerons* stormed the castle and bludgeoned Count Guy de la Trémouille to death with their mallets. This incident has earned the people of Joigny the nickname of Maillotins, and a mallet figures in the town's coat of arms.

If Villeneuve-sur-Yonne has a surprisingly grid-like street layout, this is not a result of modern town planning. Villefranche-le-Roy, as it was then known, was created from virtually nothing by Louis VII in 1163. It was to serve as a royal residence and as a stronghold protecting the southern access to the king's personal domain. Pope Alexander III, exiled in northern France at the time, laid the foundation stone of the church. Apart from some visits by Chateaubriand, Villeneuve's only modern claim to notoriety is that between 1927 and 1933 its mayor was 'the abominable Dr Petiot', one of France's most prolific mass murderers. A native of Auxerre, he was a controversial figure during his term of office. Some citizens saw him as the man of action, who had put in the main drainage, built the new schools, the day-nursery, the tennis-courts and the bowling-alley, and was equally at home curing humans and horses. Others alleged that he had not only embezzled public funds, but had stolen a cemetery cross weighing half a ton one Christmas Eve and thrown it into the Yonne. He moved to Paris, where, in 1946, he was arraigned on 27 charges of murder. He admitted to 19, but pleaded in mitigation that his victims had all been Gestapo informers. This defence failed to save him from the guillotine.

Sens, at the very limits of Burgundy, takes its name (formerly *Agedincum Senonum*) from the Senones, the Gallic tribe that invaded Italy around 390 B.C., defeated the Romans at the Allia and sacked Rome itself (though their night attack on the Capitol was foiled when the temple geese gave the alarm). It was their chief Brennus—his statue stands on the roof of the town hall at Sens—who contemptuously cried 'Woe to the conquered!' as he flung his sword on to the scales on which Rome's ransom was being weighed out.

In the Middle Ages, the archbishop of Sens was one of the most important ecclesiastical personalities in France, being the metropolitan of Chartres, Auxerre, Meaux, Paris, Orléans, Nevers and Troyes—hence the acronymic motto of his dean and chapter, CAMPONT. The Council that condemned the unorthodoxy of Abelard was held at Sens in 1140; Pope Alexander III resided there for two years during his quarrel with Frederick Barbarossa (Thomas Becket, also in exile, passed through); and on 27 May 1234 the wedding of St Louis and Margaret of Provence was celebrated in the cathedral. In 1627, Paris was given an archbishop of its own, and Meaux, Chartres and Orléans were placed under his jurisdiction. Sens relapsed into obscurity, so much so that when the archbishop toured Canada recently, he preferred to be introduced as 'the archbishop of Chablis'. Since the Bourbon Restoration, the archbishops of Sens have doubled as bishops of Auxerre, a fact which prompted Pope John XXIII to say to Monseigneur Lamy, 'My lord, you are the bishop with the beautiful churches.'

Saint-Etienne de Sens, begun in 1140 and thus almost contemporary with Suger's Saint-Denis, was the first of the great French Gothic cathedrals. The west front is squat and massive, the vaulting is kept relatively low because flying buttresses were not planned, and the Romanesque round arch is still much in evidence (especially in the ambulatory and, outside, on the north tower). But the pointed arch and the rib-vault were also used, and the sheer scale of Gothic construction made itself felt. The master mason William of Sens began his career at the cathedral, before going to England to supervise the rebuilding of the chancel at Canterbury. This link explains the close similarity of the twelfth-century work in the two churches.

The north or 'Lead' tower was begun in 1180, but never properly completed. Until 1848 it had a timber belfry covered with sheet lead, hence its name. The south or 'Stone' tower is manifestly younger than its sister, passing from the traceried windows of High Gothic to the crockets and pinnacles of Flamboyant. The original tower collapsed on Maundy Thursday 1267 (this sort of accident was alarmingly common in an age when one built by rule of thumb rather than by mathematical calculation), taking with it parts of the nave, the façade, and the adjoining synodal palace. The rebuilding went on well into the sixteenth century. As a final flourish, a little Renaissance belfry was added in 1534, giving the west front the ponderously jaunty air of a cross-gartered Malvolio. Against the mullion of the main portal stands a statue of St Stephen—not a nineteenth-century imitation but the original, spared by the revolutionaries because they thought that the book in his hands (in fact the Gospel) was the Book of the Law. They contented themselves with dressing him in a red bonnet. The transepts were built at the end of the fifteenth and beginning of the sixteenth centuries by Martin Chambiges, who was also responsible for the façade at Troyes and the transepts at Beauvais. The glorious tracery of the rose-windows, like jets of flame spurting from the centre, makes them Flamboyant in the most literal sense.

The cathedral treasury is one of the richest in Europe, with a large collection of ivories, tapestries and vestments (including the chasuble and stole of Thomas Becket). The furnishings of the church itself include a high altar and baldacchino by Servandoni (inspired by those at St Peter's in Rome), and a magnificent wrought-iron chancel-grille by Guillaume Doré (1762). There is also the monument erected by Archbishop Tristan de Salazar (who financed the construction of the transepts) to the memory of his parents. Hidden in one of the apsidal chapels, however—and unfortunately kept under lock and key—is something of much greater interest, a neglected masterpiece of French eighteenth-century sculpture. The Dauphin Louis, son of Louis XV and father of Louis XVI, died in 1765 and in his will declared his wish to be buried at Sens. The sculptor chosen for the tomb was Guillaume Coustou, who was popular at court and had worked for the king and Madame de Pompadour. The basic form of the monument was dictated by its original free-standing position in the choir; the visitor is advised to persist with the sacristan to get the apsidal chapel open, as the monument needs to be seen in the round.

The convention of the wall-tomb had been abandoned, and the Sens tomb was new in the history of funerary monuments in France. There is no image of the Dauphin, only mourning allegorical figures surrounding two urns, one for the Dauphin, the other for his wife, Marie-Josèphe of Saxony. There are four principal figures: Religion holding up a crown of stars, a grieving Conjugal Love, Immortality, and Time, who veils the Dauphine's urn, having already covered that of the Dauphin. The tomb is the first large-scale neo-classical monument to be built in France. The sentiment is Stoic resignation rather than Christian hope. It is severe, yet there is an effortlessness in the carving that removes it from the confines of academic classicism.

Depending on whether one travels from north to south or vice versa, Sens is either the first or last town in Burgundy. Which is all the more reason to treat oneself to a bit of culinary luxury, either to celebrate one's arrival or to ensure that the last memory is the best. The place to do it is the Hôtel de Paris et de la Poste, just round the corner from the cathedral and opposite the town hall. People come from Paris especially to eat at M. Sandré's, a journey of 72 miles.

8 The Morvan

Gaston Roupnel, who celebrated Burgundy in the orotund prose beloved of French academics, described the Morvan as 'the granite pillar on which the whole construction rests'. This spur of the Massif Central is a complex of ancient igneous and metamorphic rocks, raised and planed down twice in the 270 million years since the Carboniferous Age. The various *pays* of Burgundy surround it on three sides, separated by its mass of rounded hills from the Loire country to the west.

The Morvan (Celtic for 'the black mountain') is Burgundy's only highland area, a country of heath and woodland. For most of its history, it has been the poor relation of the surrounding *pays*. There are few large villages, solitary farms and remote groups of cottages being the rule. Until recently, isolated by hills, forests and superstition, the Morvan had an almost closed economy. The peasants made bread from rye and buckwheat (the only cereals that the acid soil would grow), and got milk and meat from a breed of small red cattle unique to the region. There was no industry apart from wood-cutting. For centuries, the principal export was human beings. The cold, wet climate meant that the Morvandiaux could go down to the lowlands for the harvest in August and the vintage in September, and still be finished before their own crops were ripe. Others, known as Galvachers, would leave their villages in spring with a cart and a yoke of oxen, to pick up firewood, wine, clogs and other products for Paris and the north. When they had ·made their deliveries, they would hire themselves and their teams out for transport or ploughing, not heading for home until the autumn. Wherever possible, a Galvacher would sell his oxen and return on foot. This export of able-bodied adults was balanced in the nineteenth century by the import of babes-in-arms. It was not polite practice in Paris for young mothers to suckle their children. Consequently, as wet-nurses to the *petits Paris,* the Morvandelles were able to earn more than their menfolk. It was not even necessary for them to leave home, as the babies were often sent to the Morvan and left there until they were weaned. An unmarried girl who became pregnant had no difficulty in catching a husband, as her ability to produce milk was a dowry in itself. A variation of this cottage industry was the fostering of Parisian orphans. Of course, the attraction for the peasants was the allowance money, but the proportion of foster-children who spent the rest of their lives in the Morvan was higher than that of native-born Morvandiaux. Today, as in all the poorer rural areas of France, the seasonal migration from the Morvan has become a permanent one. Rye has given place to wheat, thanks to the use of fertilisers, the wiry local cattle have been replaced by the Charollais, and the beech forests are retreating before monotonous but profitable pinewoods.

The country slopes downwards from south to north. The south is the only truly mountainous area, rising to 2,959 feet at Le Haut Folin. The two main rivers of the Morvan, the Yonne and its tributary the Cure, rise in this massif. Also in the south is the 'capital' of the Morvan, Château-Chinon. The 'little town of great renown' has no pretensions to being a *ville d'art*—its mushrooming development as an industrial centre ensures that. However, it does have a certain reflected fame through its mayor François Mitterand, leader of the Socialist Party and the 'Union of the Left', who failed by the narrowest of margins to become President of the Republic in 1974. They used to say that, as at Brest, it rained 300 days a year at Château-Chinon. In fact, the figure is more like 180—though there is still enough snow on Le Haut Folin to justify a ski resort.

The relatively low-lying northern parts of the Morvan, being less of a wilderness, are richer in associations. Clamecy, in the far north-west corner, was the birthplace of the novelist Romain Rolland (1866-1944), who wrote of it in *Colas Breugnon*. It was also, by virtue of its position on the Yonne, the former centre of the Morvan timber trade. In the sixteenth century, a Parisian merchant called Jean Rouvet pioneered the running of logs from the High Morvan to Paris by river. The logs were felled and dragged to the banks of the Cure or the Yonne, where they were stacked and given an owner's mark. On an agreed date the sluices were opened to create an artificial spate, into which the logs were thrown. Those that travelled along the upper Yonne were swept down to Clamecy, where they were halted by a dam, beached and sorted. From mid-March, when the spring thaw brought the real spate, the logs were trussed to form rafts which were coupled together to make huge 'log-trains'. These were loaded with cargo and then run down the Yonne and the Seine to the capital.

By the early years of the nineteenth century the industry had reached its peak, and as late as 1861 a new large dam was built on the Lac des Settons to facilitate log-running on the Cure. But the days of this picturesque activity were already numbered. In 1834, even before the coming of the railway, the opening of the Nivernais Canal from the Loire (at Decize) to the Yonne (just above Auxerre) simplified the process by bringing barges to within a few miles of the lumber-camps. The last log-train left Clamecy in 1923, and since then the lakes of the Morvan have served simply to regulate the mountain torrents and, ironically, to feed the Nivernais Canal. The only legacies of nearly four centuries of *flottage* are a statue on the bridge over the Yonne at Clamecy, and one of the biggest wood-processing (carbonising and distillation) plants in France.

Above the Pont de Bethléem at Clamecy, at the tip of a peninsula formed by the river and a backwater, is a bust dedicated in 1849 to the memory of Jean Rouvet. The bust's striking resemblance to Napoleon I is no coincidence. The Parisian sculptor David d'Angers, commissioned to provide the memorial, was overloaded with work. Feeling sure that the people of Clamecy had no better idea than he himself of what Rouvet looked like, he sent them an old bust of the Emperor that was lying around his workshop. The hoax was not discovered until after David had been paid.

The old town stands on the left bank of the Yonne, its medieval streets clustered round the church of Saint-Martin. But the real historical curiosity of Clamecy lies across the Pont de Bethléem, in the quarter of 'Judaea'. In 1168 Count William of Nevers died at Acre in Palestine, and requested that he should be buried at Bethlehem. In return for this privilege, he bequeathed to the bishops of Bethlehem the Hôpital de Panthenor at Clamecy, a hospice for sick pilgrims returned from the Holy Land. This property was to serve as the bishops' residence in the event of their diocese falling into the hands of the Infidel. When the crusaders' position at last became untenable in 1225, Rainier, ninth bishop of Bethlehem, became the first of 50 bishops *in partibus (infidelium)* to rule his phantom see from Clamecy. The hospital chapel (now ruined, though parts of it are incorporated in the Hôtel de la Boule d'Or, across the square from the new church) was upgraded to cathedral, a status it retained until 1793. By the Concordat of 1801, the see of Bethlehem was abolished, despite the refusal of the last bishop to resign. The title was revived in 1840, but is now held by the abbot of Saint-Maurice-en-Valais in Switzerland.

Fifteen miles by road to the east of Clamecy, in the valley of the Cure, a convent was founded in the middle of the 9th century by Girard de Roussillon, whose adventures were the basis of one of the most famous of all *chansons de geste*. Shortly afterwards the nuns were replaced by Benedictine monks, and by a papal bull of 863 the monastery was placed under the direct protection of the Holy See. In 887, bribed by Charles the Fat to raise the siege of Paris in return for a free hand elsewhere, the Norsemen descended on Burgundy and destroyed the little abbey. The monks retreated just in time to a defensive position on the top of a nearby hill, where they refounded their community. These were the beginnings of an institution whose name is among Burgundy's most evocative—Vézelay.

If one were allowed to see only one thing in the whole province, it would have to be Vézelay. From any direction, the first sight of it is breathtaking; but nothing can quite equal the view from Fontette on the road from Avallon, two towers silhouetted against the distant horizon, floating above a sea of haze in the valley.

The steep main street winds up to the basilica of Sainte-Madeleine between tightly-packed houses; Romain Rolland spent the last years of his life at No. 20. When one emerges on to the square, the plain exterior of the church is something of a disappointment. One feels a little cheated that the distant 'vision of peace and beauty' is not repeated at close quarters. The towers (one at the south corner of the façade, the other in the angle of the nave and the south transept) barely offset the horizontal emphasis of the building. Worse, the sculpture of the west front, almost completely destroyed during the Revolution, was rather unsuccessfully restored in the last century. The stone is too pale in colour, and the scenes themselves have the lifelessness of imitations.

These impressions are dispelled the moment we enter the narthex. Few church interiors can rival Vézelay as a material expression of divine joy. 'It is so harmonious,' said Lord Clark, 'that surely St Bernard, who preached the Second Crusade here, must have felt it to be an expression of the Divine Law and an aid to worship and contemplation.' St Bernard's famous visit took place in 1146, when the abbot of Clairvaux was at the height of his authority and prestige. Vézelay, too, had reached its zenith. In the early eleventh century, the monk Badilo brought back some relics which purported to be those of Mary Magdalene. In 1050 the church was re-dedicated in her name, and eight years later the authenticity of the relics was recognised by the pope. Thereafter, Vézelay became not only an object of pilgrimage in its own right, but one of the main assembly-points for the pilgrimage to Santiago de Compostela in Spain.

For most of the abbey's history, the monks jealously guarded the autonomy inherent in their direct dependence on the Holy See. They were in continual conflict with the counts of Nevers and the bishops of Autun, not to mention the townspeople themselves, often resentful of theocratic rule (one abbot was assassinated). However, Vézelay did fall briefly within the Cluniac orbit, and it was during this interlude (1096-1137) that the present abbey church was begun and largely completed. A new east end was in place by 1104, and in 1115 a western extension was started to accommodate the growing numbers of pilgrims. Then on the night of 21 July 1120, when the old Carolingian nave was packed with penitents keeping vigil for the saint's feast, fire broke out. In the ensuring panic, according to one chronicler, 1,127 people lost their lives. This disaster is commemorated by a small medallion over the keystone of the third arcade on the south side of the nave; round a figure of a woman carrying a miniature church, a Latin inscription reads: 'Though now blackened with smoke, later I shall be fair.'

A new nave was built in record time and dedicated in 1132. But Vézelay owes none of its structural elements to St Hugh's recently completed abbey church at Cluny, despite a nominal Cluniac obedience reinforced by the presence of St Hugh's great-nephew as abbot. Renaud of Semur chose instead to reproduce the design of the priory church of Anzy-le-Duc in the Brionnais, that region of southern Burgundy of which his family were *seigneurs*. Its most striking characteristic was that, instead of the conventional tunnel vault, the nave was covered by a series of groin vaults. Previously, this system had been restricted to the aisles—and in fact, it proved unsuitable for the broad span of the nave at Vézelay, and necessitated first internal tie-beams, and later flying buttresses. Pilasters and the pointed arch, both Cluniac hallmarks, were rejected in favour of half-columns and the round arch of the older Romanesque. A large three-bayed narthex was added between 1140 and 1160. The predominant colour is a delectable pale pink. In the arches, the alternation of pink blocks with white has a faintly Alhambran flavour, and may well be of Moorish inspiration. The perspective culminates in the radiant Gothic chancel, which replaced a dark Romanesque oven vault at the very end of the twelfth century.

Cluny's only gift to Vézelay is its sculpture. There seems no doubt that the carvers of Vézelay had previously worked at Cluny until the completion of the two major sculptural ensembles there around 1115. As well as the tympana of the west doors, there is a profusion of figured capitals in the nave and narthex. Unlike the abstract foliated capitals of Cluny, these delight in telling a story, and have the popular appeal appropriate to a pilgrimage church.

Scores of separate incidents are described with imagination and wit, but no obvious general scheme emerges. The Old Testament is well represented, as are the lives of SS Peter, Antony, Martin, Benedict and Eugenia (who lived in a monastery as a man, and is depicted baring her breasts to clear herself of a charge of attempted rape)—but there is not a single episode from the life of Christ nor any reference to Mary Magdalene. The clue to the underlying theme is the appearance of Satan in all his guises: demon, lion, eagle, serpent, basilisk, Golden Calf, tempter of the carnal appetites, and slanderer (the original meaning of the Greek *diabolos*). In counterpoint to this motif of ever-present spiritual danger is one of the soul's deliverance from the bondage of the flesh: St Peter released from prison by the angel, David killing Goliath, Daniel in the lions' den, Moses killing the Egyptian slave-driver, the Angel of the Passover, St Martin saving himself by a simple sign of the Cross, which stops a falling tree and hurls it back on the saint's would-be murderers. In short, Vézelay is an eloquent appeal for repentance to the pilgrims who had come to honour the patroness of penitents, a reminder that their share in the benefits of salvation had to be earned.

Every one of the figured capitals deserves detailed study (it is worth getting a comprehensive guide), but only a few of the most outstanding can be mentioned here. The second pillar from the west in the south aisle depicts Lust and Despair with savage enthusiasm. On one side, the serpents of lust devour a women's breasts and genitals; on the other, a fiend impales himself on a sword. Two pillars further along is the most vivid of all the narrative capitals, illustrating the story of Dives and Lazarus: Lazarus the beggar, who waited at the gate 'desiring to be fed with the crumbs which fell from the rich man's table', has died; angels bear his soul (a doll-like figure in a mandorla) off to heaven. In the centre, the rich man dies too, but in his bed, surrounded by harlots. Serpents consume his bags of gold as demons with pincers tear his soul from his mouth. In the last scene, beneath the trees of Paradise, Abraham gathers Lazarus to his bosom and blesses him.

The west pillar of the same pier is surmounted by the finest symbolic capital in the church, the most profound in conception as well as the most perfect in execution, the Mystic Mill. Moses empties grain into a mill representing Christ, and St Paul collects the flour. The sense of this beautiful allegory is that the Law of Moses contained the truth, but a dimly-perceived truth hidden like the flour in the grain. Through Christ's sacrifice, the grain is transformed into the flour of the New Law, which St Paul is charged to distribute to the hungry world.

The narthex is dominated by the great tympanum of the main

west door, one of Burgundy's two masterpieces of Romanesque sculpture (the other is at Autun). The archivolt, composed of medallions depicting the signs of the Zodiac and the Labours of the Months, frames one of the rarest themes in Christian iconography, the Mission of the Apostles. The only contemporary parallel is on parchment, in an illuminated lectionary from Cluny.

The tympanum is one of those few works of Christian art dedicated to the Word of God rather than the person of Christ. It recalls the gift of the Holy Spirit at Pentecost, symbolised by the rays of divine inspiration streaming from Christ's hand to the heads of the apostles. But the real message is from the end of St Mark's Gospel, 'Go ye into all the world, and preach the gospel to every creature.' The nations march round the tympanum and process across the lintel to the feet of Christ, where they are welcomed by St Peter and St Paul. The inclusion of the bizarre inventions of travellers' tales—pygmies, elephant-eared Panotii and dog-headed Cynocephali—proclaims that the church is universal and Christ's redeeming love available to all. The mutilated statue against the mullion was of St John the Baptist displaying the Paschal Lamb on a salver.

Almost eclipsed by the splendour of the central tableau, the tympana of the side-doors complete the theological scheme. They depict the mysteries that the apostles were required to expound: the Incarnation (from the Annunciation to the Adoration of the Magi) and the Resurrection (the appearance to the disciples and the supper at Emmaus). At the time the ensemble must have been conceived, the regent of the monastery school at Vézelay was Peter of Montboissier, one of the leading scholars of the day and better known to us as Peter the Venerable, abbot of Cluny. Some historians have seen his hand in the grand design of the sculpted decoration, and though the evidence is only circumstantial, the idea is attractive. The consoling theme of the great tympanum, far removed from the melodrama of the Last Judgment, accords so well with everything we know about his personality. It would have been in character for him to imagine a monument to the *Logos,* the power of Divine Reason made visible at Vézelay.

Behind the apse of the basilica is a terrace with a sweeping panorama of the Morvan. It was on the slopes below—the site is marked by a cross—that Louis VII and his followers gathered to hear St Bernard on 31 March 1146. Like all but the First, the Second Crusade was a failure, and petered out in mutual recriminations. St Bernard's prestige suffered badly, but Vézelay's outlasted the century. In 1190, it was the rendez-vous of Richard the Lionheart

and his wily overlord Philip Augustus of France at the start of the
Third Crusade. Then things began to go seriously wrong at Vézelay.
As the rôle of monasteries everywhere declined, pilgrims were
discouraged by the frequent fighting between the monks, the
townsfolk and the count of Nevers, and attendances at the fairs were
drastically reduced. A small amount of new building went on (the
upper storeys of the west tower and the pediment over the main
entrance), but in 1279 came the final ignominy: official recognition
was transferred to the rival relics of Mary Magdalene in Provence.

The Wars of Religion took their toll. When the Huguenots
captured the town in 1569, they sacked the abbey and played bowls
with the heads of their decapitated oppoents. The Revolution
completed the destruction of the monastery buildings, and by 1840
the church itself was virtually a ruin. Prosper Mérimée, Inspector of
the newly-founded Commission on Historic Monuments, offered the
job of restoring it to several seasoned architects, all of whom
refused. The challenge was taken up by the 26-year-old Eugène-
Emmanuel Viollet-le-Duc, who devoted 20 years, on and off, to the
task. It was his first commission in a career which led him, if the
credits in guide-books are anything to go by, to comment on and
restore practically every church in France.

In the valley below the basilica is the village of Saint-Père, whose
small but exquisite Gothic church stands on the site of the first
monastic settlement at Vézelay. The present building dates from the
reign of St Louis, probably about 1240, though the deep porch was
added a century later. The church has passed under the patronage
of Our Lady, but the original dedication to St Peter ad Vincula has
given its name to the village.

The triangular pediment over the façade, with its nine niches, is
supposed to have inspired the similar pediment at Vézelay, but the
statues at Saint-Père are far superior. The most exciting feature of
the building is the tower that launches itself effortlessly skywards. At
the corners of the second storey, four angels sound the last trump
and announce the Judgment portrayed over the main arch of the
portico. Just inside the porch, on the right, are two figures carved in
bas-relief, of a man carrying a church and a woman holding a book;
according to tradition, these represent the founders, Girard de
Roussillon and his wife, though they could simply be the unknown
donors of the thirteenth-century church.

There are two large hotels in Vézelay itself, but neither has quite
the charm of the Auberge à l'Espérance at Saint-Père. Among the
specialities of M. Meneau's cuisine is duck in port wine with caper
sauce, and the front bedrooms have a perfect view of the church,

floodlit at night.

A short distance upstream from Saint-Père is the site of the salt springs which were exploited from before 600 B.C. until the seventeenth century, when they were filled in by order of the administrators of the salt tax. Objects from the excavations are on display at the museum in the former presbytery of Notre-Dame de Saint-Père. Among them are the original 'pans' used by the Celts, oak-trunks hollowed out by fire and partially petrified by the mineral content of the water.

Further on, the village of Pierre-Perthuis takes its name from a natural stone arch eroded from the hillside that rises steeply from the opposite bank. Two bridges span the Cure, one modern, the other eighteenth-century and reputedly the creation (in his capacity as lord of the manor of nearby Bazoches) of the greatest military engineer of his own or any age, the marquis de Vauban.

Sébastien Le Prestre was born in 1633, into a family of minor Morvandiau gentry. His beginnings were certainly modest, but the story of how he lost his father at the age of ten, was abandoned by his mother when she remarried, evicted from his cottage by his father's creditors, and taken in as a factotum by the village priest, is sheer romance. Nor did the young Sébastien run away and become involved in the Fronde by accident; he was presented to the prince of Condé, the rebel leader, by a maternal uncle already on the prince's staff. Captured by the royalists, he switched his allegiance and was appointed by Mazarin to the suite of the Commissioner-General of Fortifications.

In the course of his career, Vauban repaired and improved 300 existing fortresses, and built 33 new ones. He introduced a repertoire of new concepts such as crossfire and ricochet, but his talent was more than just defensive: he also successfully directed 53 sieges, 20 of them in the presence of his master Louis XIV. It was said that a town defended by Vauban was impregnable, and a town besieged by him as good as lost. In 1673, the king awarded him 60,000 *livres* as a token of appreciation for the capture of Maastricht. Two years later, Vauban used the bounty to buy the château of Bazoches, almost within sight of the family seat from which the Le Prestres took their title (Vauban's father had been the losing party in a lawsuit over the inheritance).

Vauban had a special affection for his 'little provincial patrimony which requires much attention'. Among his improvements were a terrace, a new main entrance, and extensive outbuildings, but none of these refurbishments altered the château's essential character. It is still an ungainly remnant of the Middle Ages, the home of the country squire rather than the courtier. Inside, he converted the whole of the first floor of the west wing into a long gallery where he could work with his assistant engineers and designers.

Apart from being one of the originators of 'classical' warfare, Vauban wrote notes on civil engineering, agronomy, town planning, diplomacy and economics (one memorandom was entitled *Thoughts of a man with nothing much to do*). He put theory into practice on his estate at Bazoches, growing vines—the 1696 was excellent—and improving his woodland. Honours continued to pour in. In 1688, the Dauphin presented him with four cannon taken at the siege of Philippsburg (an unheard-of privilege), and the year before, Boileau had written to Racine to say, 'I think that there is more than one marshal of France who, on meeting him, blushes to see himself marshal of France.' Despite Vauban's own misgivings (he pointed out that he was an engineer, not a soldier), he was eventually awarded the marshal's baton in 1704.

'Ever miserly of men's lives,' in the words of Saint-Simon, Vauban's concern for the common people off the battlefield was his undoing. Appalled at the distress caused by years of economic mismanagement and by France's dismal performance in the War of the Spanish Succession, Vauban wrote *A Project for a Royal Tithe*, advocating a ten per cent tax on all land and trade, and backing up his arguments with the first systematic use of statistics. The nobility (who were exempt from taxation) and the profiteering revenue-farmers were scandalised, but publication went ahead secretly. Just when it was really needed, royal support was lacking. The king permitted the book to be banned by the Parlement of Paris, and all copies of it were seized and burnt. Vauban died a few weeks later, in March 1707.

His body was brought back to Bazoches and buried in the village church. In a codicil to his will, he left provision for five illegitimate children (by various mothers) of whom he was the putative father, stating in one case that although there was reason to doubt the woman's claim, 'he did not wish to risk his soul's salvation thereby'. Nevertheless, if the executors found that any of the children were no longer living, the mothers were to receive nothing, 'for I have paid them well enough not to have scruples about them'. By his own request, his heart was buried separately beneath the altar steps. In 1808, it was exhumed on Napoleon's orders, and joined the remains of France's other military heroes at Les Invalides.

Another marshal of France was born a few miles to the east at the château of Chastellux, in a picturesque forest setting overlooking the gorge of the Cure. Claude de Beauvoir, baron of Chastellux

(1386-1453), created marshal in 1418, was chamberlain to John the Fearless. His victory at Cravant in 1423 earned him a bizarre privilege, described earlier, from the dean and chapter of Auxerre. Yet a third marshal—this time a Napoleonic one, Davout—was born in the district, at Arnoux. The coincidence enables Avallon to call itself, with a certain generosity of interpretation, 'the town of the three marshals'.

Avallon, a strategically-placed hill-town like Flavigny and Semur, is the northern gate of the Morvan. It was the capital of one of the four original counties of the Capetian duchy in 1031, and was long considered one of the province's key strongholds. When the freebooter Fortépice, in the pay of Charles VII, captured Avallon by a surprise attack in 1433, Philip the Good rushed back from Flanders to direct siege operations in person. Although Fortépice's 200 men repulsed the first assault, it was clear that the duke's troops had an overwhelming superiority. Fortépice organised a festivity to divert the townspeople and his own men from their plight, and while everyone was dancing he escaped under cover of darkness, alone.

From the fifteenth-century clock-tower, where the aldermen once held their deliberations, the Rue Aristide Briand leads down to the cobbled square in front of the church of Saint-Lazare. A supposed skull of Lazarus was given to the church in the year 1000, and by the end of the century had become an object of popular veneration on account of its power to cure and ward off leprosy. A new church was consecrated by Pope Paschal II in 1106 and completed some 50 years later. The floor-level follows the slope of the hillside in such a way that the chancel is ten feet lower than the portico. The north tower caught fire several times and finally collapsed in 1633, taking the north doorway and part of the façade with it. The nondescript rebuilding has left the west front lopsided.

The two surviving portals, from about 1150, are Saint-Lazare's main attraction. The tympana have been badly mutilated, but in any case, they would have been upstaged by the exuberant carving of the arches. Both consist of five concentric bands of sculpture. The larger depicts (working from the tympanum outwards) angels, the Elders of the Apocalypse, the signs of the Zodiac interspersed with the Labours of the Months, acanthus leaves, and vines; the smaller, which is even more opulent, more than makes up for its lack of figures by a jungle of vegetation—rose blossoms, stocks, arum lilies, and vines again. Both doorways had barley-sugar and statue-columns (all but one of the latter have been destroyed and replaced by plain shafts), and the pillars of the smaller portal rest on ornamental dadoes. This turmoil and profusion of detail is typical of the last phase of Burgundian Romanesque art, aptly known in France as *roman fleuri* (Florid Romanesque). The cycle, which begins with the primitive at Saint-Bénigne and runs through the classic at Cluny, finishes in wilful elaboration and restless movement.

After Saint-Lazare the street runs out through the ramparts, and takes a hairpin bend down past terraced gardens into the valley of the Cousin. One road leads to Vézelay, the other back into the Morvan towards Saulieu.

The name of Quarré-les-Tombes has a very literal sense. The village church is surrounded by over 100 stone sarcophagi of the Merovingian period (6th-8th centuries); it is said that originally there were more than 2,000. No-one knows why or how they came to be there, though there is no shortage of suggestions. We can probably discard the hypothesis that they rained down from heaven for the decent interment of Christians killed in battle against the Saracens or Norsemen (there are two variants of the story). They may belong to pilgrims who wanted their last resting-place to be under the protection of some forgotten saint (the dedication of the church to St George is much later). Or again, they may simply be a stockpile belonging to a known sarcophagus-factor at Dissangis, 30 miles away—though this hardly explains why they should have been dumped at Quarré-les-Tombes.

Saint-Léger-Vauban (formerly Saint-Léger-de-Foucheret) was the birthplace of the marshal, but the real centre of interest in the environs lies in the depths of the forest of Saint-Léger. There on the banks of the Cousin, in one of the loneliest parts of the Morvan, Father Muard founded the abbey of La Pierre-qui-Vire in 1850. Any monastic institution is an oddity today, let alone one of such recent foundation. This one belongs to the same mid-nineteenth-century French Catholic revival as Lacordaire's Dominicans, and has become a popular centre for religious retreats. The monks not only make a cream cheese on their farm, but also run a printing press and published the excellent Zodiaque series on art and architecture. The *pierre-qui-vire* itself, or rocking-stone, stands just outside the abbey grounds. According to local legend, it revolves on its axis once a year, at midnight on Christmas Eve.

If Château-Chinon prides itself on being the 'capital' of the Morvan, Saulieu has the satisfaction of knowing that its *curé* can call himself 'bishop of the Morvan'. His 'cathedral' of Saint-Andoche derives its unusual name from an associate of Benignus, said to have been martyred at Saulieu in 177 during the persecution of Marcus Aurelius. The present church was begun in 1112 on the initiative of

Stephen of Bâgé, bishop of Autun and abbot of Saulieu, who also rebuilt Autun Cathedral. The Romanesque east end was destroyed by the English during the Hundred Years' War, and its Gothic replacement met a similar fate 200 years later at the hands of the Huguenots; the chancel was rebuilt in an austere 'Jansenist' style in 1704. The nave has pointed arches and a false triforrium in the Cluniac manner, but the local granite seems to have forced the builders to simplify the decorative elements and dispense with the usual fluted pilasters.

The special charm of Saint-Andoche is its sculptured capitals. Their chronology is disputed, some seeing them as forerunners of those at Autun and Vézelay, others as imitations. Dates of consecration (in this case 1119) are misleading as they generally indicate no more than the completion of the chancel; so the second theory is probably the correct one. Most of the capitals depict foliage, sometimes so recognisable that they must have been carved from the life. The five 'biblical' capitals (the Flight into Egypt, Temptation of Christ, Balaam and his Ass, Suicide of Judas, and Resurrection) take up themes treated at Autun. The artist of Saulieu exploits his talent for caricature to take advantage of the 'human interest' in a story. For example, Mary clutching Jesus to her breast in the Flight into Egypt, or the realism of the apparition to Mary Magdalene, which translates Christ's 'Touch me not' so much more vividly than its more refined model. The Arch-Fiend of the Temptation is a splendid creation, and the two donkeys, Mary's and Balaam's, show a surer grasp of anatomy than we find at Autun. Indeed, even though Autun's Balaam is badly damaged. we can see that Saulieu's is the more appealing version of the story. All the same, this is the art of the miniature; enlargements, as it were, of contemporary ivories. It is difficult to imagine the unknown sculptor of Saulieu attempting the grandeur of the Last Judgment at Autun.

In 1651, the States of Burgundy decided to upgrade the Paris-Lyon road via Saulieu and revive the route followed by the Roman Via Agrippa, which had fallen into disuse as Dijon grew in importance. Saulieu became a busy staging-post, and inns and taverns sprang up to minister to the needs of travellers. Rabelais had already noted, 100 years earlier, that one ate and drank well at Saulieu; and in 1677, stopping on her way from Bourbilly to Vichy, the prim Madame de Sévigné, to her shame, found herself the worse for drink after a lavish meal. She gave a statue of the Virgin to the church of Saint-Andoche by way of expiation; it stands in the north aisle.

The gastronomic reputation remains—perhaps it is the best place of all to sample the great Morvandiau dish of *jambon à la crème*—but the traffic has been spirited away by the opening of the A6 motorway. Saulieu consoles itself with woodworking and with the export of nearly a million Christmas trees a year from the nearby forest.

East of Saulieu, on the very fringes of the Morvan and the Auxois, Stephen of Bâgé acquired the château of Thoisy-la-Berchère, which remained the country residence of the bishops of Autun until 1567. It was rebuilt by the celebrated Cardinal Rolin in the fifteenth century, and radically restored in the nineteenth. Inside are the 'Falcon' tapestries from Haroué in Lorraine, a series devoted to a hawking party at various moments on its outing. The story goes that they adorned the tent of Charles the Rash when he was on campaign, though the costumes are in fact those of the first quarter of the sixteenth century.

Approached from the north, Autun is strikingly revealed against the backdrop of the Uchon massif, isolated from the rest of the Morvan by the plain of the Arroux. The two white slagheaps that one passes at Les Télots, near Saint-Forgeot, are the last (and unfortunately persistent) traces of a shale-oil extraction plant which closed down in 1957. In the last century, it actually exported petroleum to the United States.

Autun was long thought to be the original Bibracte, capital of the Aedui, but excavations 15 miles away in the Morvan have proved conclusively that Bibracte stood on the summit of Mont Beuvray. Round about the beginning of the Christian era, the Emperor Augustus decided that the best way to control this sensitive area of Gaul was to build a truly Roman (and more accessible) city to compete with Bibracte. The first historical reference to this new town, Augustodunum, occurs in Tacitus, in connexion with the abortive revolt of Sacrovir in 21. By this time Bibracte had been completely supplanted; its ancient druidic schools had been transferred to Augustodunum and were promoting Greco-Roman civilisation. With a population of 100,000 (12,000 of them students), the new town could proudly style herself 'sister and rival of Rome'. The barbarian invasions were fatal to Augustodunum. The city never recovered its importance after its first sack, in 270, by the Batavi under the command of the Imperial pretender Tetricus.

Little remains of this former splendour: a theatre (in bad repair); the ruins of a sanctuary (popularly, but probably incorrectly, known as the Temple of Janus) in a field outside the town; and two Roman gates, the Porte d'Arroux and the Porte Saint-André. The amphitheatre, which was larger than those at Arles and Nimes, had already disappeared by the seventeenth century. There is also the enigmatic Pierre de Couhard, at the village of that name just south of Autun. Archaeologists have established that it was raised in the 1st century and was once a pyramid, but we can only speculate on its purpose. It may have been a beacon, but its position in a Gallo-Roman cemetery suggests some kind of funerary monument. An attempt to investigate the interior in 1640 left the ignorant no wiser, and a large hole in one side of the object.

In the Middle Ages, the population of Autun had fallen to a tenth of what it had been in Roman times. Nevertheless, the city did retain one vital vestige of its past glory, its episcopal see. From the main square, the Champ de Mars, the Rue Saint-Saulge climbs past the wrought-iron grille of the former Jesuit college and its austerely classical chapel (1757). Bussy-Rabutin and the Bonapartes—Joseph, Napoleon and Lucien—were all educated there, though the future emperor only stayed a few months. The cathedral of Saint-Lazare stands at the highest point of the town, in the *château* or citadel, ruled by the clergy as a city within a city until 1566.

The original cathedral, founded in the 5th century, was dedicated to St Nazaire. In the 10th century it came into possession of the relics of Lazarus, but nobody thought of giving them a sanctuary of their own until the time of Bishop Stephen of Bâgé. Work on new church was in progress from 1120, and in 1146 the relics were translated with great pomp and confusion (the noblemen had to cut their way out of the press with their swords, but by a miracle no-one was fatally injured). From 1195 onwards, the two churches, standing side by side, took it in turns to be cathedral—Saint-Nazaire from All Saints to Easter, Saint-Lazare from Easter to All Saints. Saint-Nazaire was eventually ousted by the newcomer, though not demolished until 1783. All that remains of it, a single chapel, can be seen in the courtyard of the choir-school (Maître).

The Romanesque lines of Saint-Lazare are almost completely submerged by its late Gothic spire and side-chapels. Only the north transept and Viollet-le-Duc's bogusly authentic west towers (imitated from Paray-le-Monial—one of his more successful divinations of 'original intentions') prepare us for what we find inside. Stephen of Bâgé was a friend of Cluny—he retired there to die—so it is not surprising that his new cathedral should have been strongly influenced by St Hugh's great abbey church. All the hallmarks of Cluniac style are there: fluted pilasters, pointed tunnel vault, false triforium. At Autun, this last feature is consciously imitated from the upper gallery of the Porte d'Arroux, and it is even possible that Cluny's fluted pilasters and Corinthian capitals had the same inspiration. Only the lower part of the apse is original, as the oven vault was destroyed when the crossing tower was struck by lightning and burnt down during a thunderstorm in 1469.

Autun's greatest glory is its sculpture. Medieval artists have a reputation (a little exaggerated) for self-effacing anonymity, but we know the name of the Autun master because he himself placed it where it could not be missed. Between 1130 and 1140, Gilbert, or Gislebertus to give his name the latinised form by which it is better known, produced one of Europe's most important sculptural ensembles. What is more, although he must have had assistants, his hand is discernible in almost every part of the decoration. He must have been regarded with a certain amount of awe to have obtained such an exclusive commission. He also worked at Vézelay, so we can trace his career back with virtual certainty to Cluny, where the mature Romanesque style originated. At Autun, where the cathedral is of local grey sandstone, he worked in softer, finer-grained limestone brought in from outside the district.

Gislebertus' masterpiece, the great tympanum of the Last Judgment over the west door, looms dramatically at the head of a flight of steps in an open narthex. It is a perfect illustration of his personality and techniques: a superb narrative gift that relished horrors, and a fondness for distortion and exaggeration that has been described as Baroque, though perhaps Expressionistic would be nearer the mark. Nothing was spared to impress the spectator with the wrath to come and its promise of certain damnation for the vast majority of mankind.

Despite the apparent disorder, the scene is elaborately conceived and carefully organised. Christ in Majesty, his mandorla supported by four angels, presides at the Latter Day: the figure is rigid and remote, its draperies reduced to a motionless pattern. In the upper register, separated from the rest of the drama, are the three mortals who were assumed bodily into heaven at the moment of their deaths—the Virgin Mary, and the prophets Enoch and Elijah. Across the whole breadth of the lintel, the dead emerge from their tombs and are separated by the angel beneath Christ's feet; to His right the elect—including two pilgrims wearing the badges of their pilgrimages on their satchels, the cross of Jerusalem and the cockleshell of Santiago—and to His left the reprobate, who stand in attitudes of despair as they contemplate the prospect of eternal hell-fire. The miser and the drunkard carry the instruments of their perdition, a bag of gold and a wine-barrel; the harlot's breasts are devoured by serpents; and most terrifying of all, an enormous pair of talons seizes a victim by the head.

On Christ's right in the central register, the apostles intercede for man as Peter admits the saints to Paradise. 'Strait is the gate, and narrow is the way, which leadeth unto life' is a phrase that Gislebertus takes literally: and angel passes a soul up through a tiny opening, no bigger than the Needle's Eye. But the peace of God passes all understanding and, consequently, all representation. As always, and not just in medieval art, Hell and its denizens are the most exciting element in the composition. Here the artist could give his imagination free rein. A grimacing Lucifer, abetted by a demon crouched in one of the scale-pans, tries to cheat St Michael of a soul; while on the far right, another fiend thrusts a pair of horrified sinners into the mouth of the furnace. A menacing inscription is interrupted beneath Christ's feet to announce, with a justifiable absence of modesty, *'Gisdlebertus hoc fecit'*—Gislebertus made this.

Incredibly (it seems to us), the dean and chapter had the whole tympanum blocked in with plaster in 1766. The head of Christ projected too far and was struck off with a mallet. The canons claimed that Gislebertus' sculptures were crude and primitive—their own tastes can be judged from the fact that at about the same time, they covered the interior of the chancel with marble, which was much admired. Medieval man lived with such intensity that he only responded to the most powerful stimulants; rewards had to be extravagant, remedies and punishments drastic. No doubt so much passion embarrassed the urbane Catholicism of the Enlightenment. This outrageous lack or excess of sensibility did have one virtue: it protected the tympanum from mutilation during the Revolution. The plaster was removed in 1837, but it was not until 1948 that the head of Christ was identified from amongst other debris by Canon Denis Grivot (the present-day historian of Autun) and restored to its rightful place.

The pillar-capitals in the nave show Gislebertus to be fond of a good story. He seizes on the apocryphal incident of Simon Magus flying up to heaven to impress St Peter. The capital opposite catches Simon as he plummets earthward, his features contorted with fear, just a split second before impact. The artist may not have any of our illusions about the dignity of man, but he has an eye for light-hearted detail: in a scene of the Nativity, he depicts the old clown Joseph asleep at the turning-point of history.

Some of the finest (and most famous) capitals were originally in the chancel and transept, but are today more conveniently displayed in the Chapter House, directly above the Sacristy. Here the angel wakes the Three Kings, who share a bed for all the world like the three Italian aviators in 'A Night at the Opera'. The Magi adore the Infant, while a very bored Joseph waits round the corner for the end of the tedious ceremony. Best-known of all, the Holy Family flee into Egypt. The anatomy may be more accurate in the Saulieu artist's treatment of the same subject, but he could never have matched the near-humanity of the donkey's expression, or the infinite tenderness of the Virgin's face.

Among the cathedral's furniture is a work of a later and unexpected period, French neo-classicism of the nineteenth century. In the third chapel on the left of the nave is 'The Martyrdom of St Symphorian' painted for Autun by Ingres. The legend ran that the young Christian Symphorian, who lived during the reign of Marcus Aurelius, objected noisily to a procession in honour of the Great Goddess Berecynthia, and was arrested and put to death. His mother shouted encouragement to him from the top of the Porte Saint-André as he was led out to the place of execution. The mood of Ingres' painting is melodramatic, but the cool palette and frigidly immaculate technique compel admiration (as does the cool effrontery with which Ingres added a large dog in the bottom left-hand corner to conceal a blob of spilt paint).

In the chancel, by the door that leads to the Chapter House, stand the tomb effigies of Pierre Jeannin and his wife. A native of Autun, Jeannin rose in the legal profession to become President of the Dijon Parlement. It was in this capacity that in 1572 he prevailed on the governor not to issue the order which would have brought the St Bartholomew's Day massacre to Burgundy. 'When kings are angry,' he said, 'they must be obeyed slowly.' Although a Catholic Leaguer, he later accepted employment as adviser and ambassador to Henri IV; he died in 1623.

Since Stephen of Bâgé, Autun has had three famous bishops. The fifteenth century is dominated by the figure of Cardinal-Bishop Jean Rolin, son of Chancellor Nicolas Rolin and the very model of the worldly prelate. He rebuilt the chancel and crossing tower, donated a rich organ-loft and rood-screen, and encouraged the canons to vie with one another in the construction and embellishment of side-chapels. After the arts his second passion was litigation; he went to court at one time or another with practically everyone who crossed his path—not only the collegiate chapter of Notre-Dame d'Autun, but even his own father and brother. These exertions left no time for religious duties, which devolved upon his suffragan.

His examples, both good and bad, were followed enthusiastically in later years by the cathedral chapter. In 1543 the canons erected the delightful fountain on the square outside Saint-Lazare, but were not above ducking passers-by in it, or each other. Ecclesiastical discipline went by the board as it did in many other places (to the righteous indignation of the Protestants), and by the time Gabriel de Roquette became bishop in 1667 the canons were commonly to be seen dressed in the latest fashions, drinking openly in cabarets, frequenting brothels and fighting duels. The rural clergy were hardly better, painfully ignorant and often drunk or living in concubinage. Roquette did his best with this unpromising material, and even built a Seminary (today the Military Academy) to designs by Gittard, the King's Architect. But his reputation for unscrupulous ambition and his assiduous cultivation of society ladies caused him to be dismissed as a hypocrite. It was on him, according to Saint-Simon, that Molière based his sanctimonious humbug Tartuffe. Nevertheless, he enjoyed the friendship of Bussy-Rabutin and Madame de Sévigné, and was a skilful manager of the States of Burgundy of which, as bishop of Autun, he was ex officio president. Even though the dean and chapter refused to attend his funeral in 1702, his reforms seem to have improved clerical behaviour in the diocese.

The most celebrated bishop of all, however, had an effective period of office of only 30 days. Charles-Maurice de Talleyrand-Périgord, the great survivor, foreign minister of both Napoleon and Louis XVIII, was consecrated bishop of Autun in January 1789. His mother protested, knowing the dissolute life her son led in Paris, but the king simply replied, 'This will cure him.' Talleyrand did not arrive at Autun until 12 March. The investiture was held three days later, and he celebrated mass (not without a few mistakes) in Saint-Lazare. But the preoccupation of the day was the impending election of deputies for the States General, to be convened in May for the first time in 175 years. By dint of his charm, backed by lavish entertaining, Talleyrand was elected for the clergy. He returned to Paris on 12 April, and thereafter his career belongs to French history. To the increasing fury of his dean and chapter, he proposed the nationalisation of Church property, celebrated mass at the Festival of National Federation on 14 July 1790, and voted in favour of the Civil Constitution of the Clergy. Accused by his vicars-general of apostasy for having taken the oath of loyalty to the new constitution, he resigned his see in January 1791.

After a period of exile during the Terror, he returned to serve under the Directory, but was instrumental in bringing Napoleon to power in the Brumaire coup d'état. When the tide turned against the Empire, he negotiated with the Tsar on his own behalf, organised the Bourbon Restoration of 1814, and deposed the Emperor. His greatest service to France was his skilful handling of the Congress of Vienna, at which he lightened the burden of defeat by playing off the Allies against each other. His reaction to the

Hundred Days was a declaration in which the man he had helped to make was, in his own words, 'expelled from the human race'. As he was retired in September 1815, he had no opportunity to betray Louis XVIII, but made up for it by playing a prominent rôle in the overthrow of Charles X and the creation of the July Monarchy in 1830. At the last, Talleyrand did not forget Autun. When he died in 1838, he insisted on receiving the last rites as a bishop.

Almost opposite the cathedral is the Musée Rolin, housed partly in the nineteenth-century Hôtel Lacomme and partly in the surviving wing of the Hôtel Rolin, where Chancellor Nicolas was born in 1376, which he rebuilt, and where he came home to die in 1462. The large Gallo-Roman collections are overshadowed by the selection of medieval treasures across the courtyard in the Rolin mansion. On the ground floor have been assembled the fragments of the tomb of St Lazarus, notably three very fine statues of Martha, Mary and St Andrew. The tomb, sculpted by a monk known only as Brother Martin (now believed to be a contemporary of Gislebertus), stood in the centre of the chancel and was broken up in 1766 as part of the 'improvements'. At the same time, the canons did away with the sculptures of the north door. All that escaped the wreck was part of the lintel, a Temptation of Eve in which Gislebertus surpassed himself and revealed a deep-seated sensuality. His Eve is a sinuous coquette, floating amongst the foliage that hides her sex, and almost absent-mindedly plucking the fatal apple. It is one of the first sculptures since classical times to show a feeling for the beauty of the naked female form.

The first floor is devoted to painting and sculpture of the fifteenth century. The polychrome statue of the Virgin, a gift of the archaeologist Bulliot, is very different from the monumental, queenly figures of Sluter or de la Huerta. This Mary is hardly more than a girl, fetchingly girdled just beneath her breasts, and the baby she cradles in her arms is swaddled like a papoose—the appeal to sentiment is controlled, but unmistakable. The artist is unknown, though the style resembles that of known works by Claus de Werve.

The most important exhibit, however, is a small panel painting of the Nativity, commissioned from the anonymous Master of Moulins by Cardinal Rolin. Painted about 1480 in bright, strong colours, it shows the cardinal, accompanied by a small white pug, adoring the Holy Family—an activity he would have done well to indulge in more frequently. Though probably French, the artist was profoundly influenced by the art of the Netherlands, of van Eyck and Petrus Christus. The pug has a notoriety of its own. Whether it was cause or effect, the quarrelsome cardinal was acutely dyspeptic and often could not hold down his food. On these occasions, the pug happily licked up his master's vomit.

Just outside Autun, on the road to Mont Beuvray, is the little manor-house of Monthelon where St Jeanne-Françoise de Chantal spent nine years of her widowhood. Its only aristocratic feature is the carved escutcheon of the Rabutin-Chantals (her husband's family) over the door. The loggia, the small tiled belfry, and the stumpy round towers give it a warm and friendly appearance, though in fact it witnessed the least happy period of the saint's life. Following the death of her husband in a hunting accident, her father-in-law threatened to disinherit his grandchildren if they and their mother did not join him at Monthelon. Jeanne-Françoise had to fend off the lecherous old man's advances as well as put up with his dictatorial housekeeper, but she consoled herself with good works and with the education of her children. She returned to Dijon in 1604 to visit her family (her father was Bénigne Frémyot, president of the Parlement), and was introduced by her brother André, archbishop of Bourges, to St François de Sales, who was preaching a Lenten course in Dijon.

De Sales became Jeanne's director of conscience, and her love for him was sublimated in a religious vocation. In 1607, de Sales disclosed his plan for a new order designed for single women and widows who, because of age or other reasons, were unfitted for the more severe rule of existing orders. Three years later, after an angry scene with her only son Celse-Bénigne (the father of Madame de Sévigné), Jeanne left Monthelon for ever to found the first convent of the Visitation at Annecy. The village church of Monthelon has preserved the pulpit from which St François de Sales once preached to such effect that a young atheist debauchee was converted, and became a Capuchin friar.

On Mont Beuvray, one of the highest summits of the Morvan, the Aedui had their capital, Bibracte. That much was proved by the excavations conducted by Bulliot from 1867 onwards, demolishing the claims of Autun and (an even wilder conjecture) Beaune. It was at Bibracte, in 52 B.C., that Vercingetorix summoned an assembly of the Gallic tribes and was appointed commander-in-chief of their armies before the disastrous Alesia campaign. There is practically nothing to see on Beuvray today—only a slight unevenness in the ground betrays the line of the ramparts—partly because the owners of the land requested that any remains should be covered over again, and partly because there was not very much to find. Significantly, Caesar always refers to a Gallic township like Bibracte as *oppidum*, and not *urbs*. The Gauls were a rural people, living in scattered villages, who withdrew to hill-forts in times of danger. Strategic industries like metal-working were concentrated in these hill-forts (Bulliot unearthed a large forge at

Bibracte, complete with the remains of blacksmiths' tools), and markets were held in them. This put the Gauls on the bottom rung of urban civilisation, but when the Romans came they found these *oppida* still sited for defence rather than commerce. This explains Bibracte's inaccessibility, and its rapid decline in favour of Augustodunum when the country was pacified. There was also a druidic 'university' at Bibracte whose influence was exploited by the Romans. Hardly anything survives on Beuvray now to give substance to the legend of a great city whose gates could be heard groaning on their hinges 40 miles away on the banks of the Loire.

In the opposite direction from Autun, a short way off the main road to Beaune and easily missed, is something a little more imposing than the manor of Monthelon; something so magnificent that St Jeanne de Chantal's grand-daughter described it as 'the Fontainebleau of Burgundy'. The château of Sully does not enjoy the same fame as Ancy-le-Franc and Tanlay, and yet its mixture of discipline and fantasy makes it more completely satisfying than either.

There is no connection with Henri IV's great minister of the same name. The present house—probably designed by Ribonnier—was begun by Gaspard de Saulx-Tavannes, marshal of France and one of the pillars of the Catholic party, who died in 1573. One report of the massacre of St Bartholomew, no doubt apocryphal, puts into his mouth the curious phrase, 'Bleed! Bleed! The doctors say a bleeding is as good in all of August as in May!' In fact, he seems to have advocated the assassination only of the Protestant leaders.

The layout of the château is medieval, as are the moat and the four massive square angle-towers. The courtyard and the façade on the box drive date from the sixteenth century, and have a decoration reminiscent of the style of Hugues Sambin. The triangular pediment, however, is a classical addition due to Pierre de Morey, marquis de Vianges, who bought Sully in 1716. He set about transforming the east and north façades, which his predecessors seem to have left untouched. His tour-de-force is the great staircase which leads down from the centre of the north wing to a vast semi-circular terrace, flanked by landing-stages and overlooking the moat, which broadens here into an ornamental lake. The south front is a parvenu, an imitation of the Renaissance elements of the entrance façade, and replaces a mock Gothic structure which was erected in the early nineteenth century. Here the 'restorers' have indulged a taste for the picturesque, not without success, in the irregular outlines of the turrets and the projecting chapel.

By her second marriage, the widow of Vianges' eldest son brought the château into the MacMahon family (Marshal MacMahon, who succeeded Thiers as President of the Republic in 1873, was born at Sully), who have not relinquished it since. The property escaped confiscation and destruction during the Revolution by means of a macabre ruse: instead of registering the death of the châtelaine, her heirs continued to display her in bed as though she were merely ill, and preserved the corpse by pickling it in alcohol every night.

9 Le Creusot and the Charollais

The best way south from Autun is to take what the French would call 'the schoolboys' route' (the long way round) to Le Creusot. The road climbs past the grounds of the château of Montjeu, built in the early seventeenth century by Pierre Jeannin, the tanner's son who spared Burgundy the horrors of St Bartholomew's Day. He later rose to become Intendant of Finance during the minority of Louis XIII. When asked why he had chosen to build his house on top of a mountain, he replied, 'I shall always be far enough from my enemies, and my friends are perfectly capable of finding me.' His grandson, Nicolas Jeannin de Castille, was disgraced with Fouquet and spent five years in the Bastille. He was forced to restore eight million *livres* of misappropriated funds, was fined a further two million, and still managed to amass another fortune after his release. The large ponds in the park are never affected by drought, and this guaranteeed water supply no doubt determined the site of Augustodunum.

The boulder-strewn slopes around the village of Uchon offer a series of vantage-points, followed by a scenic but tortuous descent to the valley on the other side. Like a smudge on the face of the countryside, an incongruous avenue of mines and steelworks stretches north-east and south-west to form Burgundy's only concentration of heavy industry. The history of the coalfield begins in the early sixteenth century with the random quarrying of outcrops of coal around Le Creusot. The full extent of the deposits was not realised for long afterwards, and it was not until 1769 that the local combination of coal and iron-ore (which had been extracted at Couches since the Middle Ages) was exploited. By the time the Revolution broke out, there was already a thriving foundry and glassworks at Le Creusot. The two large conical structures in front of the Château de la Verrerie were kilns for firing crystal.

Another boost to industry was the opening of the Canal du Centre in 1794. The Dheune and the Bourbince both rise near Le Creusot, but flow in opposite directions along the depression; the first north-east towards the Saône, the second south-west towards the Loire. By providing the only practicable link between the latter two rivers, this freak of geography put Burgundy's black country on the main waterway between Paris and Lyon.

But Le Creusot is effectively the creation of a single entrepreneur-ial dynasty whose paternal shadow still falls over every aspect of the town's life, in the best tradition of nineteenth-century ironmasters. The Schneiders were to Le Creusot what the Krupps were to Essen. They not only built the factories, but also the schools, the hospitals, and even the churches: two of them (Saint-Henri and Saint-Eugène) are dedicated to the patron saints of Schneider patriarchs, and a third (Saint-Charles) actually belongs to the family, who have their private vault under the chancel. Most of the statues in Le Creusot are of one Schneider or another.

Since 1836, when the brothers Eugène and Adolphe took over the original foundry, the population has increased tenfold. The first fortunes were made in the railway boom, building locomotives and marine engines. In 1841 a Schneider engineer named Bourdon invented the steam-hammer, enabling the firm to forge larger individual pieces than ever before; and the introduction of steel-working in 1867 turned Schneider into France's biggest armaments manufacturer. Eugène Schneider II was president of the Comité des Forges which co-ordinated the nation's war production between 1914 and 1918; one of his grand-daughters is Mme Giscard d'Estaing.

The Schneider factories employ 10,000 workers in three separate complexes, but Le Creusot itself has ceased to be a mining town. Since 1856, its furnaces have been fed increasingly by the more extensive measures of Blanzy, which still supply four per cent of France's coal. The village of Blanzy has been vastly outgrown by its offshoot Montceau-les-Mines, whose superiority to Le Creusot any Montcellian will be glad to explain. Like the mining areas of the north, Montceau-les-Mines has a fair-sized Polish population, descended from refugees who arrived between 1921 and 1923 after the Soviet-Polish War.

The satanic mills should not discourage anyone from visiting the vicinity. Three *pays,* the Chalonnais, the Charollais and the Mâconnais, meet at Mont Saint-Vincent, where the church has a nave vaulted by the same rare system as at Tournus. Perrecy-les-Forges was formerly a priory of Saint-Benoit-sur-Loire, and the twelfth-century tower-porch shows the influence of the mother-house. The carved portal, however, featuring scenes from the Passion and a Christ in Majesty supported by six-winged seraphim, belongs to the Brionnais school, of which it is one of the most accomplished examples. One of the capitals of the porch, dated about 1125, shows four cockleshells—the earliest known representa-tion in France of the insignia of the Santiago pilgrimmage. Back in the valley of the Bourbince, the château of Digoine has a pavilion converted into a miniature theatre, where Sarah Bernhardt performed.

The Charollais today is usually taken to mean the whole of the south-west corner of Saône-et-Loire, wedged against the river Loire by the Morvan to the north and the Mâconnais and Beaujolais to the east. Under the Ancien Régime this area formed two separate baileywicks—the Charollais proper in the north, and in the south the Brionnais, the rump of an extensive feudal barony that had once straddled the Beaujolais mountains and controlled the west bank of the Loire. Both territories were brought into ducal Burgundy by Philip the Bold, who used the dowry of his daughter-in-law Margaret of Bavaria to buy them from the count of Armagnac in 1390. From the time of John the Fearless, the county of Charollais was the apanage of the heirs-apparent to the duchy of Burgundy. Both Philip the Good and Charles the Rash held the title before their accessions. Seized along with the rest of the province by Louis XI in 1477, the Charollais was among the lands surrendered by Charles VIII at the treaty of Senlis in 1493. Philip the Handsome, son of the Emperor Maximilian and grandson of Charles the Rash, took the title of count. This anomaly of a Habsburg enclave in the territory of that family's bitterest rivals persisted, incredibly, until Louis XIV adopted a 'policy of reunion, in 1684. Even then, it was made over to the house of Condé, and did not revert to the crown until 1761.

The little town of Charolles lies at the heart of its county on the banks of the Arconce, overshadowed by the ruins of its castle. The last count, Charles de Bourbon-Condé, relieved the boredom of provincial life by shooting at the tilers who worked on the roofs of houses within range of the castle—a disconcerting pastime that caused death and serious injury on more than one occasion. Each time, the count confidently awaited royal letters of pardon. Finally, even the easy-going Louis XV lost patience and informed him, 'Monsieur, I have also just signed a pardon for whoever kills you in reprisal.'

To the east is the *mauvais pays* of granite hills, heaths and woodlands, beyond which stretch the vineyards of the Mâconnais. Not far from the range's culminating point at the Butte de Suin, the château of Chaumont was begun by Pierre de La Guiche, who negotiated the marriage of the future Henri II and Catherine de Medici. His grandson Philibert rose to be governor of the Lyonnais and Grand Master of the Ordnance, and finished the château in 1584. But the passage of the nineteenth century, with its notions of 'improvement', has left the horses more magnificently housed than their owners. The stables—the largest and finest in France after Versailles and Chantilly—are the work of Philibert's daughter Henriette, duchess of Angoulême, who built them between 1648 and 1652. Her husband Louis (grandson of Charles IX and his mistress Marie Touchet) held the rank of Commander-in-Chief of the Light Cavalry of France, a fact which probably inspired this equine palace with accommodation for 99 animals. As only the king could own more than that number, the 100th horse at Chaumont is in stone, the duchess's father in the saddle, over the main entrance. La Guiche is surrounded by the field-pieces, cannonballs and ramrods appropriate to the Grand Master of the Ordnance. The most grandiose feature is the pair of double staircases outside, giving access to the guards' quarters.

Westwards, the pastures of the *bon pays* undulate down to the Loire. It was on the fertile loam of the vales of the Brionnais that Burgundian farmers first devoted themselves exclusively and systematically to fattening cattle for market. In the second half of the eighteenth century, the practice spread to all the other parts of the Charollais where the land was suitable, and rents increased so much that graziers were forced to look even further afield, notably to the Nivernais, but later to the Morvan and the Auxois. Wherever they went, they took the white Charollais cattle that are such a distinctive feature of the Burgundy countryside, and whose name is synonymous in French with the best beef in the world. Charollais bulls have been exported to improve stock in nearly all beef-producing countries, including Great Britain and Argentina. The herds are put out to grass in April, and from then until December are sold off in their thousands at the markets and fairs of Charolles, Saint-Christophe and Paray-le-Monial.

The Jurassic limestone which breaks down into this ideal topsoil is easy to extract and easy to carve. Perhaps the presence of this resplendent honey-coloured stone is enough to explain the extraordinary concentration of Romanesque churches in the Brionnais. More prosaic but probably just as important were the prestige of the *seigneurs* of Semur, the pilgrimage to Anzy-le-Duc, contacts with the Loire valley, Cluniac influence through the priories of Charlieu and Marcigny, and a supply of skilled labour from the second abbey church at Cluny, begun in 955.

Azy-le-Duc priory was founded around 876, just a few years after the abbey of Charlieu. Raoul Glaber records that its first benefactor, one Lethbald, made the pilgrimage to Jerusalem and prayed God on arrival that his soul might proceed thence to

Paradise without delay and that same evening, though he had previously been in good health, he died. Hugh of Poitiers, one of the earliest priors and a former companion of Berno, the first abbot of Cluny, died about 930 and miracles immediately began to be reported at his tomb. St Odilo, who became abbot of Cluny in 994, took a keen interest in the pilgrimage to the shrine of the Blessed Hugh, to the extent of borrowing the relics for display at one of the councils of Anse. It is therefore hardly a coincidence that there are striking similarities between the new church at Anzy-le-Duc and Odilo's rebuilding of Charlieu after 1030.

The monastery buildings have resisted the assaults of time and war remarkably well—the farmyard on the south side of the church is dominated by a great square tower and is enclosed by the outhouses that originally threw a defensive screen around the priory. The most outstanding survival is the nobly-proportioned octagon tower that rises from the crossing of the transept. In the eighteenth century, the beauty of its design and material earned it more than local celebrity and saved it from the pickaxes of revolutionary fanatics. Inside, the nave is covered by a series of groin-vaults separated by round transverse arches. Abbot Renaud, great-nephew of St Hugh of Cluny and himself a son of the *seigneur* of Semur-en-Brionnais, must have been familiar in his childhood with Anzy-le-Duc. He proved it at Vézelay by reproducing not only the vaulting plan, but also the two-storey interior elevation and applied columns (not pilasters as at Cluny) of the Brionnais priory church. This makes Anzy-le-Duc the ancestor of the Cistercian Gothic style (as seen in Burgundy at Pontigny), which is an adaptation of Vézelay for the pointed arch and the rib-vault.

As well as a rich painted decoration (now badly faded), there was plenty of sculpture. The Ascension appears twice, or indeed three times if one includes the tiny parish church at nearby Montceaux-l'Etoile; the portal there is obviously from the hand of one of the Anzy-le-Duc carvers. The most mature of the three sculptures came from the main gate of the priory grounds, and was rescued at the Revolution by being transported to the château of Arcy, hence its usual name, the 'Arcy Tympanum'. It is now is the Musée du Hiéron at Paray-le-Monial. Beneath the Ascension, of impeccable geometry despite the strained pose of the angels, is a touchingly natural scene of Mary suckling the Christ-child. The two church doors, still in situ, show the Ascension complete with spectators. The Montceaux-l'Etoile tympanum is by far the more animated and dramatic: Christ stands upright in His mandorla, holding the Cross and supported by two angels in full flight; the apostles gesticulate and turn to look at one another in amazement. The unusual unity of the scene derives from the fact that the tympanum and lintel are carved from a single block. The south postern at Anzy-le-Duc (across the farmyard and through the little gate) shows what happened in the latter half of the twelfth century, when the style had grown 'decadent'. The composition (showing the Adoration of the Magi and the Original Sin on the tympanum, and Heaven and Hell on the lintel) is confused and overloaded, though the treatment has a naïve charm.

The influence of St Hugh's third abbey church at Cluny can be seen in the pointed tunnel vaults of Bois-Sainte-Marie and Varenne-l'Arconce (both built not of limestone, but of the granite which outcrops in the eastern Brionnais). The most thorough statement of the Cluniac style in the Brionnais is at St Hugh's home town of Semur, which looks down on the Loire from its hill. The handsome village church has the typical blind triforium and clerestory, and a gallery with a corbelled balcony exactly like the St Michael Gallery at the west end of Cluny. The octagon tower, with its deep embrasures, has an air of weight and solidity that contrasts with the delicacy of Anzy-le-Duc. The west door is another example of the local carving in decline. The whole field of the tympanum is crammed with figures—Christ, angels, and the symbols of the evangelists—which seem hardly more than facile caricatures. This treatment suits the whimsical anecdote of which the later Romanesque sculptors were so fond. In this case, the story is about St Hilary of Poitiers, the great polemicist against Arianism. The saint sits on the ground, because the Arian bishops refuse to give him a seat at the council of Seleucia in 359; but an angel prepares to restore him to his rightful position by levitation.

Ironically, Cluny and its Brionnais priories, which had such profound effects on building styles in the region, are mere shadows of their former selves today. Marcigny was the site of the very first Cluniac house for women, founded by St Hugh on his family's own estates. All that remains of it is the stout, round 'Windmill Tower', which belonged to the small monastery inhabited by the monks who served the nuns' (religious) needs. The rule was one of strict seclusion. On one occasion when fire broke out in the convent, the nuns refused to break their vow and abandon the buildings, and would surely have been burnt alive if a visiting bishop had not commanded the fire to put itself out.

Just across the boundary, in the department of Loire but still in the Brionnais, the imposing narthex of the priory church at Charlieu opens on to a void. Only the westmost bays of St Odilo's early Romanesque building survive. The cloister, chapter house and prior's chapel are all late Gothic, though the six round arches in the east range of the cloister seem to have formed part of the ambulatory of a church dating back to the 10th century. The main entrance to the narthex was from the north side, where the stream of travellers between the Saône and Loire valleys could be suitably impressed by the priory's finest sculpture. The main scene in the small portal is the Wedding at Cana, and the turning of water into wine. Round the arch is depicted the Transfiguration, a feast which was introduced into the Cluniac liturgy by Peter the Venerable in 1132. The great portal is an astonishing illustration of 'Florid Romanesque' in which the sculptor exhausts a treasury of ornamental devices: tendrils, rosettes, foliated scrolls, chessboard and Greek key patterns, all help to set off an Ascension contorted by violent movement. On the inside of the left door-jamb, Lust is consumed by a snake and a huge toad. Both the architecture and carving of the narthex are clear examples of the Baroque spirit in Romanesque art, and one only has to look at the west door of the church itself (in position before 1094), lucid, understated, to gauge the distance covered in less than 50 years.

Charlieu has two surviving monastic cloisters; the other, the late Gothic Cloître des Cordeliers or Greyfriars' Cloister, is just outside the town to the west. It nearly fell victim to the American passion for dismantling buildings brick by brick and reassembling them on the other side of the Atlantic. In 1910, the antique-dealer who owned it had already accepted an offer and begun demolition, before the authorities bought back the property and rebuilt it.

North of Charlieu and half-way to Semur is the last flower of the Brionnais summer. Incorporated in the façade of the rebuilt church of Saint-Julien-de-Jonzy are an Ascension and Last Supper which are visibly by the same hand that produced the narthex portals at Charlieu. Even the exuberant foliage around the arch is a magnified version of the same motif on the great portal at Charlieu, while the folds of the table-cloth are an exact reproduction of those figured in the smaller doorway's Wedding at Cana. The church stands in a superb natural setting against a backdrop of the Beaujolais mountains.

Close against these same hills, a turnpike barred the road from the Mâconnais at La Clayette (pronounced 'La Clette'). In 1380 the toll-house was replaced by a fortress, the remains of which were turned into a meretricious fairy castle in the last century. Only the outbuildings and gatehouse are authentic. In the fifteenth century, the fief passed into the hands of the Chantemerles, important figures of the Burgundian court. The similarity between the name of the former *seigneurs* of La Clayette and that of a certain fictional village in the Beaujolais is no accident. Gabriel Chevallier, author of *Clochemerle* and its sequels, lived at La Clayette and, we can assume, drew his inspiration from its characters. The idea of setting his stories on the other side of the hills was doubtless to bathe them in the rosy glow of his readers' preconceived ideas of a Rabelaisian, wine-bibbing Beaujolais. The wisdom of his decision is proved by the fact that *Clochemerle* has never been out of print in 50 years, and is as much an institution in France as *Three Men in a Boat* in England.

La Clayette may not be a town of wine-growers, but it has developed a special version of the local art of raising animals. *Pace* the claims of Chalus in the Limousin, the white charger mounted by Henri IV the day of his victory over the Leaguers at Ivry in 1590 came from La Clayette, and horse-breeding (with an eye to the race-course rather than the battlefield) is still a major activity. The town is the smallest in France to have its own Tote office, whose takings were once, and may still be, the highest in the country per head of population served.

The nearby château of Drée is a monument to the fortune-hunter's art. It was begun about 1620 by Charles de Blanchefort de Créquy, and built of the warm-coloured Brionnais stone Créquy had married Madeleine, daughter and heiress of the Constable de Lesdiguières, and looked forward to inheriting vast wealth and a ducal title; but his wife thoughtlessly predeceased her father. Nothing daunted, Créquy buried Madeleine and married Françoise, Lesdiguières' legitimised child by the daughter of a Grenoble furrier. To make assurance doubly sure, he married his son by his first marriage to his new wife's younger sister.

Almost equidistant from Anzy-le-Duc and Charolles, Paray-le-Monial has supplanted the latter as the economic centre of the Charollais, and the former as the principal place of pilgrimage. The church of Notre-Dame, now re-dedicated as the Basilica of the Sacred Heart, is not strictly a Brionnais church, but is close enough to make a fitting climax to any tour of this corner of Burgundy. The land at Paray was given to the abbey of Cluny about 972 by Count Lambert of Chalon; by coincidence, Lambert's son Hugh, bishop of Auxerre, became great-uncle and tutor to the young Hugh of Semur, the future abbot of Cluny. Perhaps it was in honour of this family and sentimental connection that St Hugh decided to build so generously for a priory which can never have had more than 25 monks. The church, pleasantly sited on the banks of the Bourbince, dates from around 1110 and has rightly been termed a 'pocket edition' of the vanished great abbey church of Cluny. The only major difference lies in the narthex and its twin towers, which are manifestly out of proportion—in fact they belonged to the smaller eleventh-century building. The left-hand tower (slightly later than the other) was imitated by Viollet-le-Duc at Autun. Otherwise, the chevet and octagon tower are a miniature reproduction of the east end of Cluny III, and the resemblance is even clearer inside: all the vaulting arches are pointed, and pilasters, engaged columns and paired colonnettes are used in the same positions as at the mother-house. This decorative similarity reveals a technical one: the upper surfaces overhang the lower ones very slightly, bringing the walls inwards to take the thrust of the vault and preventing the splaying that often occurs between floor and roof. This ingenious system of wall-corbelling is especially noticeable in the choir. There it is reinforced by the downward tapering of the columns, the slenderest being in the bottom storey.

The symbolism of the Trinity is especially marked at Paray-le-Monial, as was pointed out by Joris-Karl Huysmans; three aisles, three bays to the nave, three apsidioles, three towers, a three-storey interior elevation, three arches in each bay of the triforium, and three windows in each bay of the clerestory. This last feature, imitated from Cluny and in contrast to the single windows of Autun, gives the nave and transepts brilliant lighting, which focuses the observer's attention on the relative obscurity of the oven-vaulted sanctuary. The painted ceiling of the oven vault, depicting Christ in Majesty and dating from the fourteenth century, was discovered in 1935 under a layer of whitewash.

Paray-le-Monial is the fountainhead of the Roman Catholic devotion of the Sacred Heart. Marguerite-Marie Alacoque was a lawyer's daughter who was professed a nun at the convent of the Visitation at Paray in 1671. She was an extreme case of what William James described as the 'theopathic' condition. From the age of four the notion of sex was so abhorrent to her that the very sight of a male person offended her modesty, and she would have run off into the wild if she had not been afraid of meeting men there too. Later she suffered from a series of illnesses—rheumatism, paralysis, pains in her side, ulcerated legs—which were to afflict her all her life, and which by their nature and their inexplicable comings and goings must have been psychosomatic. It was only to be expected that such a hypersensitive subject should progress to visions. Between 1673 and 1675, Christ appeared to her four times and charged her to promote Christian devotion to 'this heart which so loved Man'. Many of the other nuns were sarcastic about what they regarded as delusions, but with the help of the convent chaplain Claude de la Colombière, opposition had been overcome by the time of her death in 1690, at the age of 43.

The devotion of the Sacred Heart did not really gather momentum until after the Revolution. The process of Sister Marguerite-Marie's canonisation began in 1817, but was not completed until 1920. However, the feast of the Sacred Heart was made general in 1856, and 30,000 French Catholics made the first pilgrimage to Paray-le-Monial in 1873. It was on this occasion, following such evidence of divine displeasure as defeat in the Franco-Prussian War and the horrors of the Paris Commune, that the decision was taken to consecrate France to the Sacred Heart, and to raise a basilica (the Sacré-Coeur on Montmartre) as the concrete expression of this national vow.

The divine apparitions did not occur in the basilica at Paray-le-Monial, but in the chapel of the convent of the Visitation (situated in the street of the same name), where the saint's body is preserved in a silver-gilt reliquary. Other relics are displayed in the house opposite the chevet of the basilica.

Whatever the state of current ideas on the adoration of the Sacred Heart of Jesus, the cult's foundress clearly did not mean to speak metaphorically. As Father Gallifet explains, 'It concerns the heart of Jesus in its proper and natural signification . . . Christ speaks of his heart in the literal sense.' And a booklet published in 1782 confirms, 'This heart must be taken in its literal meaning. It is the material heart.' Sceptics may find this visceral devotion repellent, and may even be unmoved by the strange, sad personality of St Marguerite-Marie; their consolation is St Hugh's basilica.

10 The Chalonnais and the Mâconnais

After the Dheune gap at Chagny, which marks both the administrative and viticultural frontier of the Côte d'Or, the long, straight line of hills that has stretched from Dijon to Santenay breaks up. Wine-growing, however, is still a major activity wherever the slopes offer the favourable south-easterly exposure. This is the area known as the Côte Chalonnaise (though Chalon is way out on the plain, and has no vines), or sometimes as the 'Mercurey Region', after its largest appellation and the main centre of its trade. The soil is similar to that of the Côte d'Or, the same varieties of grapes are grown (pinot noir, chardonnay, gamay and aligoté), and the same methods of vinification are used. The wines, especially the red, possess the same qualities as those of the Côte de Beaune but not quite to the same degree. They are lighter, drinkable sooner, consequently less long-lived, but often better value.

Owing to its inclusion in the department of Saône-et-Loire in 1791, the area has not been able to share the instant recognition enjoyed by the name 'Côte d'Or'. The vineyards had great difficulty in recovering from the phylloxera, and the slaughter of young men in the First World War, followed by the Depression, nearly wiped the vine from the map. The situation was not improved by the law on appellations of origin. As was the case with many villages of the Côte de Nuits and the Côte de Beaune, low output prevented the village names becoming widely known. Only Mercurey could boast a volume of production approaching that of Beaune or Pommard, but a judicial decision of 1923 forbade Rully and Givry to benefit from their neighbour's fame by selling their wine as Mercurey. Nevertheless, their fortunes have since improved and the appearance of any of the village names (Mercurey, Givry, Rully and Montagny) on a wine-list is a sign of imaginative buying.

Northernmost of the four is Rully, where the production is mostly of a full-bodied white which is particularly suitable for conversion to sparkling wine. In 1822 a Chalon merchant, quick to take advantage of the rapidly-growing world demand for champagne and anything like it, recruited cellarmen from Champagne and set to work with the wines of Rully. The village concentrated so hard on the production of sparkling wine (and not necessarily burgundy) that the name 'Rully' became synonymous with 'champagne-type'. the still wine, which is the only one entitled to the appellation *Rully,* was edged into obscurity. Though less profitable, the naturally-fermented wine is better. It has the merit of being 100% chardonnay (or more rarely pinot), whereas sparkling burgundy can be up to 70% aligoté. The château of Rully (itself still a wine-producer) contains the great glass goblet specially made for Charles de Saint-Ligier, a sixteenth-century lord of the manor. Its capacity is over five pints, and its owner was reputedly able to drain it at one draught.

At Mercurey and Givry the colours are reversed, with red predominating. These were the 'wines of Chalon' praised by the monk Gregory of Tours in the 6th century. Today, Mercurey is the more highly-regarded (and abundant), but Givry has the more impressive pedigree. In the Middle Ages (before long vatting became the rule and changed the character of so many wines), the wines of Givry were mentioned in the same breath as those of Beaune. By a decree of 1349, Philip VI levied the same internal customs duty on Beaune and Givry entering Paris. In honour of the visit of Charles VI in 1390, Margaret of Flanders stocked the cellars of her nearby château of Germolles with 90 hogsheads of Givry (this was before the king went mad). The château is in ruins today, and no trace has been found of its finest ornament, Sluter's group of the duke and duchess playing shepherds and shepherdesses under an elm. 200 years later, Henri IV's mistress Gabrielle d'Estrées stayed at Germolles. Courtépée recounts that her royal lover became so fond of Givry that he made it his everyday table wine and exempted it from duty (which soon had to be reimposed, because suddenly there was more Givry in Paris than Givry could ever have produced—a situation not unknown with other wines today). And so, with a little help from the Thénard family, who own the village's largest single estate, Givry has been enrolled (along with Suresnes, Ay, Arbois, Pommard et al.) as the favourite drink of the *vert galant.* It would be more interesting to have a list of the ones he *didn't* like, so that people could find out what was wrong with them.

Apart from having the best stories, Givry is also the only town of the Côte Chalonnaise with any outstanding public buildings. Unusually, for a region so rich in Romanesque, Gothic and Renaissance, it is the Neo-Classicism of the eighteenth century which predominates at Givry. This is largely due to the work of Emiland Gauthey, better known as the engineer of the Canal du Centre. Gauthey was a friend and disciple of Soufflot, and his striking parish church at Givry

(1773-1791) reflects some of Soufflot's ideas for the Panthéon in Paris. For example, the pendentives of the central cupola rest on four groups of columns (a device cautiously reinforced with masonry at the Panthéon by Soufflot's successor). However, Gauthey was no plagiarist. Instead of being a conventional cruciform building with a crossing dome, the church at Givry is a rotunda. By using detached columns to receive the thrust of the cupola, the designer created a gallery between the outer wall and each of the pendentives. To lighten the effect and provide a view down into the nave, each pendentive is pierced by a large oval oculus. A domed chancel projects at the east end, though the church really demands a central altar and 'mass in the round'. The monumental gateway that houses the town hall is from the same period (1771), as is the ornamental fountain attributed to Gauthey. The round market hall, completed in 1830, seems to have been devised as a complement to the church.

The Côte Chalonnaise ends with the villages of Montagny and Buxy, which share the appellation *Montagny* and produce only white wines under that name. Just as Rully in the north resembles its neighbours on the Côte Beaune, so Montagny in the south is closer to the fresh, light wines of the Mâconnais.

Chalon-sur-Saône has been an important river-port from the earliest days of international trade in the West. Excavations of the bed of the Saône have revealed ingots of tin from Cornwall, and the tips of thousands of amphorae from Italy. The presence of so many broken amphorae is probably due to the custom of transferring their contents to less fragile containers such as wineskins for overland journeys. The town has since spread north-westwards on the right bank, but the site must have been suggested originally by the two easily-defensible islands in the middle of the river, as at Paris. Chalon was the southern terminus of the overland route from the upper Seine at Vix, and Roman merchants—no doubt following in the footsteps of Phoenicians and Greeks—were already trading there before Caesar's conquest of Gaul. Caesar himself established a food-depot at Chalon and based a flotilla there. The three Roman roads from Boulogne, Trier and Strasbourg converged on the town, to be joined 700 years later by the Canal du Centre, linking the Saône with the Loire. It was at Chalon, during his march on Rome in 312, that Constantine rested his troops before embarking them on the Saône. Not far from the port, he is supposed to have had the vision which led him to adopt the Cross as his emblem before his defeat at Maxentius at the Milvian Bridge.

In 1839, at an early stage in their career, the Schneider brothers of Le Creusot set up a subsidiary ironworks called Le Petit Creusot at Chalon. Since then, the town has attracted many other industries and grown to be the second largest in the province. Chalon is plain and functional, without pretensions to being a tourist attraction. Nevertheless, there are some old houses and the church (until 1790, cathedral) of Saint-Vincent, which is interesting by reason of its progression from a Romanesque substructure to a Gothic apse and upper storey, but is spoilt by its pseudo-Gothic west towers. The old bridge over the Saône has a parapet ornamented by pyramids, the unmistakable trade-mark of Emiland Gauthey.

Chalon's best claim to distinction is as the birthplace of Nicéphore Niepce, the true father of the daguerreotype. Niepce was the living caricature of an inventor, working interminably and at great expense on projects which generally died through lack of public interest, and which, even when they did break through the wall of apathy, brought him no profit. He only turned to photography after developing, to no avail, a marine combustion engine and a bicycle. In 1816 came the first blurred images on paper sensitised by chloride and silver nitrate, but without a fixer. This followed in 1822, and by 1828 he was using bitumen on silver plate, with iodine vapour to darken the shaded areas. Unlike Fox-Talbot's method, there was no negative and thus no possibility of reproducing an image in large numbers. In 1827 Niepce went to Paris to canvass support from Daguerre, who owned a magic-lantern entertainment called the Diorama. The two men went into partnership in 1829, and the articles of association specified the man from Chalon as the inventor of the process. But in 1833, with success at last on the horizon, Niepce died of a stroke.

His partner presented the invention to the Académie des Sciences six years later, and gained a large pension for himself and Niepce's son by selling the patent to the state. In the meantime, Niepce's widow had died destitute. Full recognition has come, belatedly, and today Niepce has his statue on the embankment at Chalon and a display of his cameras and photographs in the Musée Denon. There is another monument at Saint-Loup-de-Varenne, just south of Chalon on the N6, where the inventor conducted most of his experiments.

Across the river in the suburb of Saint-Marcel stands the former Cluniac priory church, an austere early Gothic building which encloses, in a side-chapel, the well down which the Romans threw St Marcellus to his death. That heroic figure of scholastic philosophy, Peter Abelard, retired here after his condemnation by the council of Sens in 1140. His ability to confound all opponents in straight argument was no match for the influence and mortal enmity of St

Bernard, who played on Abelard's implicit denial of the necessity of prevenient grace, and on his unorthodox view of the Trinity. Only the intervention of Peter the Venerable saved Abelard from excommunication. But the old master's spirit was broken, and though Abbot Peter moved him from Cluny to Saint-Marcel, where the climate was judged healthier, Abelard died peacefully in 1142. He left a last meditation on the Lord's Prayer unfinished. The abbot wrote to the beloved Heloïse describing Abelard's last days, and assuring her that they would soon be reunited 'where, beyond these voices, there is peace'. Heloïse, not content with the prospect of a spiritual reunion, obtained permission to exhume the body secretly and have it re-interred in the convent of which she was abbess.

Clearly visible from Saint-Marcel, the tower of Saint-Martin-de-Laives on the tip of a ridge is the first outpost of the Mâconnais. After Chalon, the Saône ceases its meandering course and flows in almost a straight line to Lyon, where it joins the Rhône. At Tournus the hills come right down to the river, and road, rail and water converge at the head of the great artery leading to the Mediterranean. Travelling south on a steamer, Stendhal noted with satisfaction that at this point the scenery, the buildings and even the climate all seemed to change, and Bard remarked that there was less difference between Tournus and Avignon than there was between Tournus and Chalon. The Mâconnais belongs to the south, by culture (it was the most northerly province speaking the *langue d'oc*), by architecture and by history. After the war of succession which installed the Capetian dukes at Dijon, the Mâconnais drifted off into a history of its own. It was bought by St Louis in 1239 and not reunited with Burgundy until Bedford, the English regent of France, was forced to surrender royal rights over it in 1424.

Tournus lies just outside the Mâconnais. It began life as the Roman staging-post between Chalon and Mâcon, and prospered with the trade in salt from Lons-le-Saunier in the Jura. In 875, the 40-year Odyssey of the monks of Noirmoutier came to an end here on the banks of the Saône. Driven from their island off the west coast of France by the growing danger of Viking raids, the monks crossed the breadth of France in five stages, taking with them the relics of their founder, St Philibert. Thanks to a gift of Charles the Bald, they were able to move in with the monks of Tournus, whose abbey was dedicated to the local martyr Valerian. By taking such pains to escape the Norsemen, the monks fell victim instead to the Hungarians who raided France from the east. In 937 the abbey was pillaged and burnt. The uneasy marriage between the two communities flared into open dispute shortly afterwards, and the

Philibertines retreated to a previous refuge, Saint-Pourçain-sur-Sioule, until 949. Under the compromise which led to their return, Valerian was effectively supplanted by the newcomer, though his relics still retained a place of honour and the annual pilgrimage remained a joint one.

The new church, whose building was to span two centuries, was surrounded by fortifications; two stout round towers still shelter the abbey close from the busy traffic of the N6. Of the late 10th-century church, only the crypt escaped a devastating fire in 1006. Saint-Philibert as we see it today can be classed as part of the 'white mantle of churches' that was cast over Christendom after the year 1000, even though the two belfries that give it its distinctive silhouette were added about 1150 and represent the very last stage of Romanesque. The vast, dark narthex is one of the rare surviving examples of the First Romanesque style often known as 'Lombard', and typified by pilaster strips and decorative blind arcades on the outside walls. In fact, the Lombards did no more than diffuse the late Roman style which they were able to admire in the Byzantine outpost of Ravenna, though they did it so successfully that *lombardus* came to mean 'stonemason' in late Latin. However, the builders of Tournus were almost certainly *Lombardi* with a capital 'L'. We know that Abbot Wago, who initiated the rebuilding, had close links with Saint-Bénigne at Dijon. It would be surprising if he had not availed himself of the services of the craftsmen imported from northern Italy by William of Volpiano.

In the old Carolingian manner, the upper storey of the narthex was dedicated as a chapel of St Michael, either because of the Archangel's association with high places, or to secure the protection of Satan's gaoler against the forces of darkness, which were supposed to have their abode in the West. After the gloom of the narthex, the nave is dazzling. The lovely pale pink stone comes from an outcrop at Préty, a little way down stream on the opposite bank of the Saône. Tall, plain columns, composed of brick-like pieces of masonry, support an ingenious vaulting system of which the only other example (Mont Saint-Vincent) is also Burgundy. The main arches carry five parallel tunnel vaults running perpendicular to the axis of the nave, like the arches of a bridge; the thrust is thus displaced longitudinally rather than laterally. This enabled the architect to use the existing structure unaltered when he replaced the original wooden roof by stone vaulting, some time after 1066. It is true that this system breaks up the perspective of the upper parts of the nave; in compensation, it gives us a subtle interplay of cylindrical volumes, enhanced by the near-absence of surface ornament. An incidental effect of the design is that the windows of the clerestory are so hidden from the view of a spectator on the ground that although the upper part of the nave is brilliantly lit, the source of the light remains invisible.

There is a marked contrast between the nave and the east end, which was almost completely rebuilt in the early twelfth century. The new work was consecrated in 1120 by Pope Calixtus II. Although richer and more sophisticated than the rest of the interior, the choir has an oddly constricted appearance, because the architect chose to reproduce the plan of the existing crypt and use its walls as foundations. The lantern-dome over the crossing is of a Moorish type, and may have been inspired by similar domes at Ainay and Le Puy, or even directly from the Mozarabic style. Like Cluny, Tournus had close links with the Christian kingdom of Castile: an abbot of Saint-Philibert negotiated the marriage of Alfonso VI to the widow of the count of Chalon.

The abbey cloisters and chapter house, which had all been embedded in later buildings, have been handsomely restored. Abutting the south range of the cloister is the great vaulted hall of the monks' refectory. When the monks were finally replaced in 1627 by canons secular (who did not live in community), the refectory became a tennis-court—hence its usual name, Le Ballon. At the very end of the fifteenth century, the last elected abbot built himself an attractive residence. It stands across the street from the eastern exit of the cloister garth.

Tournus was the birthplace in 1725 of Jean-Baptiste Greuze, the portraitist and genre painter. His career went full-circle from provincial isolation to European fame, and back to unpopularity and ruin when his brand of sentimentality was swept aside by David's neo-classicism. Greuze is commemorated in his home town by a museum that boasts a few personal mementoes and several original paintings and drawings, and more cheerfully by the Restaurant Greuze, perhaps the town's best table and certainly the most unusual with a fairground organ in full working order.

Nineteen miles downstream from Tournus is Mâcon, the *Matisco* of the Romans and seat of a powerful county in the Middle Ages. In the 6th century, the Frankish king Childebert stayed at Mâcon on his way back from a successful raid into Spain, where he had accepted the relics of St Vincent in return for raising the siege of Saragossa. He made a thank-offering of part of the relics to Mâcon Cathedral, which transferred itself to the newcomer's patronage and thus established the Spanish saint's popularity in southern Burgundy. From the very beginning, the town's growth has been hampered by the proximity of Lyon, but since the last war Mâcon really seems to have taken wing. Apart from its development as a centre of the wine trade (the French National Wine Fair is held there in the last two weeks of May), Mâcon is now benefiting from the expansion and consequent dispersal of Lyonnais industry. Another important factor will be the high-speed turbotrain, whose route will by-pass Dijon and Chalon to rejoin the existing track just north of Mâcon, putting the latter town within one hour 40 minutes of Paris and 15 minutes of Lyon.

Unfortunately, the people of Mâcon welcomed the Revolution with more than average enthusiasm, and demonstrated their devotion to the cause in a particularly thorough campaign of destruction. They not only ensured the demolition of Cluny, but were the only Burgundians to make away with their cathedral. Of the old Saint-Vincent, only the early Romanesque porch and west towers survive. In the eleventh century, the cathedral suffered from a plague of sparrows. Where modern materialist public authorities would resort to poison or lime, Bishop Landry cleared his church of vermin simply by excommunicating them. Apart from a pleasant frontage on the Saône, Mâcon has little else of historic interest, except the sixteenth-century Maison de Bois (Place aux Herbes), with its grotesquely carved timber frame. It is reputed to have been the headquarters of the Abbaye de Maugouvert (Abbey of Misrule), a society such as existed in most French towns in the late Middle Ages, devoted to the irresponsible pursuit of pleasure. At Mâcon, the association overstepped the bounds of decency so often that in 1625 the authorities suppressed it and forbade anyone ever again to take the title of Abbot of Misrule, on pain of death.

The region stretching westwards from the Saône between Tournus and Mâcon is one of the loveliest in Europe. Unlike the desiccated picturesqueness of Provence or the intimidating grandeur of the Alps, the Mâconnais is nature on a human scale. No wonder the monk Berno, summoned in 910 to found a new community on the lands of Duke William of Aquitaine (who was also count of Mâcon), chose Cluny in the Mâconnais in preference to all other sites. Since then, the hand of man—especially of the monks of Cluny—has softened and moulded the country, constantly enriching its natural variety. Between the wooded summits and the lush grazing of the valleys, the use of the land is determined by the exposure: the vine on the slopes that catch the best of the morning sunlight, and elsewhere, rough heath supporting only the goats that produce the little cheeses known locally as *chevrotons*. In contrast to the Côte d'Or, the relief is more confused and the scarps of the

The Côte Chalonnaise

Appellations contrôlées: names written in
capitals and areas enclosed in thick black line.

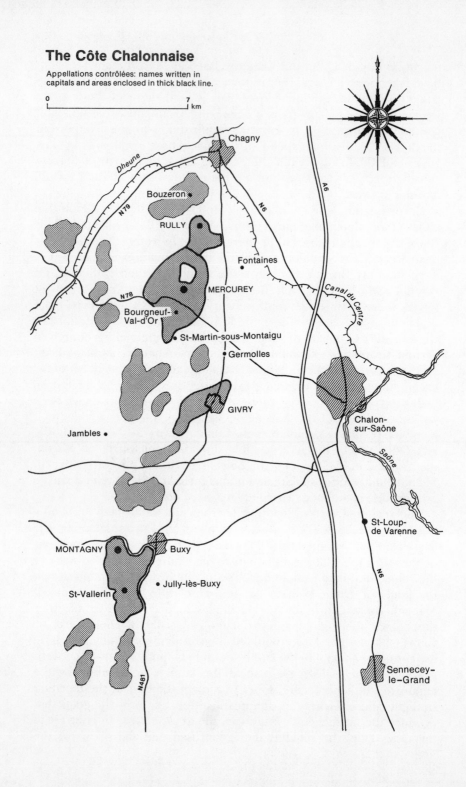

0 ____ 7
km

Mâconnais hills face west; in the south, at Solutré and Vergisson, they rear up into sheer limestone cliffs. And, instead of having exclusive possession of a narrow swathe of hillside, the vine in the Mâconnais is scattered in small patches over a vast area, wherever the soil and exposure are suitable.

Until the First World War, production was predominantly of red *vin ordinaire* made from the gamay. The pinot noir has never made much progress here, as ideal conditions are too rare to make it economic. On the other hand, because the soil is limestone, the gamay does not give of its best, and *Mâcon Rouge* cannot compete with wines grown from the same grape on the granite soil of the northern Beaujolais. Today the position is reversed, and twice as much white wine as red is produced. It is this white wine which has proved to be the region's forte, a light, fruity carafe wine with a sweetish tang, but without the unctuousness of Meursault. In defiance of conventional wisdom, this white wine is the ideal complement of the *chevrotons*, whose distinctive dry flavour would detract from any red wine. In the far south is one great name, Pouilly-Fuissé, which can stand comparison with the best of the Côte d'Or. With the exception of Saint-Véran, Loché and Vinzelles, all in the south (the latter two hyphenate their names with Pouilly), the rest of the vintage is sold as *Mâcon*—with or without qualification—and is a wine to be drunk young. An increasingly large output is handled by co-operatives, which not only guarantee a consistent quality, but enable the growers to cut overheads. The three villages whose names are most commonly met with after the appellation *Mâcon* are Viré, Clessé and Chardonnay. Viré was the altar-wine favoured by St Jean-Baptiste Vianney, the *curé* of Ars, who starved himself but insisted on the best for God; and Chardonnay was the birthplace of the grape from which all the best white burgundy, and hence the best dry white wine in the world, is made. It is difficult not to believe that the monks of Cluny, those great agriculturists, were instrumental in its selection, improvement and subsequent spread to the rest of Burgundy. Nearly all the white vines in the Mâconnais itself are chardonnay.

The late Roman poet Ausonius mentioned the wines of Tournus, but we have to wait till the middle of the 8th century for the next documentary evidence of viticulture in the area. Even then, the vineyard did not expand appreciably until the eleventh and twelfth centuries, under monastic influence. In the reign of Louis XIV, an enterprising *vigneron* of Charnay-lès-Mâcon, a giant of a man called Claude Brosse, loaded two hogsheads of his best wine on an ox-cart and set out for Paris, hoping to attract the custom of some great nobleman. The journey took him 33 days, and at the first opportunity, Claude Brosse attended high mass at Versailles. To his outrage, the king saw what he thought to be a man who remained standing when the ritual demanded that he should kneel. He sent a gentleman-in-waiting to reprimand the offender, only to discover that the gigantic Brosse had been kneeling all the time. Eager to inspect this prodigy, Louis had the peasant summoned into his presence after the service, and deigned to ask him what brought him to Paris. Brosse explained the purpose of his visit, and the king was so impressed that he asked to taste some of the wine on the spot. Louis pronounced it excellent—far better than the Suresnes and Beaugency then in use at court—and the royal seal of approval enabled Claude Brosse to make a fortune carting his wine to Versailles every year.

The hospitable countryside of the Mâconnais is dotted with Romanesque village churches, one of the densest concentrations in Europe. Most of them belong to a tradition much older than that of the great third abbey church at Cluny. The *vignerons'* houses have the shallow-pitched tiled roofs of the South, and open galleries where the family can shelter from the heat of the afternoon sun.

The usual approach to Cluny from the north is along the valley of the Grosne, continuing due south from Givry and Buxy. The château of Sercy, mirrored in a weedy pond by the road-side, has retained the medieval wooden parapet and superstructure of one of its towers. Since 1944, when the Swiss religious Roger Schutz and his companions made it the permanent home of their Protestant monastic community, the hamlet of Taizé has become an important ecumenical centre. The Church of the Reconciliation (built in 1962) has provision for the Protestant, Catholic and Orthodox cults. Young Christian enthusiasts from all over the world gather there to strum their guitars and live in love and peace, in tents. One can pause to admire the tiny Romanesque church, and be grateful to the Brothers for restoring it.

A better idea is to take a winding route over the hills from Tournus, viewing the eleventh-century towered churches at Farges and Uchizy, both closely allied to Saint-Philibert, before stopping for white wine and goat's cheese (fresh or matured) at the little café opposite the co-operative at Chardonnay. The café's two refectory tables are made entirely of vine-stocks, even the tops being formed of sections cemented together and planed level. The inhabitants of Uchizy, in common with those of a string of villages close by on the other bank of the Saône, were traditionally referred to as 'Saracens' by their neighbours. Probably no more than an abusive nickname (*sarrasin* also means 'buckwheat' in French, and jokes about other people's diet never seem to pall), it has given rise to the wildest speculation and kept historians and ethnographers harmlessly employed for 200 years.

The 'eagle's nest' of Brancion commands the most important pass linking Tournus to the Grosne valley, and was the seat of a powerful barony in medieval times. The castle is ruined now, and of the town walls only the gatehouse remains, but the small and simple late Romanesque church is decorated with fourteenth-century frescoes. It also contains the tomb effigy of Josserand IV of Brancion, killed fighting alongside St Louis in Egypt in 1250. The debts he contracted to equip himself for the fatal expedition forced his son to sell Brancion to Duke Hugues IV of Burgundy, a more fortunate crusader who had survived the rout of El Mansurah. Philip the Bold rebuilt the castle and transformed it into a ducal residence.

Half-way from Brancion to the Grosne, and clearly visible from the vantage-point in front of the west door of Brancion church, rises the high rectangular bell-tower of Saint-Martin at Chapaize. After Tournus, it is one of the finest examples of 'Lombard First Romanesque'. The exceptional height of the tower (114 feet) is due to the fact that this was no ordinary parish church but the novice-house of the abbey of Saint-Pierre at Chalon. It stood originally in a clearing of the forest that carpeted the valley floor, and must have served as a vital landmark for travellers.

According to the archaeologist Kenneth J. Conant, 'rural Burgundy is still largely Romanesque in its visual effect', meaning that although the original buildings have been replaced, the traditions have been preserved. Our route from Brancion takes us beneath the shadow of Mont Saint-Romain to Blanot, a perfect illustration of Conant's remark. With the crossing of the last ridge and the descent to the Grosne, the end of the pilgrimage comes into view.

'Amongst all the monasteries founded beyond the Alps to the glory of Almighty God and of the blessed apostles Peter and Paul, there is one which is St Peter's own, and which is united with the church of Rome by special right: Cluny. Dedicated since its foundation to the honour and defence of the Apostolic See, it has attained, under saintly abbots, by divine grace and mercy, such holiness that it surpasses all monasteries beyond the mountains in the service of God and in spiritual fervour. It has no peer, for there is not one abbot of Cluny who has not been a saint.' With these words Gregory VII, the famous 'Pope Hildebrand', celebrated the Papacy's special relationship with an ecclesiastical institution that did more than any other to shape the medieval world.

When Berno and his followers took possession of William of Aquitaine's hunting lodge in 910, they were set on a radical reform of the abuses which had plagued monastic life since Merovingian times. Outside interference—in particular, the practice of granting or selling abbacies to secular churchmen or even laymen—had drained off funds and sapped discipline and morale. This was why Cluny's foundation charter, like Vézelay's, placed it under direct responsibility to the Holy See, and exempted it from both feudal obedience and episcopal visitation. Under St Odo (927-942), the custom of 'plurality of abbacies', whereby abbots could create a personal union of monasteries during their lifetime, was extended (with papel permission) so that other Benedictine houses could be brought under the permanent control of the abbots of Cluny. The shortcomings of this system—local hostility to an expanding supranational organisation, over-centralisation, and excessive reliance on the personality of one man—only became apparent later. In the beginning, the advantage lay in the formation of a firmly-regulated élite corps that could be sent out to reform other houses. Later, the Cluniac congregation became a potent weapon in the campaign to establish a papal theocracy, and was the most active promoter of the Santiago pilgrimage and the reconquest of Moorish Spain. The abbey itself served as a papal headquarters when the activities of a succession of antipopes, installed by the Emperors during the quarrel over episcopal investitures, made Rome unsafe.

Under the blind abbot Aymard (942-965) and his successors St Mayeul (965-994) and St Odilo (994-1048), the influence of Cluny grew. Mayeul was the friend and confidant of Otto the Great, while Odilo was a zealous supporter of the peace movement known as 'The Truce of God', and the first to observe All Souls' Day (2 November) as a feast in honour of all the faithful departed. But even their long reigns are eclipsed by that of St Hugh, the first native-born Burgundian to be abbot of Cluny. Elected at the age of 25, he ruled for 60 years and brought Cluny to its peak. Popes turned to him for advice and sent him on important missions; St Anselm sought his help after falling out with William Rufus; and as Henry IV's godfather, Hugh was almost certainly instrumental in reconciling the Emperor (albeit temporarily) with Gregory VII at Canossa in 1077. But for us his political rôle is surpassed by his work as one of the greatest builders of all time.

Cluny had always been in the forefront of artistic progress. The Romanesque religious ideal found its true expression in Gregorian chant, and St Odo—an accomplished musician and choirmaster—was concerned not only to enrich the chant, but to display it to the best possible advantage. He encouraged the replacement of wooden ceilings by stone tunnel vaulting, which is not only fire-proof, but has a more reverberant acoustic. The second abbey church at Cluny, built by St Mayeul after 955, had greatly influenced building styles; but it was already too small for the 200 resident monks and the assemblies of the chapters general. A visit to Monte Cassino in 1083, where Abbot Desiderius had recently rebuilt the monastery with the help of Byzantine artists, resolved St Hugh on making Cluny the Monte Cassino of Gaul. The necessary money became available two years later, when Alfonso VI sent Hugh a thank-offering of 10,000 talents for the capture of Toledo. Work was able to start immediately, as the workforce was already on site, finishing off the enlarged monastery buildings begun under Odilo.

The avowed endeavour of every monastery was to create a replica of Heaven on earth, and by the mid-eleventh century the name of Cluny had become synonymous with achieved spiritual life. 'And what else can I call the monastery of Cluny,' wrote St Peter Damian to St Hugh in 1063, 'but a field of the Lord, where such a great company living in charity stands like a harvest of heavenly corn? The field is hoed with holy counsel and the seeds of heavenly discourse are sown in it. There the harvest of spiritual grain is collected for gathering into heavenly barns.' The Cluniac pope Urban II told St Hugh, 'You are the light of the world.' The new church at Cluny was to be not only the visible expression of the order's prestige, but the physical counterpart of a less tangible reality—the Heavenly City built of earthly stone.

With the foundation of Cîteaux yet to come, Benedictine monks still shared the assumptions of the feudal aristocracy from which they were drawn: it was a great lord's duty to spend, and his greatest glory was to spend lavishly. In exchange for individual self-denial, the great monasteries provided corporate magnificence. The general scheme of St Hugh's church was the work of Gunzo, a retired abbot of Baume, and the executive architect was the mathematician Hézelon of Liège. In the relationship of its parts, the church displayed elaborate mathematical ratios derived from a study of Vitruvius. The scope and sheer scale of the architects' efforts were sensational. Cluny III was to be a summary of the mature Romanesque style, nothing less than the largest and most beautiful church in the world. In its vastness, its soaring vaults shored up by forerunners of the flying buttress, and in its conscious evocation of Heaven through the senses, it announced the principles of the Gothic style.

The plan chosen was that of the patriarchal cross, with a major and a minor transept at the east end. The chevet was visually the most exciting feature, a mountain of masonry rising in steps from the radiating apsidal chapels to the four huge crossing and transept towers. The main church (completed in 1121) was 504 feet long, and would have accommodated, standing, the entire 10,000-strong membership of the order. With the addition of the narthex a century later, bringing the length up to 608 feet, Cluny became the biggest church in Christendom until the construction of the new St Peter's.

It provoked ecstasies of admiration from contemporaries. It was 'a place where the dwellers on high would tread, if it could be believed that human abodes of this sort are pleasing to them', and the monks 'celebrate as if at Easter every day, because they have merited to go into that Galilee'. It was the vision that inspired Bernard de Morlaas to write his hymn *Jerusalem the Golden*.

We can only take the eulogists' word for it. Between 1798 and 1823, this masterpiece was senselessly and almost completely destroyed by a consortium from Mâcon (one of them a renegade priest), who used it as a quarry for building materials. They pulled down the nave and that extraordinary *promenoir des anges*, the chancel; they blew up the great narthex towers, the Barabans, with gunpowder. Only the south transept, with its octagon and flanking clock tower, escaped the wreck. The great American scholar Kenneth J. Conant has succeeded in bringing Cluny to life again through his work, but this only increases the poignancy of our loss, by making us more conscious of the glory that was.

Even as the monks celebrated their good fortune at being admitted to Cluny, the 'light of the world' began to shine less brightly. The very conditions that the monasteries had helped to create were about to make them obsolete. St Hugh died in 1109, and the tempestuous career of his successor, Pons de Melgueil, was a foretaste of the coming decline in standards. Abbot Pons was a great patron of the arts, but his worldliness was a little ahead of its time, and he lacked the tact to maintain his position. He resigned in 1122 in a moment of anger, changed his mind, staged a coup, and eventually died in prison, excommunicate. Under its last great abbot, Peter the Venerable (1122–1156), Cluny enjoyed an Indian summer. Cluniac monasteries still formed the artistic avant-garde, and Abbot Peter crowned Cluny's reputation for scholarship by his protection of Abelard, his translation of the Koran, and his voluminous correspondence. Privately, he even got the better of his order's most outspoken opponent, St Bernard, gently reproving him for lack of Christian charity. 'Surely you are making fun of me!' replied the abbot of Clairvaux huffily, but in the end even he was won over by the beauty of Peter's personality. Nevertheless, vocations and, more important, the endowments to support them, were increasingly going elsewhere: first to the Cistercians and the Augustinian canons, and afterwards to the mendicant friars. The fact that Abbot Peter was not canonised, though his life was no less saintly than those of Odo, Mayeul, Odilo and Hugh, is an indication of Cluny's reduced prestige.

The abbots remained influential, but more and more of the abbey income found its way into their pockets, to enable them to maintain their state. From the middle of the fourteenth century they had a palace of their own in Paris (now the Cluny Museum, just off the Boulevard Saint-Michel). After the appointment of abbots became a royal prerogative in 1515, the abbacy of Cluny was one of the richest gifts the monarch could bestow. Up to two-thirds of the revenues went direct to the abbot; the Guises, Richelieu, Mazarin and La Rochefoucauld all held this lucrative sinecure. By the time of the Revolution, there was only enough revenue left over to support 40 monks, whereas under Peter the Venerable there had been 600. In 1750 the resident prior, Dom Dathoze, decided to replace the monks' existing quarters by something more comfortable and spacious. The result is a little cold, though certainly grander and more elegant than what went before; except for the churches, Romanesque monastic buildings were plain and unpretentious.

Visiting Cluny today requires an effort of the imagination. If one stands level with the Palace of Jacques d'Amboise (now the town hall) and looks eastwards along the street named appropriately after Kenneth J. Conant, one is in fact standing at the entrance to the narthex and looking down the nave. The far end of the church was over 50 yards east of the Clocher de l'Eau Bénite, the only surviving landmark.

The great south transept is reached along Dom Dathoze's airy cloister. Paray-le-Monial is a clearer example of the decorative style employed, but only the fragment at Cluny itself can give us an idea of the massive scale of the original. Well over 100 feet separate the pavement from the crown of the vault. Another remnant is one of the chapels of the small south transept, rebuilt in Flamboyant Gothic by Abbot Jean de Bourbon around 1456. Fifteen consoles project from the walls, each sculpted in the form of one of the prophets of the Old Testament. The intention was to draw an elaborate parallel between the two Testaments, each prophet being regarded as a precursor of the apostle who stood on the console (the three extra spaces were for Christ, John the Baptist and St Paul). Legend claims that the statues were in solid silver, and were hidden—never to be found again—during the Wars of Religion. There seems no reason to suppose that they were ever completed.

The thirteenth-century abbey granary houses a collection of the first importance, the capitals of the chancel pillars. Although their protests against the demolition of the abbey church had been vain, the people of Cluny obtained the right to appropriate any sculpture that might be worth preserving. The mutilation of the capitals is due to the fact that they fell 30 feet when the chancel was blown up, and were only subsequently rescued from the rubble. These sculptures from around 1095 represent the first flowering of the Romanesque Renaissance, and establish Cluny as the source of the school which went on to carve Vézelay, Autun and Saulieu. The semicircle of capitals conveys a complex symbolic message: between the Original Sin and the Redemption (in the guise of the Sacrifice of Isaac) runs an allegory that begins with virgin Nature (the unfigured Corinthian capital), continues through the works of monastic life, the theological and cardinal virtues, the fruitful seasons of Spring and Summer, the Four Rivers of Paradise, and culminates with the praise of God—symbolised by the eight tones of plainsong, the art so much in honour at Cluny.

The basement of the granary was the cellar in which the monks assembled their vintage and nurtured it until fermentation was complete. The large windows are an innovation; the building was originally cooler and darker, and a small stream was diverted through it to provide running water for cleaning out the barrels. From the fourteenth century onwards, the abbey marketed its wine in Paris. No doubt the taverns of the Latin Quarter, where the abbots had built their palace, were the principal outlet.

The southern approaches to Cluny are commanded by the castle of Berzé-le-Châtel, in its ravishing site. In the early nineteenth century, the discovery of a human skeleton and some ox-bones on different floors of one of the towers gave rise to the story that a baron of Berzé had, at some time in the Middle Ages, locked up a man and an ox in order to find out which would starve to death first. We have no record of the result of this interesting experiment.

It would be strange if this Arcadian countryside had not captured the imagination of some poet. Alphonse de Lamartine is out of fashion now, but in his day he was one of the outstanding figures of French Romanticism. Born at Mâcon in 1790, he mixed literature with politics and the life of a country squire to his own ultimate ruin. He became a deputy in 1833 and followed an individualistic policy of opposition to the July Monarchy. Solemn warnings that his day would surely come drew from one wit the remark, 'Monsieur de

Lamartine is a comet whose orbit has not yet been calculated.'
Fifteen years he waited, and actually became foreign minister after
the fall of Louis Philippe in February 1848; but as a moderate
radical he was overtaken by events, failed to avert the class war of
the 'June Days', and finished up equally unacceptable to Left and
Right. When he stood for president against Louis Napoleon in
December 1848, he polled only two votes in every 1000. He lived in
retirement in this beloved corner of the Mâconnais until his death in
1869, harassed by creditors, bereavements, and resentment of what
he regarded as his country's ingratitude.

At Milly, always referred to by Lamartine as the *terre natale*
(though in fact he lived at Mâcon until he was four), stands the
house he immortalised with the words,

> *O objets inanimés, avez-vous donc une âme*
> *Qui s'attache à notre âme et la force d'aimer?*

It is a plain, square villa such as belonged to many a prosperous
peasant, and is remarkable only as the setting for Lamartine's
blissful childhood. In 1860 he was forced to sell it 'at a distress price
which represents neither its spiritual nor its material value'. The
nearby château of Pierreclos and the little church at Bussières
appear in *Jocelyn,* a love-story based on the real-life adventures of
Father Dumont, curate at Bussières, and Mademoiselle de Milly,
daughter of the owner of Pierreclos.

The château of Monceau, inherited by Lamartine in 1833, was
where the poet liked to imagine himself as a son of the land,
planting vines and adding to his patrimony—though his capital was
exhausted long before he could expect a reasonable return from it.
In a gazebo in the garden at Monceau he wrote his most important
prose work, his *History of the Girondins* (published in 1847), in which
he called for a 'revolution of contempt' against the July Monarchy.
His favourite residence, however, was Saint-Point, a wedding
present from his father. Lamartine and his English wife 'improved'
the old manor-house by additions in the prevailing pseudo-Gothic
taste, for which the French have coined the happy term *troubadour.*
Here they received such luminaries as Victor Hugo, Liszt, the
song-writer Béranger and the Catholic liberals Lamennais and
Lacordaire. The poet's study has been preserved as it was during his
lifetime, and the stone bench on which he used to meditate still
stands under a tree in the garden. Lamartine lies with his wife,
daughter, mother and niece in the family chapel in the village
church.

Almost within sight of Milly is the former monastic grange of

Berzé-la-Ville, where St Hugh often came during the last decade of his life to rest from his heavy responsibilities. During one of his visits, a terrible thunderstorm broke over Berzé in the middle of the night. The grange was hit by lightning and burnt down, but the abbot was miraculously preserved from the flames. In his will, Hugh entrusted Brother Seguin with the completion of the rebuilding. The saint's special affection for Berzé explains the lavishness with which its chapel was decorated under his successor, the ill-fated Pons de Melgueil.

The rustic surroundings provide an unlikely home for the only large-scale group of Romanesque paintings to survive from Cluny. A farmyard, a huddle of barns, and the chapel—a single nave and apse, over a crypt which more likely served as a wine-cellar than a reliquary. Inside, all the interest resides in the tiny oven-vaulted chancel. Providentially, the frescoes of the apse were whitewashed over and hidden until 1887, when the *curé* of Berzé, Father Jolivet, investigated a faint outline which turned out to be that of Christ's head. When a few careful scrapes of his penknife had confirmed his suspicions, Jolivet painstakingly cleaned the rest and discovered the colours, ochre, dark blue and purple, glowing almost as they had done seven centuries before.

The main subject, that of the oven vault, is Christ in Majesty, seated on an embroidered cushion and proffering a scroll to St Peter. Peter and Paul were the patron saints of Cluny, so that the theme of the Mission of the Apostles was an indirect reference to the divine mission of Cluny. Apart from the apostles, there are two smaller figures on each side: the deacons Lawrence and Vincent on our left, and on the right a pair of unidentified bishops. On the spandrels of the window-arches beneath the vault appear six obscure female martyrs with upraised hands, several bearing jars of precious ointment. Here, direct Byzantine influence is beyond dispute; with their crowns and elaborate coiffures, these figures might almost have been copied from the mosaics of the Empress Theodora at Ravenna. It has even been suggested that St Hugh recruited some of the Greeks he had met at Monte Cassino to work in Burgundy. However that may be, the sudden developments in fresco-painting and manuscript illumination of that period were closely connected with the renewal of contact between East and West that occurred around the time of the First Crusade. On the wall beneath the windows, nine busts of saints (some Oriental, some Roman) emerge from behind a curtain, again in the Byzantine manner.

The blind arches on either side of the apse windows are devoted to the stories of two saints of whom Cluny owned relics, and here the artists, freed from the restrictions of convention, have given free rein to their imagination. On the left, St Blaise blesses the widow who visits him in prison; she has brought him the head and trotters of her pig, that he himself had lately saved from a wolf. In the lower scene the saint is beheaded. On the right, in a splendidly dynamic composition, is the martyrdom of St Vincent of Saragossa, roasted alive like St Lawrence.

From the lane which runs past the gate of the grange, the toppling wave-crests of the rocks of Vergisson and Solutré are silhouetted against the south-eastern horizon. Close to, the rock of Solutré has an even more dramatic profile, that of the prow of some great ship sinking by the stern. It has given its name to the Solutrean culture of the Upper Palaeolithic (15,000-12,000 B.C.), characterised by the perfection of stone-flaking and, towards its end, by the appearance of eyed needles that indicate that clothes were being made. Oddly enough, no skeletons of Solutrean man have ever been found at Solutré—only his artefacts, and the remains of the Aurignacians who preceded him and his Magdalenian, Neolithic and Bronze Age successors. But it was the Solutreans who left the feature for which Solutré is really famous—two and a half acres of heath known as 'The Charnel-House', at the very foot of the rock. In 1866, excavations revealed that just beneath the surface of this area lay a three-and-a-half-foot-deep magma of clay and horse-bones, the remains of an estimated 100,000 individual animals. They were certainly dismembered and eaten there by human beings, but the more imaginative archaeologists have gone further, and have conjured up a nightmare vision of vision of hunters manoeuvring whole herds of wild horses on to the rock and stampeding them over the cliff.

Here, just before limestone gives place to granite, the viticultural Mâconnais makes a final flourish with the white wines of Pouilly. 'You don't just *sell* a wine like that,' said a *vigneron* of the district, 'you part with it.' Of course, notes Pierre Forgeot, the value of such regret is included in the bill. Chasselas is the home of an eating grape; most of the vines that cling to the south-facing walls of the *vignerons'* houses belong to this variety. The most southerly *cru* of Burgundy proper is Saint-Véran; just over the hill, the Beaujolais begins at Saint-Amour.

11 The Sâone Valley

The Saône and the Vingeanne were the original eastern frontiers of French Burgundy; for centuries, they were also the eastern frontiers of France. Rivers, of course, are never satisfactory boundaries; mountains divide, but rivers unite. As early as the eleventh century, the counts of Chalon had extended their sway across the plain of northern Bresse to the foothills of the Jura. But with that exception the anomaly of a river border persisted in Burgundy until the seventeenth century. In 1601, Henri IV forced the duke of Savoy to give up all his territory between the Saône and Lake Geneva, including southern Bresse. These lands, which today form the department of Ain, were placed under the jurisdiction of the Dijon Parlement (which is why Voltaire, at Ferney, had so many contacts with high court officers in the provincial capital). By the treaty of Nymegen in 1678, Louis XIV finally acquired Franche-Comté and advanced the limits of his kingdom to the Alps; the Saône ceased to be a national frontier. Nevertheless, the psychological barrier created by centuries of divergent traditions remains to this day—and for years after Nymegen, the Franc-Comtois showed their disgust with the French conquest by having themselves buried face down.

At the northern end of the Burgundian plain, the valley of the Vingeanne is within easy reach of Dijon. The calm of the eighteenth century still hangs over the countryside. The notable châteaux all date from the reign of Louis XV, and even the landscape might be from a canvas by Watteau or Fragonard. Fontaine-Française, built in the neo-classical style when rococo was still the rage, was the home of Madame de Saint-Julien, Voltaire's 'philosophical butterfly'. Close by, on 5 June 1595, Henri IV led a squadron of 510 horsemen to victory over 15,000 Spaniards and Leaguers, thus writing one of the last chapters of a civil war that had lasted more than 30 years. That same night he slept at the old castle of Fontaine-Française (demolished in 1754), whence he wrote to his sister, 'On other occasions I have fought for glory, but on this one I fought for my life.'

Talmay is a more typical product of its age, an exquisite piece of

rococo chinoiserie by d'Aviler dating from 1762. A happy inspiration allowed the architect to indulge the style's taste for piquant
contrasts and asymmetry; as an annexe, he retained one of the
forbidding square towers of the medieval fortress. At nearby
Renève, the octogenarian Queen Brunnhild, whom we have met
before at Epoisses and Montréal, was put to death in 613. She had
fallen into the hands of the Frankish noblemen who had revolted in
favour of Clothair II of Neustria. They tied her by an arm and a leg
to the tail of a horse and dragged her to death. History has given
her a bad press, but perhaps her only real offence lay in curbing
aristocratic anarchy with its own weapons.

Of all Burgundy's country houses, none has quite the charm of
Beaumont-sur-Vingeanne. This delightful château in miniature—really a large pavilion or 'folly'—was planned by a worldly
ecclesiastic as a refuge from the stifling etiquette of Versailles. The
result is the ultimate in informality, haunted by the likable genius of
the king's chaplain Claude Jolyot. The house was built in 1724 to
designs by a Parisian architect; the discreet exterior conceals three
habitable storeys. Here Father Jolyot and his intimates were able to
enjoy a bottle of burgundy at their leisure, in surroundings still
redolent of the *douceur de vivre* that disappeared for ever with the
Revolution.

Bèze was the site of the long-vanished abbey that gave its name to
the *clos* adjoining the Chambertin at Gevrey, and can justly claim to
have created the first *grand cru* on the Côte de Nuits. The comforts
appreciated by the owner of Beaumont-sur-Vingeanne live on in
Bèze, at the Hostellerie du Raisin d'Or. On the corner of the square,
opposite a pair of thirteenth-century houses, M. Chambrette—a
personality straight out of a painting by Brueghel—serves meals of
classic simplicity and heroic dimensions. Those who find *truite
meunière* dull have yet to eat it at Bèze. The experience will also give
the lie to the notion that flavour is necessarily in inverse proportion
to size. The wines are impeccably chosen, and the *patron*'s advice can
be relied upon. He once persuaded us to take a 1970 Chambolle-
Musigny instead of a 1964 Corton, a decision we had no reason to
regret. Incredible though it may seem, the Guide Michelin recently
withdrew its mention of the Raisin d'Or, on the ground that the
interior was 'antiquated' (it has the authentic atmosphere of what it
is—a traditional family *bistrot* and restaurant, where the food and
drink are the first considerations). This is proof, if any were
required, that no guide is authoritative or free from quirks. Decency
demands that M. Chambrette should receive his due.

The dead flat plain south-east of Dijon is a land of sugar-beet and, nearer the river, market gardens. The leeks and asparagus of Auxonne are famous. Auxonne itself, a bridgehead on the far bank of the Saône, has lost the aspect of a frontier-post, despite remnants of fortifications by Vauban and earlier builders. In a sheltered square just off the busy main road to Geneva, the church has some interesting items of sculpture. The statues in the porch may seem oddly familiar; six are nineteenth-century free adaptations of the prophets of the Well of Moses at Dijon. Inside, the gauche but appealing Madonna of the Grapes is a perfect example of what generally happened when native Burgundians took over Sluter's style. The drapery becomes pointlessly elaborate, weighing the figure down instead of giving it movement. In contrast is the crowned Virgin in another chapel, a rare work by the elusive Juan de la Huerta. The statue is badly weathered; from 1855 till lately, it stood on the peak of the gable over the main porch, and before the Revolution it adorned one of the town gates. Just such a commission was given to de la Huerta by the town in 1447.

From 1788 to 1791, when Auxonne still had a garrison, the young Napoleon Bonaparte was stationed there. As at Valence, his previous posting, his passion for study set him apart from his comrades-in-arms. What is less well known is that he nevertheless found time to begin his sentimental education. He fell in love with the daughter of a rich timber-merchant; but her father considered a gaunt, puny artillery subaltern of Corsican extraction and no prospects to be an unambitious match. Bonaparte, deprived at a single blow of a bride and a promising career in the timber trade, was heartbroken. He asked to be transferred back to Valence, and took to soldiering in good earnest.

Saint-Jean-de-Losne, at the head of the Burgundy and Rhine-Rhône Canals, bears the proudest battle honours of all the Saône towns. In 1636, following France's intervention in the Thirty Years' War, an Imperial army under Matthias Gallas counter-attacked across the river and ravaged the plain. The few hundred defenders of Saint-Jean-de-Losne held out desperately against their 60,000 besiegers, and succeeded in denying Gallas a permanent stronghold.

The Saône from Auxonne to Mâcon is the water of the *pochouse*. This freshwater equivalent of *bouillabaisse* has a pedigree going back to at least 1598, when it is mentioned in the accounts of the hospital at Chalon. The fish used should be pike, perch, tench, carp and eels, cut into thick slices. The sauce is prepared from fat bacon cut into slivers, chopped onions, the heads of the fish, a clove of garlic, a bouquet of mixed herbs, and a generous helping of white burgundy after the other ingredients have browned. The mixture is strained off over the fish—which has itself been previously browned in butter—and brought to the boil. A glass of *marc* is added and set light to, and the whole is left to cook for 20 minutes. At the end of that time, the fish should be taken out and kept warm while the sauce is reduced and thickened with cream (some people prefer to add butter gradually during the cooking). When the stew is finally ready, it should be served on croûtons of bread fried in butter and rubbed with garlic. Unfortunately, owing to the general English apathy about food, such a recipe is beyond our capacity in this country. The rivers swarm with the ingredients, but no fishmonger bothers to stock them.

Somewhere along the Saône is a little riverside restaurant, where you can dine on a terrace overlooking a lawn that runs down to the water's edge. All round, fish-traps hang up to dry. The only means of crossing the river used to be an old bailey bridge. Now there is a gracefully-arched concrete structure, though the traffic in this remote spot hardly justifies a bridge at all. They serve *pochouse* in season; but even better is to be there on a midsummer's day dumb with heat, with nothing stirring for miles and miles, eating *friture* of baby roach followed by goat's cheese, and drinking long, cool draughts of Mâcon-Chardonnay. As for the location—well, we are all entitled to one secret.

Bresse is a neglected region of Burgundy, but no less rewarding than the others for anyone who loves rural France. Between the Saône and the Revermont of the Jura, a vast, languid plain stretches southwards, dotted with woods and ponds. The staple crops in these regions used to be buckwheat and millet (the latter eaten as *gaudes*, a sort of porridge), but these have made way for maize, which is grown in large quantities.

With the limestone hills so far away on either side, the great houses—Pierre-de-Bresse, Montcoy, Montcony—are of brick. The most splendidly-proportioned is Pierre-de-Bresse, with its domed towers and balconied façade. Cardinal de Bissy, the influential friend of Madame de Maintenon and implacable enemy of the Jansenists, was born at Pierre before his father began the present château in 1680. Brick has also replaced the daub and thatch of humbler dwellings. The isolated farmhouses, a few of which still keep their 'Saracen chimneys' (the outlets of large oven-hearths) extend their eaves to form awnings for the hanging and drying of maize.

The abundance of cereals probably explains why Bresse has a reputation founded on poultry. During its first months, the Bresse chicken traditionally ranges free. Then it is put into a fattening coop and crammed with maize and buckwheat before being killed, and soaked in a bath of milk. The old market towns of Louhans and Bourg are the centres of distribution. Mère Fillioux, the famous Lyonnais cordon bleu, ordered 25,000 birds a year from Louhans for her *poularde demi-deuil* speciality, and Bourg holds an annual poultry fair in its covered market on the third Saturday in December. Dairying is also carried on, and Bleu de Bresse is one of France's best-known blue cheeses.

The gastronomic attractions of Bourg-en-Bresse, however, are almost totally eclipsed by the church at Brou. This extraordinary mausoleum, ostensibly a monument to conjugal fidelity, embodies the spirit of an age and is a reminder of the often sad reality behind the pomp of princes. A Benedictine priory had existed at Brou since at least the early twelfth century, but for our purposes the story begins in 1480. In that year, Count Philip of Bresse (later to be duke of Savoy) was paralysed by a fall from his horse while out hunting. His wife, Margaret of Bourbon, vowed to transform the priory at Brou into a monastery if his strength was restored. Her prayers were answered, but she died before she could fulfil the vow. In her will, she laid the responsibility on her husband and her baby son Philibert, but in the end it was left to the latter's widow to repay the debt of piety.

Margaret of Austria was the daughter of Maximilian of Habsburg (Holy Roman Emperor 1493-1519) and Mary of Burgundy, only child of Charles the Rash. Mary died after a riding accident in 1482, when Margaret was only two; and in the following year, the little princess left for France in fulfilment of one of the clauses of the second treaty of Arras. At Amboise, she was officially betrothed to the young Charles VIII, who had just succeeded his father, the sly and unscrupulous Louis XI. Her dowry was to be the provinces of Artois and Franche-Comté, that Louis had failed to take by force in 1477. For ten years, Margaret remained a virtual hostage at the French court on the banks of the Loire, though admittedly the captivity was well gilded—she had a suite of 100 maids of honour. Among her playfellows were Philibert and Louise of Savoy, also exiled as pledges of their father's good faith. Louise later married the duke of Angoulême and gave birth to the future Francis I. But Margaret was never to be truly queen of France.

In 1488 the duchy of Brittany was inherited by an unmarried eleven-year-old girl, Anne. The eligible duchess was overwhelmed with suitors, of whom she favoured Maximilian of Habsburg. The wedding was duly celebrated by proxy, but lack of funds prevented Maximilian from making good his title (the problem was not new—his first wife had had to finance their wedding). Anne of Beaujeu, Charles VIII's elder sister and regent during his minority, decided that Brittany was more important at that stage than Artois and Franche-Comté. Heavy pressures were brought to bear on the Bretons, and the two unconsummated marriages were declared null and void. Charles married the Duchess Anne, and Maximilian was doubly humiliated, both as father and prospective husband. When he heard the news, he flew into such a rage that his life was thought to be in danger.

Margaret was finally able to return home when peace between France and the Empire was restored by the treaty of Senlis in 1493. Two years later she was a political pawn again, this time in her father's anti-French alliance with Spain. A double marriage was arranged between her and Crown Prince Juan, and her brother Philip the Handsome and the Infanta Juana. In 1497 she sailed from Flushing to join her fiancé, narrowly escaping shipwreck on the way. But the throne of Spain eluded her too, Don Juan died after only six months of marriage, and Margaret's child by him died after only a few days of life.

Determined to get some more mileage out of his daughter, Maximilian married her in 1501 to the young Duke Philibert of Savoy, also nicknamed 'the Handsome', the same she had known at Amboise. Now for the first time Margaret tasted the power which was to compensate her for the disappointments of her private life. The lazy, pleasure-loving duke regarded his wife as intelligent enough for both of them, and was content to let her govern in his name. Then in 1504 misfortune struck again: while out hunting one blazing hot day, Philibert caught a chill from drinking ice-cold spring-water. Several days later he was dead of pleurisy, at the age of 24.

Having obtained the usufruct of the county of Bresse, Margaret set about putting her mother-in-law's vow into effect. Her declared reason was that Philibert's untimely death had been a sign of divine displeasure, though motives of personal prestige certainly played an important part. Subsequent events turned Brou into an exercise in self-aggrandisement. Scarcely had Margaret been widowed than her father suggested that she should cement the English alliance by marrying Henry VII. This time she flatly refused. Henry Tudor's stinginess and overbearing attitudes were well known, and after being a de facto ruler, Margaret had no intention of sacrificing the substance for the title. In 1509, Maximilian at last showed recognition of his daughter's worth by making her regent of the Netherlands and Franche-Comté. The premature death of Philip the

Handsome in 1506 (as a result of an over-energetic game of tennis) sent Juana—'Joanna the Mad'—out of her mind. Margaret was appointed guardian of their children. Her chief responsibility was the upbringing of her nephew Charles. Already he had succeeded his father as king of Castile; in 1516 he succeeded his grandfather Ferdinand V as king of Aragon and Naples; and in 1519, with the aid of massive bribes arranged by his aunt, he succeeded his other grandfather Maximilian as the Holy Roman Emperor Charles V, on whose European and American empire the sun never set.

The new monastery buildings at Brou, begun in 1506, were complete two years later. Margaret's appointment as regent of the Netherlands and guardian of her brother's children radically altered her conception of the church and tombs. Not only was there vast new wealth at her disposal, but her natural Burgundian antipathy to the house of France was aggravated by the fact that her sister-in-law Louise of Savoy was mother of the heir presumptive to the French crown. Like her ancestor Philip the Bold at Dijon, Margaret now envisaged Brou as a symbol of her independence and glory, an extension of her own rivalry with Louise and of that between her two nephews. The tombs, originally conceived of as 'fine and decent', were now to be almost overpoweringly exotic, and their setting no less so.

The basic plans of the church were the work of the Frenchman Jean Perréal, whom Margaret had known at Amboise. The execution and most of the credit, however, is due to the Flemish master mason Loys van Boghem, commissioned in 1512. The tombs were originally entrusted to Perréal and Michel Colombe, the greatest French sculptor of his day, who had collaborated with Perréal before on the tomb of Francis of Brittany. Colombe died in 1512, and it seems that nothing carved by him or designed by Perréal was included in the final version of the Brou tombs. These were the work of Jan van Room of Brussels, who provided life-size blueprints, and the German Conrad Meyt, who sculpted the effigies and supervised a crowd of assistants, mainly Flemings, but also Frenchman and Italians. Van Boghem promised in 1512 that the church would be finished in five years, but when Margaret offered him a £500 bonus in 1528 to finish within 30 months, the work was still four years away from completion.

Margaret was never to see the monument on which she had lavished such thought and care. Van Boghem had returned to Malines twice a year in search of funds and craftsmen, and to give progress reports to the regent. By 1530, Margaret was ready to make a personal tour of inspection when the bad luck that had dogged her struck again. One morning at her toilet, a lady-in-waiting dropped a glass jug and a splinter flew unseen into the princess's slipper. Margaret cut herself when she put the slipper on, and the wound turned septic. To prevent the gangrene reaching the rest of the body, her doctors decided to amputate. Margaret died on 1 December, most probably from an overdose of the laudanum administered as an anaesthetic.

Brou has come down to us almost intact. It escaped the Wars of Religion through not being on French soil until 1601, and was saved from the *enragés* of Bourg in the dark days of 1792-3 by a prominent local revolutionary, who placed the church under armed guard. Nevertheless, until the abbey was restored to religious uses in 1823, it had a dubious career as a fodder-store, a pigsty, a prison for non-juring priests, a veterans' barracks, a solitary confinement jail, a cavalry barracks, a workhouse, and finally a lunatic asylum. The two major alterations to the exterior are not due to the Revolution. The tower originally carried an Imperial crown to emphasise Margaret's connexion with Charles V, but in 1659 it began to split under the excessive weight. Indeed, the addition of the crown worried van Boghem enough to make him abandon the original idea of a crossing-tower. The offending load was replaced by a timber spire, which itself disappeared at the end of the eighteenth century. In 1759, the Augustinian canons undertook a major restoration of the roof to obtain better drainage; the Burgundian polychrome tiles were replaced by plain brown ones.

The great basket arch of the main portal frames an Ecce Homo with Philibert and Margaret presented by their patron saints. The central mullion is occupied by St Nicholas of Tolentino, to whom the church is dedicated (his feast-day was the anniversary of Philibert's death). The dominating feature of the composition is the statue of St Andrew, patron of the house of Burgundy, which surmounts the balustrade. It recalls Margaret's last advice to her nephew, 'Be sure, for the universal good of Christendom and the safety of your realms, to maintain and preserve peace and friendship with the kings of France and England, and above all do not abolish the name of the house of Burgundy.'

Inside, in the true Flamboyant manner, the clustered piers of the nave rise without capitals to a series of lierne vaults. The brilliant white stone of the Jura foothills has never needed cleaning, probably because Brou's isolation has protected it from soot and smoke. This first impression of coolness finds a violent contrast in the rood-screen and loft, designed by van Boghem as a gallery linking the duchess's apartments in the monastery with her private chapel on the north side of the chancel. Most French rood-screens fell victims to reform sentiment during the eighteenth century, when it became fashionable to give the congregation an unobstructed view of the high altar. The screen at Brou has survived because the church was never turned over to public worship.

The surface of the stone erupts in a riot of decoration. As well as the wilful loops, curves and fretwork of the arches and balustrade, a wealth of symbolic motifs is introduced—palms interwoven with marguerites, St Andrew's crosses, the initials P and M joined by a love-knot, quills (perhaps a reference to Margaret's fondness for writing sentimental poetry), the house of Savoy's motto FERT (the acronym of *'Fortitudo eius Rhodum tenuit'*, 'His courage held Rhodes'), and Margaret's own wrily punning device, *'Fortune infortune fort une'*, which can be interpreted either as 'Fortune is very cruel to one woman', or 'In fortune or misfortune, I remain strong and whole'.

The extravagance of the rood-screen, which jars with the restraint of the nave, makes sense as soon as one enters the chancel. The artists' aim is plainly to take the spectator's breath away with a bravura display of technique, to overwhelm him with the sheer profusion of detail. The 74 oak choir-stalls, probably also designed by Jan van Room, were carved in the record time of two years (1530-2), when van Boghem was under orders from Charles V to make an end. But nothing is botched; woodworking has always been a speciality of the region—Bourg is a centre for reproduction furniture, and Saint-Claude, up in the Jura, is the home of the briar pipe—and from the canopies to the misericords, the choir-stalls of Brou are the most princely in France. On the south side, the main subjects range across the Old Testament from the Creation to the Coronation of Solomon, while on the north, the theme is the New Testament from the Nativity to the Entry into Jerusalem. But the local carvers, under the direction of Pierre Berchod, have introduced Rabelaisian details of their own—a bearded soldier offers to warm a shivering girl, a monk empties a wineskin, another whips a schoolboy's naked backside.

On the north side of the chancel, behind the choir-screen, are Margaret's oratories, one above the other. Each is provided with a fireplace for her comfort in winter, and with a squint offering a view of the high altar so that she could follow the services. The ground-floor oratory opens on to a Lady Chapel communicating directly with the choir. The east wall of the chapel is decorated with an altarpiece recording the Seven Joys of the Virgin, an array of white marble miniatures framed in an architecture more like starched lace than stone. The north window represents the Assumption, executed by Lyonnais craftsmen to Flemish designs. The inspiration for these came from an engraving by Dürer; the almost abstract decorative effects of High Medieval glass have given place to the greater clarity and popular appeal suitable for the 'mass market' aimed at by engravers. The cameo frieze of the Triumph of the Faith is derived, again via engravings, from a drawing composed by Titian for his bedroom. At the foot of the central scene, Philibert and Margaret are presented by their patron saints.

The tall lancet windows of the choir display, amid a mass of blazonry, the duke and duchess observing the Apparitions of Christ, taken from Dürer's *'Little Passion'* engravings. There is more fine stained glass in the transepts, where Margaret's confessor, Father Montecuto, and her governor of Bresse, Laurent de Gorrevod, set up chantry chapels. The white cross on a red ground—the arms of Savoy—recurs again and again. It may well seem familiar: the dukes of Savoy later became kings of Sardinia and, after 1860, of Italy. As such, their coat of arms was superimposed on the Italian tricolour until the fall of the monarchy in 1946.

One element of the splendour of the chancel at Brou did not survive the vicissitudes of history. The pavement, of which only a few fragments remain round the tomb of Margaret of Austria, was irreparably damaged by the abuses of the Revolutionary and Empire periods. It consisted of glazed tiles covered with blue and white medallion-designs, and the effect was so beautiful that, according to one chronicler, 'it was almost a shame to walk on it'. The same writer records, 'I remember that when I was there, there was a gentleman who, scrupling to spit on this pavement, spat in the face of a great peasant, saying that there was no place in all the church dirtier than that to spit on.'

The pièces de résistance, however, the justification of the whole building, are the tombs of the three people most closely involved with the vow of Brou. The effigies are in the hard Carrara marble favoured by Michelangelo; but they are practically submerged by the architecture (in the softer marble of Saint-Lothain)—a prodigy of patience and invention which typifies the final stage of Gothic art, and recalls a whole lost sculptor's repertoire of finials, crockets, fleurons, arabesques, accolades and pinnacles. As Prosper Mérimée noted, 'everything which would seem difficult to execute in metal has here been executed in marble'.

The tomb of Margaret of Bourbon, the least striking of the three, is set in an alcove in the south wall of the choir-screen. In the arcades beneath the black marble slab, cowled mourners, reminiscent of those on the ducal tombs at Dijon, alternate with cherubs. In the centre of the chancel stands the tomb of Philibert the Handsome. The young duke is represented twice, a device known in the late fifteenth century and repeated in the contemporary tomb of Louis XII, now at Saint-Denis. On the upper slab, surrounded by plump cherubs, Philibert appears in full state dress over his armour. The soft, self-indulgent good looks are already running to fat, and the head is tilted towards his wife's tomb as though seeking guidance even in death. Underneath, half hidden by the elaborate arcades, reposes his corpse, stripped now of its worldly finery, and food for worms—which, true to the late Gothic obsession with the physical details of mortality, can be seen crawling on his flesh.

The bombastic magnificence of the largest tomb of all, that of Margaret of Austria, reveals her true but unavowed motive, the determination to rule even from beyond the grave. Here, the motif of the altar-tomb reaches its ultimate expression with the addition of the grandiose baldacchino forming an eastward extension of the choir-screen. The arches are heavy with symbolic marguerites, quills, St Andrew's crosses and monograms, and round the cornice runs Margaret's wistful comment on her life, *'Fortune infortune fort une'*. Like her husband, the duchess is shown above at her lying-in-state, and below as prepared for her coffin. Meyt makes no attempt to flatter the fleshy nose or the stubborn Habsburg lip, made grotesque by inbreeding in later generations. But the lower figure, its unpinned hair coiling over a voluminous winding-sheet, has a feeling for the pathetic dignity of death which might almost be termed Renaissance. However, the medieval penchant for anecdote has the last word: on the sole of Margaret's left foot, Meyt has carved the fatal wound.

From an aesthetic point of view, Brou has never found much favour from writers brought up on post-Gothic ideals. After initial bewilderment, Mérimée feels bound to assert, 'These marvels of skill and patience are not art,' and quotes with approval the opinion of the buxom servant-girl at the inn where he stayed: *'C'est très superbe et bien joli'*. Prettiness was also the feature singled out by Joris-Karl Huysmans when he described Brou as 'a masterpiece of the pretty, the tortuous, the finicky, the dainty'. Of the whole style exemplified by Brou, the historian Johan Huizinga wrote, 'It decomposes all the formal elements endlessly; it interlaces all the details; there is not a line which has not its counter-line. The form develops at the expense of the idea, the ornament grows rank, hiding all the lines and all the surfaces. A *horror vacui* reigns, always a symptom of artistic decline.'

In more recent years, however, informed appreciation has made us more sympathetic to 'fully-developed' styles in all the arts—for example, rococo architecture or baroque music. Perhaps the turn of Flamboyant is already overdue, and the current revival of interest in the music of the period may spread to its visual arts. If so, Brou will no longer seem the pedantic and affected product of a culture in decline, but the exuberant embodiment of a dynamic civilisation exploring the extreme possibilities of static medieval styles and institutions, while evolving an approach of its own. The stained glass, the 'basket' arches (tentatively replacing the pointed arch which had reigned supreme for over 300 years) and the frankly Italianate *putti* are all pointers towards the Renaissance. One feels that des Esseintes, the decadent hero of Huysmans' *Against Nature*, who so appreciated 'the special gamy flavour' acquired by late Latin as it evolved into national dialects, would have thoroughly approved of Brou, pointing out to his creator that ripeness is all.

12   The Beaujolais

This chapter is a *bonne bouche* for those whose interest is in the wines of Burgundy. Historically, the Beaujolais has never belonged to Burgundy, but to the Lyonnais. Our claim to it is based on a court decision of 1930, by which viticultural Burgundy was adjudged to include the *arrondissement* of Villefranche in the department of Rhône. To leave this district out would be a major misrepresentation by omission: the 40,000 acres of the Beaujolais vineyards account for half Burgundy's total area under vines, half its total wine production, and two-thirds of its average annual output of red wine (four times more than the Côte d'Or).

The 1930 judgment has both geographical and practical justifications: geographical, in that the Beaujolais vineyards run on without a break from those of the Mâconnais; practical, in that the plant used is the *gamay noir à jus blanc,* with a tiny proportion (one per cent) of chardonnay. These considerations separate the Beaujolais quite clearly from the Côtes du Rhône vineyards which begin south of Lyon.

The district takes its name from the town of Beaujeu, whose *seigneurs* controlled the area's key fortress. In 1400, the *seigneurie* was acquired by the duke of Bourbon. One of his descendants, Pierre, married Louis XI's daughter; this lady subsequently became regent during the minority of Charles VIII, and is known to history as Anne of Beaujeu. Pierre and Anne's daughter brought the barony to the Montpensier branch of the Bourbons, in the person of the celebrated Charles de Bourbon-Montpensier, constable of France. After covering himself with glory at the battle of Marignano in 1515, he fell out with Francis I, went over to Charles V, and was killed at the Sack of Rome in 1527. The last heiresss of the Montpensiers married Gaston d'Orléans, brother of Louis XIII. Their daughter, the Grande Mademoiselle whom we have met at Saint-Fargeau, was, among her many other titles, baroness of Beaujolais. Dying without issue, she was succeeded by Louis XIV's brother, Philippe d'Orléans. The last baron of the house of Orléans espoused the Revolutionary cause and is better known as Philippe-Egalité. The fact that he had voted for the death of his cousin Louis XVI did not save him from

Robespierre's purges in 1793.

The principal towns are Belleville and Villefranche, on the banks of the Saône. The latter has replaced Beaujeu as the regional capital and has captured the sub-prefecture, so that the *sous-préfet* of Villefranche is known familiarly as the 'Prefect of the Beaujolais'. The town grew up near a ford, and acquired its name during the thirteenth century as a result of privileges granted by the barons of Beaujolais, who had a toll-post there. These were confirmed and added to by Baron Guichard's great charter of 1260. Among the more conventional provisions of the 68 articles (such as complete exemption from seigneurial dues, even for the brothel-keeper) are some curiosities: people taken in, or reasonably suspected (by reason of their state of undress) of adultery were to run naked through the town, or pay the baron a fine in lieu; and the good burghers of Villefranche were free to beat their wives as much as they liked, provided the results were not fatal.

The church of Notre-Dame des Marais was built on reclaimed swamp, as its name indicates, and has been the victim of many piecemeal alterations over the centuries. The apse has a set of sixteenth-century gargoyles, one of which represents a goat fornicating with a witch. The square in front of the church is paved with large flagstones called *calades* in the *langue d'oc*. As this was also the market square, *aller à la calade* came to mean 'to go to market at Villefranche', and the citizens to be known as *Caladois*.

Across the Saône from Villefranche, the land rises to the lonely, waterlogged plateau of Dombes. Ars-sur-Formans, just off the main road from Villefranche to Bourg-en-Bresse, witnessed the ministry of St Jean-Baptiste Vianney from 1818 till his death in 1859. This strange personality, a simple peasant's son without academic gifts (his seminary report read 'Extremely weak'), despised by his parishioners and tormented by self-doubt, was torn from the obscurity he would so much have preferred by his amazing power of individual conversion. At the height of his fame, the stream of pilgrims was so great that he sometimes had to spend up to 18 hours a day in the confessional. The *curé* of Ars, who was so discouraged by his own shortcomings that more than once he almost abandoned his charge, was named the patron saint of parish priests in 1929. Despite an unseemly controversy with his native Dardilly (in Rhône), Ars retained his lucrative relics and built a basilica to house them. The true significance of the saint's life has been lost under a welter of doubtful miracles, and the many have turned Ars into a miniature Lourdes.

The Beaujolais includes all the country between the Loire and the

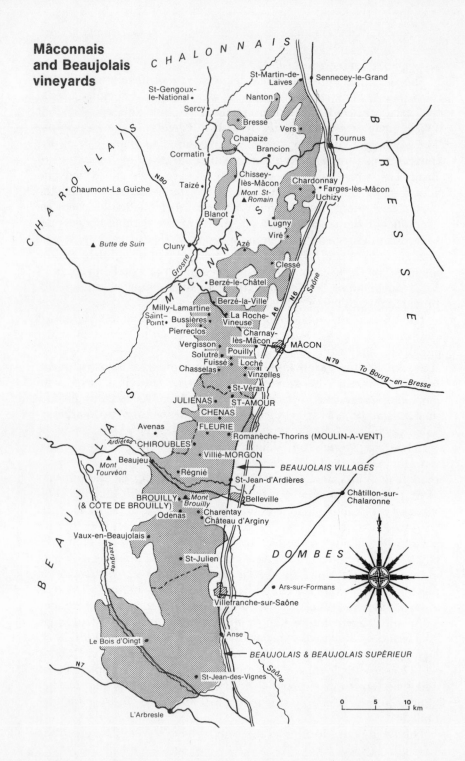

Mâconnais and Beaujolais vineyards

CHALONNAIS

CHAROLLAIS

BRESSE

St-Gengoux-le-National
Sercy
St-Martin-de-Laives
Sennecey-le-Grand
Nanton
Bresse
Vers
Chapaize
Brancion
Cormatin
Tournus
Chaumont-La Guiche
Taizé
Chissey-lès-Mâcon
Chardonnay
Farges-lès-Mâcon
Mont St-Romain
Uchizy
Blanot
Lugny
Viré
Butte de Suin
Cluny
Azé
Clessé
Berzé-le-Châtel
Berzé-la-Ville
Milly-Lamartine
Saint-Point
Bussières
La Roche-Vineuse
Pierreclos
Charnay-lès-Mâcon
Vergisson
MÂCON
Solutré
Pouilly
Fuissé
Loché
Chasselas
Vinzelles
St-Véran
To Bourg-en-Bresse
JULIENAS
ST-AMOUR
CHENAS
Avenas
FLEURIE
Ardières
Romanèche-Thorins (MOULIN-A-VENT)
CHIROUBLES
Beaujeu
Villié-MORGON
BEAUJOLAIS VILLAGES
Mont Tourvéon
Régnié
St-Jean-d'Ardières
BROUILLY
(& CÔTE DE BROUILLY)
Mont Brouilly
Belleville
Châtillon-sur-Chalaronne
Odenas
Charentay
Château d'Arginy
Vaux-en-Beaujolais
DOMBES
St-Julien
Ars-sur-Formans
Azergues
Villefranche-sur-Saône
Le Bois d'Oingt
Anse
BEAUJOLAIS & BEAUJOLAIS SUPÉRIEUR
St-Jean-des-Vignes
L'Arbresle

BEAUJOLAIS

MÂCONNAIS

Grosne

Saône

N 80
N 6
A 6
N 79
N 7

0   5   10 km

Saône, south of the Mâconnais and the Charollais. Most of it is occupied by the Montagne, but what really concerns us is the vineyard, which clings to the eastern slopes of this high ground. Henri IV situated the most beautiful place in France amongst the high, forested hills of the Beaujolais; and with due allowance for alcoholic euphoria, one can sympathise with him. The countryside is more rugged than in Burgundy proper, though one is never far from signs of human habitation. The neatness of the Côte d'Or and the Mâconnais is missing; the whole personality of the land is more expansive.

The vine has been cultivated here since Roman times, though its fortunes have fluctuated considerably over 2,000-odd years. In the Middle Ages, a time of great prosperity, the city of Lyon consumed the region's entire production, giving rise to the saying that 'Lyon is watered by three rivers: the Rhône, the Saône, and the Beaujolais'. The opening of the Briare Canal (linking the Loire and the Seine) in 1642 also gave beaujolais a Parisian clientèle; but Louis XIV's wars ruined the peasantry and prevented this new potential from being immediately exploited. The vineyard's recovery during the eighteenth century was helped first by the suppression of internal customs duties on wine (1776), and later by the large-scale redistribution of property during the Revolution. Despite modern *appellation contrôlée* laws, beaujolais is still considered a 'much imitated' wine, especially by those who claim to have driven from Mâcon to Lyon by the motorway without seeing a single vine-stock (as is perfectly possible, since these roads cross land which is too low-lying for the vine). If only these motorists lifted up their eyes to the hills, they would find the vine occupying every square foot of the slopes, between 500 and 1,700 feet above sea level—representing an average output of 90 million bottles a year.

The essential quality of beaujolais is summed up by the onomatopoeic but untranslatable word *gouleyant:* tender, easy on the stomach, sweet rather than savoury, slightly effervescent, refreshing, and above all 'quaffable' without the unpleasant after-effects of stronger wines. Beaujolais is still regarded as a *vin de primeur,* and its particular tender fruitiness is the result of deliberately keeping the tannin content low. This is done by allowing the juice to be squeezed out in the vat by the grapes' own weight, rather than by using a *fouloir* beforehand, and by vatting for only three or four days, just long enough to give the wine its colour. Even after heavier wines for laying down became fashionable, beaujolais remained a carafe wine, drunk up in the year following the vintage. Until recently, the notion of bottling it would have been unthinkable—the restaurateurs of Lyon and Paris served it from the wood, in *pots* or *pichets* of pewter or earthenware. Beaujolais possesses the rare distinction, for a red wine, of needing to be served at cellar temperature.

The vineyard looks on a map like a short, stubby thermometer. The bulb, near Lyon, has a soil composed mainly of clay and limestone. This is the area of the plain *Beaujolais* (nine degrees minimum alcoholic content) or *Beaujolais Supérieur* (ten degrees) which is the mainstay of cafés all over France. The stem (the top end of which is in Saône-et-Loire) contains the granite and metamorphic soils best suited to the gamay. The nine named village wines of this area—Saint-Amour, Juliénas, Chénas, Moulin-à-Vent, Fleurie, Chiroubles, Morgon, Brouilly and Côte de Brouilly—can lay claim to real distinction. While obviously not in the same class as the pinot noir wines of the Côte d'Or, they gain appreciably from two or three years in bottle and are the only beaujolais which can be declassified into *Bourgogne.* The names of the *grand cru* villages are appellations in their own right, like those of the Côte d'Or; the other wines of the *grand cru* district bear the collective appellation of *Beaujolais-Villages.*

In this region, the grip of the merchants of Beaune and Mâcon has eased since the last war. The smaller peasant proprietors have increasingly come together for the production and marketing of their quality wines. There are eight co-operatives and 15 *caveaux de dégustation,* many of them converted from old cellars, where the local product can be tasted. The Maison des Beaujolais, on the N6 at Saint-Jean d'Ardières near Belleville, offers an opportunity to taste the entire range of *grands crus* with cheese and *charcuterie.* The route of the *Beaujolais-Villages* is worth a more detailed description.

There is no perceptible dividing-line between the Mâconnais and the Beaujolais. Somewhere near Saint-Véran, on the southernmost fringes of Saône-et-Loire, the chardonnay gives place to the gamay and the frontier is crossed. Saint-Amour is the first outpost. The very name arouses thoughts of dalliance and seduction, though no-one ever seems to have recommended the wine as an aphrodisiac. It is said, however, that the canons of Mâcon Cathedral (who owned the village) did not allow their priestly status to stand in the way of full enjoyment of their *droits de seigneur.* There is in fact a St 'Amour' (Amadour or Amator) in the calendar; his feast falls on 20 August. Like its companions at the very top of the thermometer, the wine of Saint-Amour has a very full flavour and, especially when young, a distinct purple colour.

The adjoining commune of Juliénas is one of the best-known beaujolais names. It was supposed to be the favourite tipple of Gnafron, the red-nosed crony of the Lyonnais puppet-character

Guignol.

Chénas is the smallest of the named growths, but the village also has a stake in Moulin-à-Vent, the most distinguished beaujolais of all, which it shares with Romanèche-Thorins. A soil rich in manganese is one of the factors which have put Moulin-à-Vent in a class by itself. It is exceptionally long-lived, and comes close to rivalling the *grands crus* of the Côte d'Or. The windmill that has lent its name to the wine is the last one left in the Beaujolais. Shorn of its sails, it stands at the side of the road leading down to the plain from Chénas.

Romanèche-Thorins is content to be part-producer of Moulin-à-Vent, and has no appellation of its own. Its most illustrious son was the *vigneron* Benoît Raclet, saviour of the vineyard, in whose honour the new wine festival is celebrated at Romanèche. In the 1820's, the Beaujolais vines were being devastated by a parasite called the *pyrale*. In some areas whole vintages were lost. Then in 1829 Raclet noticed that a vine-stock planted close to the outlet-pipe of his kitchen sink had not been attacked. He experimented with deliberate scalding of his vine-stocks during the grubs' hibernation, a policy that met with instant success. Yet his friends refused to take him seriously, and his technique was not generally adopted until 1841.

At Fleurie, the strong character of the northernmost *crus* changes into something more feminine. The colour mellows from purple to ruby, the flavour becomes lighter and the perfume acquires, appropriately enough, a hint of spring flowers. A steep climb leads to Chiroubles, whose lower vineyards produce a wine similar to that of Fleurie. Higher up the mountainside the altitude begins to tell, and a certain harshness creeps in. It was at Chiroubles, during the phylloxera years of the 1870's, that the wine expert Victor Pulliat planted the first French vine grafted on to an American root.

Many other fruits have been called in to describe the distinctive flavour of Morgon (which is in fact a *lieu-dit* in the commune of Villié, now renamed Villié-Morgon): apricots, cherries, even gooseberries. The locals avoid doubtful comparisons and say simply '*il morgonne*'. Its uniqueness derives from a soil of decomposed schist, called *roche pourrie* or 'rotten stone'. As at Moulin-à-Vent, the earth is rich in manganese, and the wines of Morgon, especially Le Py, have the same reputation for longevity. A detour from the route of the *crus* takes us to Régnié and the Grange Charton, a communal housing project for *vignerons* built in the early nineteenth century.

'*A tout venant, beau jeu*' reads the bonhomous motto of the Beaujolais' former capital, strung out along the narrow valley of the Ardières. From here, the D136 and the D26 climb to the Col du Fût d'Avenas, which affords a panorama of mountains and vineyards, and a view across the plateau of Dombes to the Alps. Mont Blanc may well be visible on a clear day through a very long telescope. The church at Avenas possesses a carved stone altar, on one side of which a king presents the church to St Vincent (i.e. to the dean and chapter of Mâcon). The reference beneath this scene to *Ludovicus Pius* has led the monarch to be wrongly identified as either Louis the Pious (the son of Charlemagne) or St Louis. The inscription is actually a chronogram (a phrase whose Roman-numeral letters added give a date) indicating that the donation took place in 1180 under the reign of Louis VII.

In the other direction from Beaujeu, the road leads to Charlieu via the pass of Les Echarmeaux. Overlooking Chénelette is Mont Tourvéon, from whose summit, according to legend, the astrologer Nostradamus observed the stars. Formerly it had been the stronghold of Ganelon, the jealous paladin who conspired with the Moors to destroy Roland and Oliver at Roncesvalles. Despite the traitor's boasts, the castle was eventually taken and razed to the ground by Louis the Pious. Ganelon himself is said to have been rolled down Tourvéon in a barrel full of iron spikes.

Returning to the vineyards, our route leads from Beaujeu to the conspicuous isolated hill of Mont Brouilly and its chapel of Notre-Dame du Raisin. The building, dating from 1857, is of no architectual interest but is nevertheless an object of pilgrimage for *vignerons* on 8 September every year. If the official reason is to secure the Virgin's blessing for the vintage, the long climb is also an excuse for a picnic and a devotional bottle-party. The appellation *Côte de Brouilly* applies only to vines grown on the south-facing slopes of the hill. This wine's dark colour and full body give it a more than passing resemblance to the *crus* of the northern end of the Beaujolais; it is unique in having its minimum alcoholic content set at 10.5° rather than ten. *Brouilly,* on the other hand, is the largest named growth of all. It surrounds the hill on all sides and gives a lighter wine, more typical of the area. Some of it, however, can come close to the standards of *Côte de Brouilly*—like the unflatteringly-named Pisse-Vieille at Cercié.

The village of Charentay is one of many which sell their wine as Brouilly, but is especially remarkable for two odd buildings. One is a nineteenth-century folly, a 114-foot-high tower said to have been built by a mother-in-law as a look-out post from which she could spy on her daughter's husband. The other is the decaying château of Arginy. Most of it dates back only to the sixteenth century, but its faintly sinister appearance has helped to confuse history with romance. It would seem that the tall brick tower was originally only one of 22 and dates from the thirteenth century, when the castle belonged to the powerful Order of the Temple. In this 'Tower of the Seven Beatitudes', new Templars underwent nameless initiation ceremonies. Then in 1311 the order was condemned en masse at the instance of Philip the Fair, and on the strength of fantastic allegations. Its organisation was dissolved, its members dispersed, and its lands, of course, confiscated. In 1314 the Grand Master, Jacques de Molay, was burnt at the stake after uttering his eminently successful curse on the king, his sons, his advisers, and his pope. The Templars fled from Arginy, and never returned to claim the fabulous treasure hidden within its walls.

The present owner of Arginy, the comte de Rosemont, is convinced that the treasure lies there undisturbed. 'Beneath my château, according to expert investigations, is a layer of salt within which are located three underground chambers, one on top of the other. These are protected by booby-traps operated by enormous stones. The treasure is contained in jars of Egyptian design; heaps of gold, coins, ingots and dust weighing more than several tons. There are also, in the very centre, mysterious objects emitting extraordinarily intense vibrations; perhaps the very ones that came from the Holy of Holies of the Temple at Jerusalem, and that the Jews seek in vain.'

After this, it hardly comes as a surprise to find an entire village where fiction has subdued fact. Vaux-en-Beaujolais prides itself on being the original of Clochemerle, despite the claims of several rivals. The topographical details are right enough: there is a *haut-bourg* and a *bas-bourg,* and in the valley below the village there was even once a pump-room whose waters were reputed sovereign against anaemia, jaundice and venereal disease—a fact which undoubtedly inspired *Clochemerle*'s sequel *Clochemerle-les-Bains.* As we have already noted, Gabriel Chevallier drew the characters and even the name of his imaginary community from his associations with La Clayette, in the Charollais. But the people of Vaux were insistent, and the author eventually gave them his official blessing. On 26 October 1956, he inaugurated their municipal *caveau* and became the first signatory of its Visitors' Book. Vaux has its own 'bacchic brotherhood', the Compagnons du Gosier Sec or 'Fellowship of the Parched Throat'.

Index